THE MAGPIES

For Sue Plant

Different species and races of magpies. Top left: Yellow-billed magpie Pica nuttalli. *All other magpies shown here are various races of* Pica pica. *From top to bottom: North American Black-billed magpie* P.p.hudsonia, *the race from the Asir Mountains, Saudi Arabia* P.p.asirensis, *the North African race* P.p.mauritanica, *the race from Kamchatka, USSR* P.p.camtschatica, *and the largest of all races, from Tibet,* P.p.bottanensis. *Paintings by David Quinn.*

THE MAGPIES

The Ecology and Behaviour of Black-billed
and Yellow-billed Magpies

by Tim Birkhead

Illustrated by

DAVID QUINN

T & A D POYSER

London

© T & A D Poyser 1991

ISBN 0 85661 067 4

First published in 1991 by T & A D Poyser Ltd
24–28 Oval Road, London NW1

United States Edition published by
ACADEMIC PRESS INC.
San Diego, CA 92101

Text set in Linotron Baskerville
Printed and bound in Great Britain by
Mackays of Chatham PLC, Chatham, Kent

A catalogue record for this book
is available from the British Library

Contents

List of Photographs

7

List of Figures

List of Tables

Acknowledgements

A number of people have helped in a variety of ways in the production of this book. My first debt is to Keith Clarkson, Simon Eden and Sandy Goodburn, ex-research students who collected much of the information presented here. Their enthusiasm, diligence and competence kept the magpie study going, and I thank them for allowing me to use their data, and for their stimulating discussions and friendship. I am especially grateful to Sandy Goodburn for extracting much of the information for Chapters 7, 8 and 9. Their research and my own were supported by the Natural Environment Research Council, the Science and Engineering Research Council, the Royal Society, the Nuffield Foundation, the British Ecological Society and the Royal Society for Protection of Birds.

I am also indebted to the landowners in the Rivelin Valley who generously allowed us to work on their land. Without their cooperation there would have been no study. Although lying just a few miles from the centre of Sheffield, the Rivelin Valley was (and still is) very much a microcosm of traditional rural England, apparently untouched by the 20th century. The combination of the location and its occupants made it a great place to conduct fieldwork. Unfortunately, most of the people who helped us are now dead; they include: Horace White who told me on our very first meeting, at the outset of the study that he was 'snided with magpies', but doubting my ability, added 'I'll give thee a shilling for every one thou catches'. He died owing me relatively little. Also Frank Revitts and his wife, who kept us up to date with 'her' colour-ringed magpie, while Frank described the various ways in which he dealt with vermin (excluding magpies). Willie Guites and his sister lived in the Rivelin for over 95 years each and were a rich source of stories from the past. Dougie Birch and his family (still going strong), and Mr A. H. Thompson also helped in numerous ways, and tolerated our persistent presence.

My observations of Black-billed and Yellow-billed Magpies in North America were made with Keith Clarkson: I thank him for tireless fieldwork and great companionship. Our visit was made possible by the generous cooperation and hospitality of the following people: in Pocatello, Idaho, Charles (Chuck) Trost and Cheryl Webb, together with Eric Stone and Lisa Reed were tremendous hosts and provided great insight into Black-billed Magpie ways; at Hastings Reservation, California, Walt Koenig and Janis Dickinson, and Mark Reynolds ensured that our stay there was both productive and immensely enjoyable.

Several people in what used to be the Zoology Department at the University of Sheffield deserve special thanks for their contribution to the magpie study, especially Pete Jackson, Jayne Pellatt and Len Hill, who helped in various ingenious ways. Special thanks to Dave Hollingworth for tremendous help and advice with photography.

I am also very grateful to those magpie enthusiasts and others less enthusiastic, who have generously allowed me to use their unpublished information: F. Alvarez, Gert Baeyens, D. A. Boag, Deborah Buitron, J. Gasperetti, Steve Gooch, Derek Goodwin, Wes Hochachka, Göran Högstedt, Fred Hustings, Leszek Jerzak, Brendan Kavanagh, Walter Koenig, Les May, T. Mizera, Anders Møller, B. Pambour, Tomas Redondo, Kerry Reese, Mark Reynolds, Tore Slagsvold, M. Soler, Stephen Sutcliffe, Steve Tapper (Game Conservancy), Charles (Chuck) Trost, J. Walters, Cheryl Webb, Klaus Witt, The US Fish & Wildlife Banding Office, and the British Trust for Ornithology. I am especially grateful to Peter Enggist-Dublin who provided the magpie sonagrams and allowed me to cross-examine him about Magpie vocalizations.

Thanks are also due to Linda Birch (EGI library), Mike Birkhead, Lee Callander (Museum of the North American Indian, New York), Euan Dunn, Erick Greene, Paul Hodges, P. A. D. Hollom, Pete Hudson, Richard Porter and Mike Rands for answering various queries relating to magpies. I'm grateful to Angela Saxby and Julie Thorpe who relieved me of the tedious task of typing the references and tables, and to Jayne Pellatt for producing all the figures.

It is a pleasure to acknowledge David Quinn for his outstanding illustrations. He (and the author) are grateful to Clem Fisher and Dr Malcolm Largen of Liverpool Museum and to Dr Mike Hounsome of Manchester University Museum for the loan of skins.

I am extremely grateful to Michael Brooke, Keith Clarkson, Sandy Goodburn and Anders Møller for giving up their time to read and constructively criticize a first draft of the manuscript. Any errors remaining are entirely my own. Andy Richford of T & A. D. Poyser provided some hard-headed and enthusiastic encouragement throughout.

Finally I thank my parents and Miriam, Nick, Laurie and Francesca for their contribution.

CHAPTER 1

Magpies

In spite of his evil reputation the magpie is regarded by most persons who are not breeders of pheasants with exceptional interest.

W.H. Hudson (1934)

Attractive, artful and aggressive are all terms which have been used to describe magpies, and they are all accurate. Few bird species outside the tropics can compete with the magpie for looks: its crisp, iridescent black and white plumage together with its elongated tail gives it a distinctly exotic appearance. The magpie's artfulness may be the result of human persecution. Two or three hundred years ago the magpie was a popular bird in Europe, but as soon as it came into conflict with man's interests over the preservation of gamebirds it was heavily persecuted. Not surprisingly the magpie had to adopt a more clandestine life-style in order to survive, hence its reputation for furtiveness. The recent expansion of European magpies into urban areas has led to concern for songbird populations, and magpies certainly appear to be aggressive in the way they take fledgeling birds. However, as always, there are two sides to this story.

Considering how common and widespread the magpie is in Europe, Asia and western North America, surprisingly little was known about its ecology and behaviour until recently. Although there was a mass of anecdotal information available, it was not until the mid-1970s, when several detailed field studies were initiated, that we started to appreciate the intricacies of magpie ways. These studies have revealed, for example, the magpie's rather loose marital arrangements; the complex hierarchical relationships among young, non-breeding birds; and the various strategies that they use in the intense competition for breeding space.

The magpie is a member of the crow family (Corvidae), of which there are some 102 species (Goodwin 1986). The magpie's name is

> a contraction of Magot Pie, a Middle English name for the bird . . . the first part of the name appears to have no reference to the birds' habit of picking maggots from the backs of sheep . . ., but it is derived from the French Margot, a diminutive of Marguerite, but also signifying a Magpie, perhaps from its noisy chattering, in which it is popularly supposed to resemble a talkative woman. The second part of the name is supposed to come through French from Latin *pica* which refers to the black and white coloration of the birds.
>
> (Linsdale 1937)

The magpie's present name was first recorded in 1605 and gradually replaced the French 'pie' (used since at least 1200), and 'piannet' of northern England. The latter term is a combination of 'pie' and 'Annet' a pet form of the once common Christian name Agnes. After the publication of Thomas Pennant's *British Zoology (Birds)* in 1768 the name 'Magpie' became standard (Lockwood 1984).

There are two species of magpie, the Black-billed *Pica pica*, which occurs throughout much of the northern hemisphere (Fig. 1), and the Yellow-billed *Pica nuttalli* which is restricted to a small area in California. John James Audubon wrote: 'I have conferred on this beautiful bird the name of a most zealous, learned and enterprising naturalist, my friend Thomas Nuttall'. Nuttall (1786–1859) was a Yorkshire ornithologist who travelled widely in the western United States, including California.

My aim in this book is to consider both species and to summarize and compare what is known about their biology. However, I make no apologies for emphasizing those aspects which have interested me most, namely their social behaviour and breeding ecology. I have also used my long-term study of magpies conducted near Sheffield, England, as a base-line with which to compare other studies, not because this study is better than any others, but because many of the results have not previously been published.

The present range of the Black-billed Magpie in the Palearctic Region extends from Ireland in the west to the Kamchatka Peninsula in the eastern USSR. On the basis of some fossil evidence Voous (1960) suggested that magpies originally occurred throughout the Northern Hemisphere, but that during the Pleistocene period, 1 to 10 million years ago, they became extinct in North America, except for a small, relict population in California. These subsequently became the present-day Yellow-billed Magpie. The Black-billed Magpie is thought to have recolonized North America from Asia some time after the last glaciation, and probably around 40,000 years ago when there was

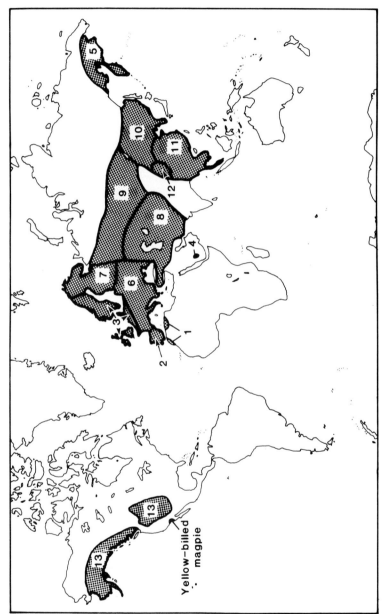

Fig. 1.   *Distribution of Black-billed and Yellow-billed Magpies, showing the approximate range of thirteen races of* Pica pica: *1.* mauritanica, *2.* melanotos, *3.* pica, *4.* asirensis, *5.* camtschatica, *6.* galliae, *7.* fennorum, *8.* bactriana, *9.* hemileucoptera, *10.* leucoptera, *11.* sericea, *12.* bottanensis, *13.* hudsonia.

Portrait of European Black-billed Magpie. (Photo: M. Wilkes).

a land-bridge between the two continents. The ranges of the two species of magpie in North America do not overlap: the closest they get is about 50 miles (80 km). Even if they did meet, the birds have been isolated for so long that they are probably now sufficiently distinct to avoid interbreeding. Despite the differences between Black-billed and Yellow-billed Magpies it is clear that they share a great many characteristics. Indeed, the morphological feature which now separates the two species, namely the yellow bill of *nuttalli*, may be due to a very small genetic difference. Support for this idea comes from the fact that there are several records of European magpies possessing yellow beaks (Linsdale 1937).

When I started writing this book I decided to treat the North American Black-billed Magpie *Pica pica hudsonia* and Eurasian *Pica pica* as a single species, as others have done. However, on making a few comparisons it became clear that these two forms are very different from each other. Goodwin (1986) made a similar point by suggesting that the Yellow-billed Magpie and North American Black-billed Magpie are more similar to each other than they are to the Eurasian one. As we shall see, there is now good evidence for this. I have therefore tried to make it quite clear throughout this book when I am discussing the North American Black-billed Magpie or the Eurasian form. However, to save writing these names out in full each time I sometimes refer to them as 'North American magpies' and 'Eurasian magpies', and use the term 'magpie' to cover both of them. If I discuss some aspect of the biology of Eurasian magpies based on studies made in Europe I use the term 'European magpie'. Yellow-billed Magpies are referred to by their full name.

Portrait of Yellow-billed Magpie. (Photo: T. R. Birkhead).

DISTRIBUTION

The magpie occurs across much of the Northern Hemisphere (Fig. 1). In the Old World it has a continuous range from Britain and Ireland in the west, through Europe and the USSR to China and Kamchatka in the east. It occurs as far north as 70°N in Europe and as far south as 15°N in Saudi Arabia. In North America the magpie is confined mainly to the western side of the continent, from north-western Alaska to northern Arizona, New Mexico and western Texas (Fig. 2). The Yellow-billed Magpie has a small, restricted range, occurring only in California in the Sacramento and San Joaquin valleys, and in coastal valleys south of San Francisco Bay (Fig. 2). Both species are sedentary throughout much of their range.

At first sight it seems odd that the magpie should be confined to the western part of North America. However, Linsdale (1937) noticed that its range coincides almost exactly with what has been described as a 'Cold Type Steppe Dry Climate'. Within this range magpies typically breed at altitudes up to 3000 m in areas of sagebrush, woodland along river courses adjacent to meadows and fields. A detailed analysis, using Christmas bird counts and climatological information, showed that summer temperatures and humidity were the factors limiting the magpie's abundance and distribution (Bock & Lepthien 1975). Although suitable habitat exists to the south of its present range, summer temperatures in those desert regions are apparently too high. Again, areas of suitable habitat occur on the Central Plains to the east, but

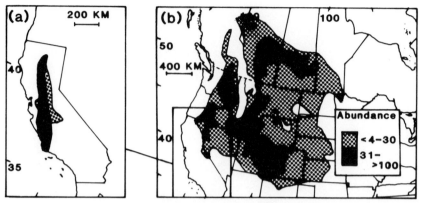

Fig. 2.   *Distribution and density of (a) Yellow-billed Magpie and (b) Black-billed Magpie in North America. Note that the data for Black-billed Magpies show only that part of the range for which most information on abundance is available. The intensity of shading reflects population density (shaded areas: 4–30 birds per route; black areas: 31–100 birds per route). Redrawn from Robbins* et al. *(1986).*

these are probably too humid. To the north the magpie's distribution is limited by dense boreal forest, which it does not penetrate.

The Yellow-billed Magpie occupies much warmer areas than the Black-billed Magpie in North America, and its range is described as having a 'Hot Summer Mediterranean Type Climate' (Linsdale 1937). Restricted to California and oak-savannah habitat, the Yellow-billed Magpie's geographic range is about 150 miles (240 km) wide by 500 miles (800 km) north to south. Summer temperatures enjoyed by Yellow-billed Magpies are about 8 °C hotter than those experienced by Black-billed Magpies. Conversely the latter species is exposed to winter temperatures at least 20 °C colder than Yellow-billed Magpies ever experience. The factors which determine why particular bird species occur where they do are often obscure, and the distribution of the two North American magpies could be due either to the direct effects of climate on the birds themselves, or to its indirect effects on their food supply. Some elegant experimental studies by Hayworth and Weathers (1984), involving the measurements of magpie body temperatures and metabolic rates under a range of conditions, showed quite clearly that each species is physiologically adapted to its own type of summer climate.

There have been no comparable studies of climate and the distribution of magpies in the Old World. Such an investigation would be interesting especially if it included *mauritanica* and *asirensis*, the races of magpie occupying North Africa and Saudi Arabia, respectively, where it is considerably hotter and more arid than elsewhere in the range. Detailed information on the distribution of the magpie exists for various parts of western Europe, derived from atlas studies conducted during the past twenty years. The British Trust for Ornithology's Atlas survey (Sharrock 1976) conducted between 1968 and 1972, shows (Fig. 3) that the magpie is widespread in England and Wales, but absent from many parts of Scotland. The lack of magpies in Scotland may be

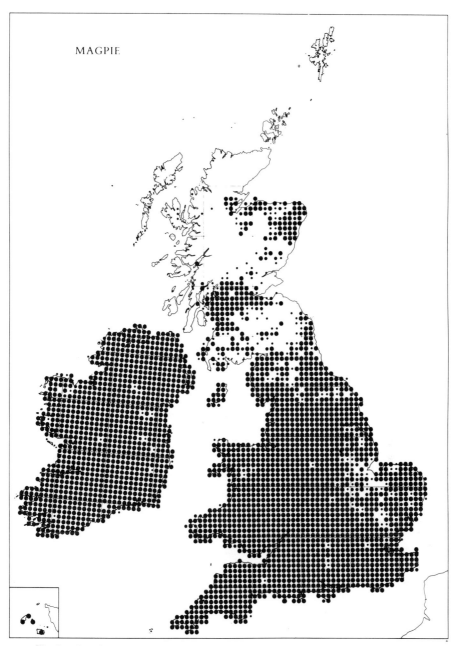

MAGPIE

Fig. 3. *Distribution of the magpie in Britain and Ireland in the years 1968 to 1972, based on 10 × 10 km squares. Large circles: confirmed breeding; medium circles: probable breeding; small circles: possible breeding. From Sharrock (1976).*

partly due to there being less suitable habitat, but also to intensive persecution by gamekeepers during the last century. Over much of Britain magpie numbers have increased dramatically since the 1960s (see Chapter 6). The exception is eastern England, where numbers had been kept low by game-keepers, but were further reduced during the 1950s and 1960s by changes in agricultural practices, including the use of pesticides, the loss of hedgerows and the widespread loss of grassland resulting from an increase in arable farming. A decrease in grassland which magpies rely on for foraging (see Chapter 10), and the loss of suitable nesting trees inevitably led to a massive reduction in magpie numbers in that region (Cooke 1979).

RACES OF MAGPIES

Thirteen races or subspecies of the Black-billed Magpie are recognized by Vaurie (1959), and their ranges are shown in Fig. 1. The North American Black-billed Magpie *Pica p. hudsonia* has a range which is isolated from all others. The same is true of the Arabian Magpie *P. p. asirensis*, *P. p. mauritanica* of north-west Africa, and *P. p. camtschatica* of the Sea of Okhotsk region. The various subspecies differ from each other in a number of ways, including body size, the relative size of their wings, tail and bill, and the relative amounts of black and white in the plumage. Within Europe and North Africa there is a trend for magpies to increase in size, and to have more white on their wing and rump, as one goes from the southern to the northern parts of their range. There is also a trend as one moves from Europe eastwards across Asia for magpies to have much more white on the wing, longer wings, and a greener gloss on the black feathers. Descriptions of the different races can be found in Stegmann (1927), Linsdale (1937), Vaurie (1959) and Goodwin (1986). My own measurements and descriptions of all races, based on material in the British Museum, are presented in Appendix 1.

The north–south trend in magpie size within Europe suggests that like many other bird species, body size is correlated with temperature, being larger in cooler areas. I checked for this kind of effect using data on wing lengths from the British Museum for all 13 races of *P. pica* and the Yellow-billed Magpie. Although there was a negative correlation in the expected direction between wing length and July temperature (mean daily maxima) it was not significant ($r = -0.480$, 12 d.f., $p < 0.1$, > 0.05). The correlation between wing length and winter temperature was even weaker, so some factor(s) other than temperature must help to explain the variation in magpie body size.

Unfortunately there has been no recent study of the taxonomic status of the different races based on morphological features, appearance, or biochemistry. Nor have there been many studies of the ecology or social behaviour of Asian magpies. As will become apparent later in the book, ecological conditions play a central role in determining the social aspects of any species' lives. Some of the Asian races of magpies live in ecologically severe climates and would be

Breeding habitat of Pica pica asirensis *in the Asir Mountains, Saudi Arabia. (Photo: M. Jennings, left). Nest of Arabian magpie. (Photo: J. Gasperetti, right).*

particularly interesting in this respect. For example *bottanensis*, which lives high up in the Himalayas in Tibet, and the Arabian race *asirensis*, occupying the mountainous regions of Saudi Arabia, are just waiting to be studied!

Relatively little is known about Eurasian magpies outside western Europe (but see Eigelis 1964; Kekilova 1978; Doo-Pyo and Koo 1986), and all the Asian races would repay further study. In this book I will, through necessity, concentrate on the North American and European races of the Black-billed Magpie and on the Yellow-billed Magpie. European and North American Black-billed Magpies differ morphologically in several respects: notably in body size (see Appendices 1–4) and iris colour. The Old World Magpies have uniformly dark brown irides, whereas the relatively small American race *hudsonia* has a brown iris with a white outer ring. On the basis of this feature and the difference in voice between the two forms, Brooks (1931) felt that they should be considered separate species. This is discussed further in Chapter 12.

MORPHOMETRICS: SEX AND AGE DIFFERENCES IN BODY SIZE

There are no differences in the plumage of the two sexes: male and female magpies of both species are virtually identical in appearance. However, in all populations that have been examined males are larger than females. Most of the information which is available is for European and North American birds; few data exist for magpies in other areas (see Linsdale 1937). The most frequently taken measurements are body weight, wing length (chord), maximum tail length, bill length and depth; and for these, females are about 10% smaller than males (Fig. 4). In all studies the differences in body weight and linear measurements between the sexes were statistically significant (Appendix 2). However, as Fig. 4 shows, some overlap in measurements exists between the sexes, so no single measurement can be used to sex magpies. However, by taking several measurements in combination, using a procedure dauntingly referred to as discriminant function analysis (DFA), it is possible to determine the sex of a magpie much more accurately. The simplest form of DFA uses two characters, such as body weight and wing length. These are plotted against each other and a line calculated which best separates the two sexes. This technique has been used successfully for both Black-billed and Yellow-billed Magpies (Fig. 4). Mark Reynolds was able accurately to determine the sex of 96% of the Yellow-billed Magpies he caught in this way, and Scharf (1987) had a similar success for Black-billed Magpies in Edmonton, Canada. In the studies of Kavanagh (1986, 1988) and Reese and Kadlec (1982) the differences between the sexes were slightly less marked, but by using five different measurements 93% and 89% respectively of all adult birds could be sexed correctly.

The Yellow-billed Magpie is about 10% smaller than the smallest populations of North American Black-billed Magpie. The sexes also differ in body size: Linsdale (1937) gives the mean weight of males as 175 g ± 9.1 ($N = 17$) and females as 146.1 g ± 12.1 ($N = 15$). In his study of Yellow-billed Magpies

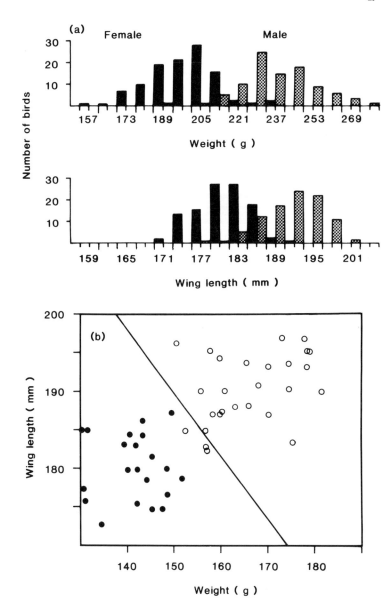

Fig. 4. *(a) Frequency distribution of body weight (upper) and wing length (lower), in male (shaded) and female (black) magpies from Ireland. Males are larger than females on average, but there is some overlap between the sexes in both measurements. From Kavanagh (1986). (b) Using weight and wing length to separate male and female magpies. The data here are for Yellow-billed Magpies (M. D. Reynolds, unpublished). Males tend to be heavier and have longer wings, and the line is the discriminant function that best separates the two groups (equation: wing length = (36.2112 − 0.09466 × weight)/ 0.1156). The discriminant score (DS) can also be used to distinguish the sexes (DS = 0.09466 × weight + 0.1156 × wing length): if it is positive the bird is likely to be a male, if the score is negative or zero it is a female.*

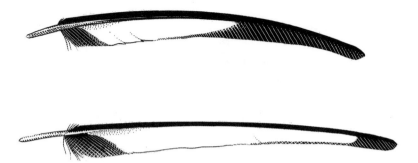

Fig. 5.   *Outermost primaries from magpies from the Sheffield area, to show the difference in the amount of black on first-year (upper) and adult birds (lower).*

Nico Verbeek (1973) found no overlap in the weights of male and female: the lightest male weighed 165 g and the heaviest female 158 g (see also Fig. 4). Despite this, Yellow-billed Magpies are no more sexually dimorphic than some populations of magpies elsewhere (see Appendix 3).

If a mated pair of magpies is seen side by side, the size difference between the sexes is almost always apparent. When I was catching adult magpies to colour-mark them, I tried to predict their sex by eye, by comparing their size with that of their partner. On checking which bird incubated (only the female incubates), I found that my visual size assessment could always separate the sexes accurately. There are also differences in the behaviour of the two sexes, including their position during courtship and copulation, and begging by females (Baeyens 1979). However, if these were the only differences, field workers might have to wait a long time to sex their birds.

It is possible to distinguish first-year from older magpies from the shape and appearance of the first (outermost) primary (Linsdale 1937; Erpino 1968a). The sickle-shaped first primary is unique to magpies (*Pica*), and in adults has a relatively small black tip, whereas in first-year birds this feather is less curved and has much more black on the tip (Fig. 5; see also Appendix 1). Young magpies do not moult their wing and tail feathers until the summer after they are hatched, so the amount of black on the first primary separates birds in their first calendar year from older ones. In addition, the feathers of first-year birds are usually more abraded, less glossy and slightly more brownish in colour than those of adults. One consequence of the difference in abrasion is that first-year birds usually have rounded tips to their outermost tail feathers, whereas in adults these are always square.

First-year magpies also differ from older birds by being about 5–10% lighter in weight, and having a shorter tail (by about 10%). For a sample of Irish birds the size differences between these two age categories, treating each sex separately, were all statistically significant (Kavanagh 1986). In contrast, a sample of North American magpies showed very few significant differences between age classes (Scharf 1987). However, for both samples the greatest difference was in tail length (Appendix 3).

Plumage differences in first-year (left) and older (right) Black-billed Magpies. The amount of black on the primary and secondary feathers of first-year birds is clearly much greater than in the older bird. (Photo: D. Hollingworth).

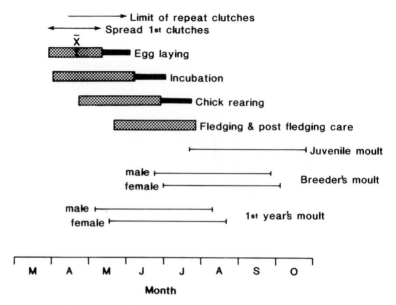

Fig. 6.   *Annual breeding and moult cycle of magpies near Sheffield.*

Chuck Trost and Cheryl Webb (personal communication) noticed a number of other differences between young and old North American Black-billed Magpies. First-year birds have pink mouths (dark in older birds), a grey iris (dark brown in older birds), a white tip to their bill (dark in older birds), and a dark nictitating membrane, without an orange spot (see below). Interestingly, they found that adult birds reverted to this juvenile plumage during the autumn when they were moulting – the possible reasons for this are discussed later (Chapter 12).

PLUMAGE AND MOULT

The magpie's striking black and white plumage hardly requires a detailed description. The black feathers of both species usually have a high gloss, appearing blue, purple, bronze, or green in different lighting conditions. For further information see Appendix 1, Linsdale (1937) and Goodwin (1986). In juvenile Eurasian and North American magpies there is often a bare patch of bluish-grey skin behind the eye (see Chapter 12). In the North African race *mauritanica* this patch is present in adult birds and is a bright cobalt blue. Its function is unknown. A smaller patch of skin in the same area is yellow in the Yellow-billed Magpie, along with the beak and, according to Linsdale (1946), the claws and soles of the feet. However, I never saw either of the two latter features in my examination of birds during the breeding season: the claws and

*Head of a North American Black-billed Magpie showing the nictitating membrane drawn across the eye.
(Photo: C. Trost).*

soles were black. In adults of both species the nictitating membrane is white and bears a small, bright orange spot. Exposure of this membrane is used in courtship and aggressive displays, but its precise function is unknown (Gwinner 1966).

The sequence of moults in North American and European Magpies is apparently identical (Linsdale 1937). As in almost all corvids, adult magpies undergo a single, annual moult after breeding, and within a few weeks of fledging young birds undergo an incomplete post-juvenile moult (see Fig. 6). This involves the replacement of the entire body plumage, but not the wing and tail feathers, which are replaced only when the birds are about 12 months old. The first full moult at the end of their first year usually starts about one month before that of older birds (Holyoak 1974a). In both first-year and older birds the replacement of the primaries takes about 95 days to complete. The body feathers are also replaced over this period, but mainly during the middle three or four weeks. Holyoak (1974a) has pointed out that magpies start their moult rather later than most other British corvids and suggests that this is due to the relatively long period (four to six weeks) of care they provide for their young after fledging. In Britain the annual moult of adult birds starts towards the end of June and is completed sometime in September, with females moulting about a week later than males (Seel 1976). Since moulting birds sometimes have a conspicuous lack of feathers on the head, the difference in the timing of moult between the sexes was often apparent among my colour-marked birds.

Albino North American Black-billed Magpie (courtesy of Cheryl Webb and Chuck Trost: Photo: T. R. Birkhead).

The pattern of moult and sequence of plumages in the Yellow-billed Magpie is similar to that for the Black-billed Magpie (Verbeek 1973). Moult starts towards the end of the nestling period in late May, continues through the period of post-fledging care and is completed by late September or October. From start to finish the moult of an individual bird lasts about 4.5 months. Juveniles start their body moult in early August but, because they do not moult their wing or tail feathers, can complete it within 3.5 months, by October.

Black-billed Magpies with abnormally coloured plumage have been recorded quite frequently in both North America and Europe. These include uniformly white, fawn and grey birds, but the most common colour aberrations involve birds in which the areas which are usually black are grey or brown (Linsdale 1937; Vader *et al.* 1979).

STUDIES OF MAGPIES

This book is based to a large extent on relatively recent studies made of Black-billed and Yellow-billed Magpies in North America, and magpies in Europe. Those studies made over a number of years and involving individually marked birds have yielded the most detailed information on breeding biology and social behaviour. A list of the main studies and the type of information they have provided is presented in Table 1 and their locations are

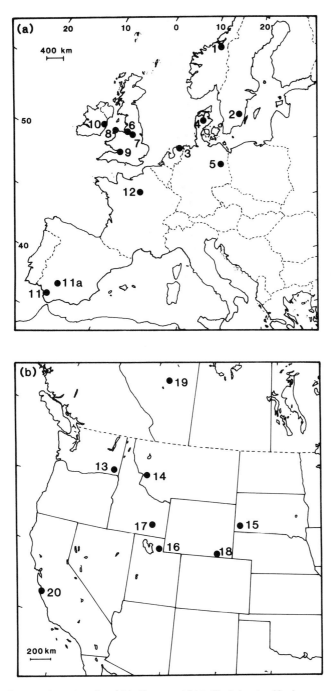

Fig. 7. *Location of magpie studies: (a) in Europe, and (b) in North America. Numbers correspond to those in Table 1.*

TABLE 1: *The main studies of magpies in Europe and North America*

Species	Number	Location	Number of years	Colour rings	Main type of information	Workers
Black-billed Magpie	1	Norway, Trondheim	—	—	Breeding biology Egg size; brood reduction	T. Slagsvold, M. Husby
	2	Sweden, Revinge	11+	+	Breeding biology Interspecific competition Territory quality	G. Högstedt
	3	Netherlands, Groningen	5	+	Breeding biology Social behaviour	G. Baeyens
	4	Denmark, Jutland	12	some	Habitats, territory quality Roosting	A. P. Møller
	5	Poland, Zielona Gora	Several	—	Habitat, breeding biology	L. Jerzak
	6	UK, Manchester	3	—	Urban breeding ecology Growth, diet	P. Tatner
	7	UK, Sheffield	10	+	Social behaviour Breeding biology Survival rates Food hoarding	This study: T. R. Birkhead K. Clarkson, S. F. Eden S. F. Goodburn
	8	UK, Anglesey	3	—	Breeding biology	D. Seel
	9	UK, Bristol	2	—	Social behaviour	G. Vines
	10	Ireland, Dublin	3	—	Breeding biology Population biology	B. Kavanagh

11	Spain, Coto Doñana	Several	—	Brood parasitism	F. A. Alvarez, L. Arias de Reyna
11a	Spain, Cordoba	4	—	Breeding biology Chick development	T. Redondo, L. Arias de Reyna, J. Carranza
12	France, Samois	2	—	Habitat, diet, breeding biology	G. Balança
13	USA, Washington State	2	—	Energetics	J. N. Mugaas, J. R. King
14	USA, Montana	2	some	Breeding biology	R. L. Brown
15	USA, South Dakota	4	+	Breeding biology Parental care Food hoarding	D. Buitron
16	USA, Utah	2	—	Breeding biology	K. P. Reese, J. A. Kadlec
17	USA, Idaho	10	—	Breeding biology	C. Trost, C. Webb
18	USA, Wyoming	2	—	Breeding biology Reproductive physiology	M. Erpino
19	Canada, Alberta	4+	—	Breeding biology Captive birds: dominance Pair formation, nest placement, mate choice	D. A. Boag, W. Hochachka, P. Komers, M. Dhindsa
Yellow-billed Magpie					
20	USA, California Hastings Reservation	8+	+	Breeding biology Social behaviour	J. Linsdale, N. Verbeek, W. D. Koenig, M. D. Reynolds

Notes: Numbers in left-hand column refer to locations in Fig. 7. In the colour-rings column, + indicates colour-marked birds were used in the study, dash (—) indicates no colour-marked birds.

The Rivelin Valley study area on the outskirts of Sheffield looking north, showing the wooded valley bottom, and in the far distance the virtually treeless tops. (Photo: D. Hollingworth).

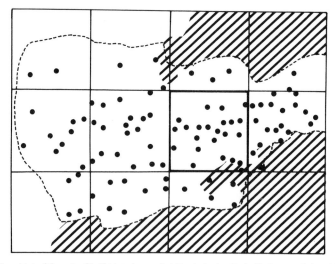

Fig. 8.   *Map of the entire Sheffield study area (within the broken line). Each square is 1 × 1 km, and the bold square is the main part of the study area. Black dots show the position of all (first) nests in 1981 to show the variation in breeding density. The hatched region represents built-up areas. From Birkhead et al. (1986).*

shown in Fig. 7. For those interested in earlier published work on both species of magpie, Linsdale's (1937) book provides a wonderfully comprehensive account.

The aim of this section is to provide a feel for the methods which I and my research students used during our study of magpies. The study started in the spring of 1977 and continued through the hard work of three research students, Keith Clarkson, Simon Eden and Sandy Goodburn, until the end of the 1986 breeding season. Because the study was very much a joint venture, I refer to it as 'our' study. We worked in the Rivelin Valley, on the eastern side of Sheffield, which is known to have supported a high density of magpies at least since about 1890 (Dixon 1900). The area consists of farmland devoted to grazing cattle and horses. The fields are relatively small and separated by drystone walls, typical of northern England. The valley bottom contains a small stream along the length of which is an area of mixed woodland. Throughout the area there are other small patches of woodland as well as numerous isolated bushes and trees. The altitudinal range of the study area is from 110 m in the valley bottom to 300 m on the top. The main part of the study area was 1 square kilometre in area, but we also searched for nests and colour-marked birds in surrounding areas (Fig. 8).

In order to examine the magpie's social behaviour it was essential to have individually recognizable birds. When the study started I attempted to catch adults with large baited crow traps, but without success. Magpies were extremely wary about any kind of trap, and even during hard winters they never entered traps to obtain food. This situation contrasts markedly with North American Black-billed Magpies, which are much more amenable to trapping. Robert Brown (1957), for example, in his two-year study trapped no fewer than 540 magpies using baited traps. Having abandoned this trapping method I started to use the same technique that Gert Baeyens developed in her study (described subsequently by Scharf 1985). This involved presenting territorial birds with a decoy magpie in a small cage surrounded by monofilament nooses. The territory owners responded by attempting to attack or court the caged decoy, and in the process got their feet caught in the nooses. When this happened I sprinted towards the bird to grab it before it extricated itself. The 'sprint' was an essential, if somewhat undignified part of the procedure, since if left to its own devices a magpie could often remove the nooses from its feet within a few seconds. On some occasions this technique worked extremely well and I caught both members of a pair simultaneously. Unfortunately, this happened all too rarely; at other times the birds would either fail to see the decoy, or would call to it from a safe distance, or even worse, the wild magpies would attack the decoy without getting caught. The quality of the decoy made a large difference too; the most effective bird I had was a wild-caught female given to me by Gert Baeyens. This bird called noisily as soon as I placed her in

Eric Stone and Chuck Trost's Black-billed Magpie study area south of Pocatello, Idaho. (Photo: T. R. Birkhead).

Magpie breeding habitat Coto Doñana, southern Spain. (Photo: F. Alvarez).

the decoy cage, attracting the wild birds. As a female she had the advantage of attracting both sexes: wild females approached in order to attack, but interestingly, a male's behaviour differed according to the location of his mate. If the male was alone, he would approach the decoy and court her, but if while doing this his partner started to approach, his behaviour would switch instantly to aggression . . . Scientists are not supposed to be anthropomorphic, but the human analogy is obvious. Other decoys which I used included hand-reared males and females and none of these was very effective. I estimated that I caught one bird for every ten hours of trapping using this technique. Moreover since the decoy could not be left unattended, it was not very efficient! Consequently, we more or less stopped trapping in this way but relied on colour-marking every nestling in and around the study area. This involved a large number of colour-ring combinations, but it worked well, mainly because young Magpies in our study area dispersed very little.

All birds were given metal, numbered British Trust for Ornithology rings. In addition, nestling magpies were given a unique combination of three Darvic colour rings: a total of 854 chicks were ringed during the study. The relatively small number (37) of full-grown birds we caught was marked with colour rings and sometimes patagial wing tags. Wing tags were ideal for identifying birds at a distance (we could read tags up to 1 km away through a telescope), but they did not last as long as colour rings and we gave up using them after a few years. We rarely had trouble reading colour rings, mainly because the grass in the whole area was kept quite short by livestock, and the birds were relatively tame and allowed us to approach to within 10 metres or less in a car. Magpies have remarkably strong beaks and to minimize the chance of them removing colour rings we always sealed them with glue: very few colour rings were ever lost even after six or more years of wear. Overall, from about 1980 we had 60–70% of the population colour-marked and were able to follow the fortunes of many birds throughout their entire lives.

The magpie's annual cycle (Fig. 6) determined our seasonal pattern of fieldwork, most of which was conducted between October and June. During this period the central square of the study area was visited every second day on average. Our routine was to make use of the numerous roads and tracks to slowly drive through and scan the entire study area looking for magpies. The position of colour-marked birds was recorded on large-scale maps of the area, and at regular intervals these results were used to determine the location and size of territories and home ranges (see Chapter 2). Fifty sightings of each marked bird were needed to determine accurately its territory boundaries, using the maximum polygon method (Odum & Kuenzler 1955). We made few observations between July and September mainly because the birds, which were moulting during these months, spent much of their time sitting quietly in dense vegetation and were difficult to see. Throughout the winter we created small feeding stations at various locations, providing soaked wheat grain to attract the birds. This allowed us to conduct a roll-call of the non-breeding birds. We also used feeding stations to examine the magpie's food-hoarding behaviour.

During the breeding season we located every nest in the main part of the study area, and as many nests as possible in the surrounding area. Nests were found before egg laying started by simply looking for birds carrying nest material. In the early part of the season, before the trees came into leaf, this was relatively easy, but later we had to check trees and bushes individually for nests. Magpies in our study area nested either in dense hawthorn bushes less than 5 metres above the ground, or in the tops of large trees like beeches or oaks, 25 metres or more above the ground. Checking nests in these types of situation required different tactics, but both were particularly hard on trousers: my research students always said that tree-climbing claimed three or four pairs of trousers each season. ·Hawthorns required a thick coat and stout footwear, whereas tall trees required trainers and rock-climbing equipment. At the outset I climbed trees without ropes or any other aids, but soon realized the stupidity of this. Several rock-climbers made suggestions about the equipment and techniques we could use to climb trees, but all were rather reluctant to demonstrate these themselves. We ended up using a helmet, harness, caving rope, slings and ascenders, making sure we were attached to the tree at all times. With these items, experience, and sometimes a lot of nerve, there was no nest in the study area we couldn't reach. However, gaining access to the nest was only part of the operation; once there we had to count, weigh and measure the eggs or chicks. Even just getting the eggs or chicks out of a nest at the top of a tall tree with a stiff breeze blowing could induce horrible knee tremors (accurately referred to as 'sewing-machine leg' by Mark Reynolds). In these conditions it was usually necessary to bring the nest contents to the bottom of the tree to make measurements, although we avoided this

wherever possible since it disturbed the birds more and doubled the amount of climbing to be done. This was a serious consideration since with over one hundred nests to check, there were sometimes 20 to 30 tall trees to be climbed each day. One of the worst aspects of tree-climbing was having an audience: several nests were located in the grounds of a small, rural hospital and on warm spring days the patients were sometimes wheeled outside in their beds to watch us climb. We could sometimes overhear them asking each other if they thought we would fall . . . with the usual jokes about our being in the right place if we did.

We kept our nest checks to a minimum to reduce disturbance, and on average each nest was checked four times: twice during laying, once at the time of hatching, and a final visit to ring and weigh the chicks 14 days after hatching.

A NOTE ON STATISTICS

I have tried throughout the text to keep the use of statistics to a minimum and I hope the text is readable despite their occasional inclusion. Statistics are used primarily in conjunction with results not published elsewhere. Means are presented ± one standard deviation (SD).

SUMMARY

The derivation and history of the magpie's name is described. There are two closely related species: the Black-billed Magpie and the Yellow-billed Magpie. The former has a wide geographic range across much of the Northern Hemisphere. The Yellow-billed Magpie is confined to California. Thirteen races of Black-billed Magpie are currently recognized, some being better differentiated than others. Sex and age differences in body measurements are described: in both species males are larger than females. Among European populations first-year birds are smaller than adults. The sequence of moult and the annual cycle are described. All recent major field studies of magpies are tabulated. The various trapping, marking and observation techniques used in studying magpies are presented.

CHAPTER 2

Nest spacing and territorial behaviour

*The Rivelin Valley . . . Nowhere else in our experience were the magpies
allowed to live in such peace as they enjoyed in this romantic valley.*
Charles Dixon (1900)

A major feature of any species' social organization is the way in which
individuals space themselves out within their habitat. Some birds, like the
Common Guillemot or Murre are highly social and breed colonially at very
high densities. Others, like many North American and European warblers,
live as solitary pairs in relatively large territories. One of the most interesting
aspects of magpie social organization is the remarkable variability in their
nest-spacing patterns.

Both magpie species defend a territory in which to breed, but the nature of
the territory differs markedly between populations, and even within populations. At one extreme magpies in northern Europe usually defend a relatively
large, all-purpose territory in which they nest, feed and spend most of their
time. As a consequence nests are regularly spaced out within the breeding

habitat. In contrast, Black-billed Magpies in North America show either no territorial behaviour, or defend only a small area around the nest. The distance between adjacent nests may be much less than for European magpies, and in some areas the birds appear to breed colonially as does the Yellow-billed Magpie.

I will discuss these three situations separately, starting with magpies in Europe. Several studies have shown that territories average about 5 hectares in extent and the boundaries of adjacent territories are often contiguous (Fig. 9a). In our study area territories were 4.9 ha (Fig. 10), while in Baeyens's (1979, 1981a) area they averaged 5.8 ha and in Vines's (1981) study area they were about 6 ha. The similarity in the size of area defended may seem remarkable considering that the overall population density in these studies varied by a factor of seven. However, this effect occurs because of the existence of unoccupied areas in Baeyens's and Vines's studies, which simply did not occur in the main part of our study area (Fig. 9b).

The spacing of territories within our study area varied dramatically. In the central part of the area the density was as high as 32 pairs/km^2 (Fig. 10), but

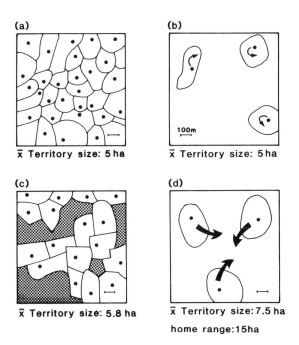

Fig. 9. *Different patterns of territoriality and nest spacing in European magpies. Filled circles = nest location. (a) Central square of the Sheffield study area: high density, contiguous boundaries, no unoccupied space. (b) High-altitude part of the Sheffield study area: low density, isolated territories. Lines represent edges of magpies' home ranges: no territorial interactions were seen between neighbours. (c) Baeyens's study area in the Netherlands; note the unoccupied space (no man's land: shaded). (d) Fochteloo, Netherlands: low breeding density but birds had large territories (7.5 ha) and fed outside their territories (indicated by arrows) in 15 ha home ranges (from Baeyens 1981a). Scale bar = 100 m.*

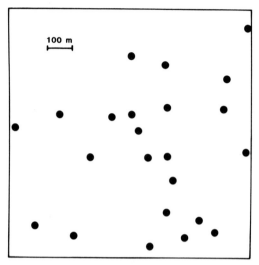

Fig. 10.   *Central square kilometre of the Sheffield study area showing the regular spacing of nests (filled circles) in one year: 1985.*

on higher ground on the valley tops, just 0.5 km away, a different system prevailed. Here there were relatively few trees and magpie numbers may have been kept low because nest sites were limiting. While the magpies occupied areas of similar size to those in the valley bottom, adjacent territories on this high ground were separated by wide tracts of unoccupied land (Fig. 9). As a result the rate of territorial interactions between pairs was extremely low. The difference between these two areas so close together was striking, and had we concentrated on only one of them we would have ended up with an unbalanced view of the magpie's territorial system. A similar difference in territorial systems was recorded by Baeyens (1981a) in the Netherlands. In her study area at Haren most territories had boundaries that abutted, but there were also some areas without breeding magpies, which Baeyens referred to as 'no-man's land'. In a nearby area, Fochteloo, which consisted of wide open meadows, the density of breeding magpies was relatively low and territories were well separated (Fig. 9d).

In other areas where nest sites are clumped magpies sometimes give the impression of breeding colonially. Under these circumstances the birds defend relatively small territories. Deckert (1968) for example, in Germany recorded a mean territory size of 3.25 ha, approximately half that in Haren or Fochteloo. But the birds left their territories in order to feed. Aggregated nest distributions also occur among magpies in the Camargue in southern France (R. Britton, pers. comm.), and in southern Spain (Alvarez & Arias de Reyna 1974; Arias de Reyna *et al.* 1984). In North Africa, magpies are said to breed colonially by a number of authors (Jourdain 1915; Heim de Balsac 1926; Valverde 1957; Etchecopar & Hue 1967). In the spring of 1990 David Gosney went to check whether this was true, and found no evidence for coloniality; nests were well spaced out (average nearest neighbour distance: 264 m).

Aerial view of the Rivelin Valley study area, looking west. Note the wooded valley bottom, with the road running alongside it, and the low density of trees on the north (right-hand) side of the valley.

Magpie breeding habitat near Taroudant, Morocco. (Photo: D. Gosney).

Deborah Buitron's magpie study area in South Dakota, USA. (Photo: D. Buitron).

Aerial view of Chuck Trost's study area, Pocatello, Idaho, USA. Note the restriction of breeding habitat (mainly Russian olives) to the banks of the Portneuf River. (Photo: C. Trost).

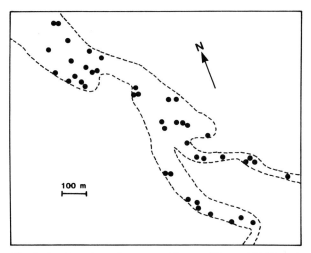

Fig. 11.   *Distribution of magpie nests in one square kilometre of Trost and Webb's study area in Idaho, USA. The dotted line indicates the boundary of suitable nesting habitat. Considering the entire square, nests are aggregated; considering only the suitable breeding habitat, they are regularly spaced (see text). From C. Trost & C. Webb, pers. comm.*

However, he did find that magpies were very patchily distributed. It therefore seems likely that the term 'coloniality' used by previous authors simply refers to this irregular distribution.

The territorial system among magpies in North America seems to be different from that in central and northern Europe. Erpino (1968b) found that magpies in Wyoming showed very little territorial behaviour. Brown (1957) found that the magpies in his study area in Montana were definitely territorial and kept other magpies from the vicinity of the nest. More detailed observations by Buitron (1988) in South Dakota confirmed that magpies there defended an area within about 30 m of the nest, although they did not confine their activities to this area. In their study of magpies in Utah Reese and Kadlec (1985) found that the average inter-nest distance was just 80 m, and the birds defended areas of about 0.5 ha around the nest. As in Buitron's study the territory was rarely used for foraging. In addition, despite the proximity of adjacent nests, territorial interactions were infrequent, just 0.1 per hour, about ten times less frequent than in our study (see below).

The highest breeding density of magpies recorded, occurs in Idaho, where Chuck Trost and Cheryl Webb (pers. comm.) found densities of up to 200 pairs per square kilometre! This figure must be interpreted with caution since the density is calculated from the number of nests found within areas of suitable habitat. None the less, the density is high, with an average nearest-neighbour distance of just 55 m (Fig. 11). Chuck Trost and Cheryl Webb (pers. comm.) considered the Black-billed Magpies in their study area to be as colonial as Yellow-billed Magpies (see below). Indeed, following Keith Clarkson's and my visit to Idaho, one of Chuck's graduate students, Eric

Stone, examined the magpies' spacing system in detail, and found that it was remarkably like that of the Yellow-billed Magpie (E. Stone, pers. comm.).

These studies suggest a marked difference between most northern European magpie populations and those of North America in terms of nest spacing and territoriality. Only in some southern parts of their range do European magpies nest in such close proximity as North American magpies. European magpies also appear to be remarkably flexible in their use of space, and birds in nearby areas can have territorial systems which are quite different. These differences appear to be dictated by ecological conditions, such as the availability of nest sites and feeding areas.

It is possible to determine statistically whether nests are aggregated, spaced randomly or evenly (Clark & Evans 1954) and I have done this for a number of European and North American magpie populations. The results (Table 2) indicate that in North America magpies' nests tend to be spatially aggregated, while in Europe nests are more evenly distributed. Unfortunately the results are not quite this clear-cut, for several reasons. First, the method used to determine these spacing patterns assumes that the habitat is uniformly suitable for nesting. Obviously this is not true; with a few exceptions, where there are no trees, there can be no magpie nests. In most cases I did not have information on the distribution of nesting habitat, and even if I had, it would still have been difficult in some instances to decide how to treat the data. Our study area is a good example of this since it is a complex mosaic of feeding and nesting areas. On the other hand, in Trost and Webb's study area in southern Idaho (Fig. 11) it is quite clear that nesting habitat is restricted to the area along the river. The density of birds calculated for the whole area is considerably less (35 pairs/km^2) than if one uses only the nesting habitat (109 pairs/km^2). In addition, if the entire area is used in calculating the spacing pattern, as in Table 2, this indicates that nests are highly aggregated ($R = 0.65$). If, however, only the nesting habitat is considered, nests are evenly spaced ($R = 1.22$). Reese and Kadlec (1985 and pers. comm.) indicate that a similar situation occurred in their two study areas. If Trost and Webb's study area is typical of magpie habitat in North America and nesting habitat is clumped, this could explain the tendency for nests to appear aggregated and the different spacing system from European birds.

On the other hand, several other aspects of the territorial behaviour of magpies in North America suggest that the differences might be due to more than habitat differences. For example, the fact that North American magpies do not defend exclusive territories during the breeding season, but have overlapping home ranges and use communal areas for feeding. In addition, the seasonal pattern of territoriality differs between European and North American magpies. In our study area most territories were occupied throughout the year although they were actively defended mainly during the breeding season. Similarly many birds in Baeyens's study remained on their territories continuously. In contrast, all studies of North American Black-billed Magpies have reported that territories are abandoned after breeding (Mugaas and King 1981; Buitron 1988). Presumably the low winter temperatures (see Chapter 1)

Yellow-billed Magpie breeding habitat near Hastings Reservation, Carmel Valley, California. (Photo: T. R. Birkhead).

over much of the Black-bill's range are such that remaining on the territory is not a viable option and the birds have to forage more widely to find sufficient food.

The milder winter conditions which Yellow-billed Magpies experience probably allows them to remain on or near their territories throughout the year. Verbeek (1973) has described the seasonal pattern of territorial defence in this species. At the end of the breeding season the territory is smallest and defence is weak and limited to the nest tree. In addition, the birds spend relatively little of the day in the territory. However, from September to January the birds spend more time in the territory which also increases in size. By the end of November the next season's territories have been established, and interactions between territorial neighbours are relatively infrequent. Territories were most intensively defended during the breeding season and reached their maximum size at this time (mean: 1.2 ha, range 0.6 to 1.9 ha). This aspect of Yellow-billed Magpie behaviour is discussed further below.

Yellow-billed Magpies are generally considered to be colonial (Table 2). However, they show a complete gradient from colonial breeding (up to 30 pairs) to solitary nesting pairs. Mark Reynolds (1990; pers. comm.) found that at the Hastings Reservation in California the mean nearest-neighbour distance between nests averaged just 38 m (Fig. 12). However, pairs sometimes nested in the same tree and the closest active nests were just 7 m apart. Verbeek noted that four discrete colonies at Hastings were separated by

TABLE 2: *Spacing patterns of magpie nests in Europe and North America*

Location	Mean nearest neighbour distance (m)	SD	Density breeding (pairs/km²)	R[1]	Spacing	Reference
Black-billed Magpie						
UK, Sheffield	111	44.8	26.0	1.13	R	This study[2]
	145	46.6	19.0	1.26	E	
UK, South	222–233	?	3.6	0.87	R	Vines (1981)[3]
Netherlands	264	116.4	7.3	1.42	E	G. Baeyens, pers. comm.
Germany, Berlin	331	121.4	3.4	1.23	E	Witt (1985)[4]
	378	138.8	2.4	1.16	E	
Germany, southwest	839	537.7	0.3	0.93	R	Ellenberg et al. (1984)[7]
Sweden	166	94.0	7.1	0.89	R	G. Högstedt, pers. comm.
Spain, Coto Doñana	126	65.9	10.0	0.79	C	Alvarez & Arias de Reyna (1974)
Morocco	264	32.1	7.0	1.40	E	T.R. Birkhead & D. Gosney, unpublished
USA, Idaho	55	33.9	35.0	0.65	C	C. Trost & C. Webb, pers. comm.[5]
USA, South Dakota	300	?	2.0	0.85	C	D. Buitron (1988; pers. comm.)
USA, Utah	79	91.0	16.1	0.63	C	Reese & Kadlec[4] (1985; pers. comm.)[6]
	109	61.9	10.4	0.70	C	
Yellow-billed Magpie						
USA, Hastings	38	21.3	46.0	0.51	C	M. D. Reynolds (1990; pers. comm.)

Notes: (1) *R* is calculated from Clark and Evans (1954): 1 = random (R), <1 = clumped (C) and >1 = even (E). Spacing: C or E indicates that the value of *R* differs significantly from random.
(2) The two values are for the range of densities in our study: in 5 out of the 6 years spacing was E.
(3) Vines (1981) used another method and found spacing to be E, but this was due to an arithmetic error.
(4) Two separate areas.
(5) But see text.
(6) These authors say nests were 'evenly distributed', presumably they meant within nesting habitat (see text).
(7) Nest distribution strongly affected by active Goshawk nests.

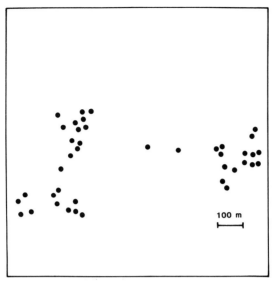

Fig. 12. *Aggregated distribution of Yellow-billed Magpie nests in one square kilometre on and adjacent to the Hastings Reservation, California. From M. D. Reynolds & W. D. Koenig, pers. comm.*

distances of 757 to 1515 metres. Most feeding takes place outside the territory, sometimes up to 3.5 km from the colony, and most colony members forage together. To determine just how large an area they used Mark Reynolds (pers. comm.) radio-tracked Yellow-bills throughout the year. He found that during the breeding season adult birds spent 95% of their time within a 22-hectare area.

The differences in the pattern of nest spacing between Yellow-billed and Black-billed Magpies can be seen by comparing Figs 10–12. It is interesting to note that the variation in different populations of Black-billed Magpies appears to be due to the spatial distribution of nesting habitat, so that in areas where trees are clumped, nests are also aggregated. For the Yellow-billed Magpie however this is not the case. Instead, breeding in colonies, albeit small ones, has arisen either in response to the risk of nest predation by snakes (Chapter 7), or because of the spatial distribution of the food supply. Verbeek (1973) argued that this species' insect food (see Chapter 5) is patchily distributed, in both space and time, so that from one week to the next the birds cannot predict where they will be able to find food. This is why so much of their feeding occurs outside the territory, and why colony members feed together in a flock. Once a patch of food, such as an outbreak of caterpillars or grasshoppers, has been located there is sufficient for a number of birds. With such a clumped and shifting food supply the best option is to breed together in the centre of all potential food patches (Horn 1968). Following on from Verbeek's study, Mark Reynolds (1990) has tested this idea, with clear results: Yellow-billed Magpies breed colonially because this minimizes the average distance that birds have to travel in order to forage.

TABLE 3: *Summary of differences in territorial behaviour of magpies in good and poor quality territories near Sheffield (percentages)*

Measure	Good quality territory	Poor quality territory
Time spent in territorial activity[1]	7.0	4.7
Time spent tree-topping	3	2
Territorial incidents/hour[2]	1.9	0.9
Types of incident:[3]		
Fly-in	21	3
Boundary	57	85
Forage-in	22	12
Response to intruders[4]		
Approach: Fly-in intruder	80	
Boundary intruder	74	
Forage-in intruder	33	
Chase: Fly-in intruder	50	
Boundary intruder	21	
Forage-in intruder	0	

Notes: (1) Difference is significant ($\chi^2 = 3.94$, 1 d.f., $p < 0.05$). (2) $p < 0.02$. (3) $\chi^2 = 8.8$, 2 d.f., $p < 0.01$. (4) There were no differences between territory types so data have been combined. Percentages refer to the percentage of incidents with a particular response.

TERRITORIAL DEFENCE

Since territoriality is either non-existent or minimal among North American Black-billed Magpies, most of the information on territory defence comes from studies of European birds. In this section most of the quantitative information is derived from 80 hours of observation which I made of six pairs of magpies during the pre-laying period of one season. These pairs occupied three good and three poor-quality territories (see Chapter 10) so that I could compare territorial behaviour between them.

European magpies signal their ownership and defend their territory by means of a number of displays (Chapter 3), and the most important of these are tree-topping and parallel walking along the territory boundary. Overall, magpies spent 6% of their time engaged in territorial behaviour, with a small but significant difference between birds in good and poor territories. This arose because birds in good territories had a significantly higher rate of territorial intrusion than birds in poor territories (Table 3), a result which Møller (1982a) also obtained in his study.

The type of intruder differed between the two types of territory. Birds which flew directly into the territory (fly-in intruders) were significantly more frequent in good territories than in poor, and there were correspondingly fewer boundary incidents among good territory birds than poor ones. Intruders which came into a territory to feed (forage-in intruders) were more frequent in good territories. Since these intruders constituted different types of threat to territory owners it was not surprising to find that owners responded to different types of intruders in different ways. Forage-in intruders were often ignored or undetected (67% of observations), whereas fly-in and boundary intruders were rarely ignored (3%), and almost always evoked some response, such as tree-topping and less frequently, chasing (Table 3).

The most common response to an intruder was tree-topping, and Bahrmann (1956) suggested that this behaviour was a territorial display. I used my data to test this idea. During the pre-laying period birds spent on average 2–3% of their total time tree-topping. Baeyens (1981a) recorded tree-topping throughout the year, although it was less common outside the breeding season. I found that the number of tree-topping incidents per hour was positively correlated with the number of territorial intrusions per hour ($r = 0.632$). However, on looking at this in more detail it was clear that while tree-topping increased with the number of fly-in intrusions ($p < 0.01$) and boundary incidents ($p < 0.02$), it was not related to the number of forage-in intruders. In other words the first two types of incident independently evoked tree-topping from territory owners. Tree-topping occurred both before and after an intrusion. For example, on seeing a boundary intruder the territory owner might tree-top, then approach for a parallel walk or to chase the intruder away, and then return to tree-topping. Before an approach the duration of tree-topping was much shorter (1.3 minutes ± 0.9) than after the incident (7.5 $\pm$ 7.1; $p < 0.02$). The same effect occurred after fly-in intruders, but not forage-in intruders.

Not all tree-topping incidents involved other magpies and on 24% of occasions it appeared to occur spontaneously. Most (74%) tree-topping incidents, however, occurred in response to conspecifics, and a few (2%) occurred when a bird of prey, such as a Sparrowhawk (a potential predator), flew over. Slightly less than half (42%) of all tree-topping incidents were followed by some further action, such as an approach or chasing. Often, though, the bird or birds simply resumed their feeding or other maintenance activities.

Both members of the pair help to defend the territory but as in most territorial species the male magpie plays a slightly more active role. In 80% (63 out of 78) territorial incidents both pair members responded to intruders by approaching them. In 9 instances the male approached the intruder alone and in 6 cases the female did so. In 12 incidents where both members of the pair approached an intruder, the male initiated the approach in 10 cases and the female in 2 ($p < 0.02$). Males also tree-topped more frequently and for longer per bout than females. Baeyens (1979) noted that if one member of a pair tree-topped alone it was most likely to be the male, and when the pair tree-topped together the male was more likely to be higher in the tree than the female. During confrontations with territory neighbours birds of the same sex usually display to each other. In other words males take care of male intruders and females look after female intruders. This was also true when a caged decoy was presented in a pair's territory (Baeyens 1979, 1981a; Birkhead 1979).

Although tree-topping does not, at first sight, look like a territorial display, the evidence shows that it undoubtedly is. Basically it is an effective and economical equivalent to song in other passerines. The display is effective because the magpies' black and white plumage makes them so conspicuous, and tree-topping has the advantage that it allows a magpie both to advertise territory ownership and overlook its own and its neighbour's territories.

Most territorial incidents are resolved peacefully, but if the intruder does not retreat a fight might ensue. Fights usually involve only males. While the females look on, the protagonists grapple with their feet and stab at each other with their beaks. Since I know from painful experience how hard a magpie can peck, birds must inflict considerable damage on each other during serious fights.

Both Yellow-billed Magpies and North American Black-billed Magpies perform the tree-topping display, but it is less clearly associated with territoriality than it is among European birds. Verbeek (1973) states that in Yellow-billed Magpies tree-topping occurs throughout the year. In September, when territories are re-established following a quiet period after breeding, the birds roosted communally away from the colony. On their return in the early morning, all territory owners immediately flew to the top of the tallest tree in their territory and sat there for 30 minutes or so, prior to going off to feed. During encounters with neighbours at a territory boundary Yellow-bills also perform a parallel walk, usually with a tail-up display. This display does not occur in European magpies (and probably not in North American Black-bills either), although it is similar to aggressive tail-flirting. The difference is that instead of merely flicking the tail up for a fraction of a second the Yellow-billed Magpie maintains the tail-up posture for several seconds, and the greater the intensity of the interaction the more nearly vertical the tail is held.

TERRITORY ACQUISITION

The transition from being a member of the non-breeding segment of the population (Chapter 6) to being a territory holder is a crucial one. Indeed, it is one of the most significant phases of any magpie's life since it effectively provides a permit to breed. Having said that, the opportunities for becoming part of the breeding population may be extremely limited and many members of the non-breeding flock simply do not make this step. There were three main ways in our study in which magpies could obtain a territory: by replacing a lost mate, by 'squeezing in' and through the so-called 'ceremonial gatherings' (Birkhead and Clarkson 1985a).

Several early observers of European magpies (e.g. Raspail 1901; Niethammer and Merzinger 1943; Minton 1958; Shannon 1958) noted that when one member of a pair was shot, the dead mate was replaced very rapidly. In virtually all cases replacement occurred within 48 hours and sometimes the same day (Selby 1833; Thompson 1849). Even more remarkably, within a single season as many as six females have been shot in the same territory and replaced each time (MacGillivray 1837; Raspail 1901). Replacement of a dead mate is therefore one way in which a magpie can achieve breeding status.

However, this method is probably more important for females than it is for males, for two reasons: (i) the mortality rate of breeding females is higher than that of males (Chapter 6), and (ii) a breeding male magpie that loses his partner is more likely to retain his territory and re-pair, than a female is. Because male magpies are larger and more aggressive than females they are much more capable of defending a territory alone than females are. In our study we recorded male replacement twice and female replacement eight times. The latter involved birds from the non-breeding flock replacing dead or injured territory owners, but other replacements included female breeders which divorced in order to re-pair. This is demonstrated by the fact that females were three times as likely to breed in more than one territory than were males (males: 5 out of 69 (7.2%), females: 13 out of 61 (21.3%) ($\chi^2 = 5.4$, 1 d.f., $p < 0.025$). Baeyens (1981b) also recorded divorce and territory switching in her magpies. She was able to show that divorce occurred more frequently following a breeding failure, and when birds switched territories they usually moved up-market, into better territories (see Chapter 10). Both these behaviours are adaptive and will increase the likelihood of the divorcee producing offspring. Undoubtedly some of the cases of rapid mate replacement described in the older literature must also include cases where the male was shot (Raspail 1901) and the territory taken over by a new pair.

The second method of territory acquisition, referred to as 'squeezing in', involved just that. As described in Chapter 3 the territorial aggression of breeding magpies declines markedly once incubation had started, and some non-breeders appeared to take advantage of this to establish small territories of their own. Usually these territories were located on the boundaries of two or three existing territories, where aggression from the established birds was least. Initially these 'squeezed in' territories were small, and were established so late in the season that the occupants had little chance of successful breeding. However, these birds were sometimes able to retain and expand their territory, and the following year commence breeding on time. Based on relatively small samples we estimated that about one-third of all territories were established by squeezing in.

The third method of territory establishment is the most interesting and involves noisy, conspicuous gatherings of birds. These 'ceremonial gatherings' were referred to by Darwin (1871), and by virtually every student of European magpies thereafter! Gatherings consist of aggregations of birds, either on the ground or in the tops of trees, calling, displaying and chasing each other in a noisy and extrovert manner. As many as one hundred birds have been recorded in such gatherings, but they usually contain many fewer than this. Brown (1924) described a typical gathering, as follows: 'There were seven magpies in the top branches of a tree, chattering a good deal and pursuing one another about the branches. Now and again a bird would give expression to some musical sounding notes like "Chook, chook"'. Similarly, Stubbs (1910) wrote: 'They [the magpies] were jumping about and parading in a most ludicrous manner. It would be impossible to describe in a few words the actions of these birds, but there was no room for doubt as to the real meaning of

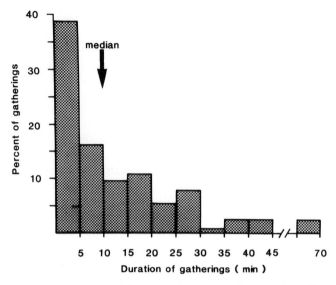

Fig. 13.   *Frequency distribution of the duration of 72 magpie gatherings in the Sheffield study. The arrow indicates the median duration (i.e. 10 minutes). From Birkhead & Clarkson (1985a).*

the function'. In fact the true function of magpie gatherings was not clear for a long time. However, many early writers thought that gatherings were mating ceremonies since they occurred mainly in late winter and spring (e.g. Stubbs 1910; Brown 1924). It was also supposed that if a breeding bird lost its partner a gathering would occur in the territory enabling the bereaved bird to re-mate (Raspail 1901). This idea was tested by Baeyens (1979) who experimentally removed one member of a pair for a few days, but there was no evidence that gatherings occurred any more frequently in these territories than elsewhere.

Later observers suggested that since many of the magpies involved in gatherings appeared to behave aggressively towards each other they might constitute fights for nest sites (Bahrmann 1956). Baeyens (1979) also suggested that gatherings might be associated with the establishment of territories. We looked at gatherings in some detail in our study to test the idea that they were associated with competition for space and the opportunity to breed. As described earlier the population density in our study area was extremely high, territories were tightly packed and there were relatively few territorial vacancies. Under such circumstances we might well expect intense competition for territories (Birkhead & Clarkson 1985a).

We found, as Baeyens (1979) had done, that gatherings were initiated by members of the non-breeding flock. Usually one or two birds started the gathering, but sometimes as many as six individuals seemed to be involved. Their behaviour typically consisted of a high, floating flight as they approached an established territory. They then swooped down into it, where they were met by the territory owners, who attempted to chase them away. The noise and display associated with this aggression soon attracted other

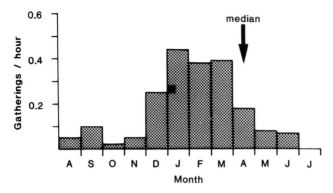

Fig. 14. *Seasonal pattern of occurrence of 255 magpie gatherings in the Sheffield study, based on 1020 hours of observation between 1978 and 1982. The arrow indicates the median laying date for the breeding population: gatherings are most frequent in the three months before this. From Birkhead & Clarkson (1985a).*

magpies, both neighbouring territorial birds and other non-breeders. The response of these other birds was surprisingly rapid and gatherings usually reached their full size within a minute. Although other observers have reported gatherings consisting of one hundred or so birds, we never saw more than 24 individuals involved, despite the high population density. It is possible that early observers sometimes referred to the activity which sometimes happens at pre-roost assemblies (see Chapter 3), as gatherings. The average number of birds we saw in 225 gatherings was 5.1 ± 3.5 (range 3 to 24).

The duration of individual gatherings varied from less than one minute to over an hour. Most lasted five minutes or less and the median duration was ten minutes (Fig. 13). In general the more magpies there were involved, the longer the gathering lasted ($r = 0.360$, 65 d.f., $p < 0.01$). Gatherings were followed by the initiators returning to their normal home range in about half the cases (120 out of 225). In the remaining cases they went on to start another gathering nearby. In 70% of cases there was one further gathering, in 16% two more, and in one instance we saw the same birds start seven successive gatherings.

Gatherings occurred in most months of the year, but as noted by previous workers they were most frequent in late winter and early spring, just before the onset of breeding (Fig. 14). They were also more frequent in the morning than the afternoon, and on bright, cold mornings in late winter one could almost guarantee to see one or more gatherings in our study area. This was especially true on the first bright day following a period of cloudy or wet weather. Magpies always seemed to dislike poor weather and spent a lot of time sitting in trees doing very little. However, as soon as there was a good day they appeared to make up for lost time and were particularly active.

Baeyens (1979) recorded gatherings occurring within territories, occasionally in her unoccupied 'no-man's land', and along territory boundaries. We also found that gatherings were much more common than expected within 10

TABLE 4: *Relationships between dominance, gathering initiation and territory acquisition in non-breeding magpies*

	Dominance rank		
	High (N = 8)	Medium (N = 9)	Low (N = 5)
No. of gatherings initiated[1]	3.5 ± 4.75	0.2 ± 0.4	0
No. of gatherings involved in[2]	9.6 ± 6.7	3.3 ± 1.7	1.4 ± 3.1
No. of birds acquiring territory[3]	7 (87.5%)	2 (22.2%)	0 (0)

Notes: Values are means ± SD. (1) Kruskal–Wallis $H = 10.38$, $P < 0.01$; (2) Kruskal–Wallis $H = 7.38$, $P < 0.05$, (3) $\chi^2 = 11.96$, 2 d.f., $p < 0.01$. From Birkhead & Clarkson (1985a).

metres of a territory boundary. Of 194 gatherings, 143 (74%) were on boundaries and 51 (26%) occurred within a territory. This is markedly different from what we would have expected if they had been distributed in the same proportions as the area of boundaries and territories ($\chi^2 = 377$, 2 d.f., $p < 0.001$).

The initiators of gatherings were always non-breeding birds. We saw 24 cases where a single bird started the gathering and in each case it was a male. When two birds started a gathering they usually comprised a pair (8 out of 10 cases). Once we saw two females, and once two unpaired birds (male and female) start gatherings. The most striking aspect of the birds which started gatherings was their social status within the non-breeding flock. As described later in Chapter 4, we categorized these birds as high, medium, or low ranking. High-ranking birds initiated significantly more gatherings and were involved in more gatherings than medium or low-ranking birds. In addition, they were more likely to obtain a territory as a result of the gathering (Table 4).

This leads us to the function of gatherings. In most cases (215 out of 225; 95%), gatherings ended with the initiators being evicted by the breeders. Two other outcomes occurred. In three cases the initiators became involved in a serious fight with the territory owners. The gathering initiators won, displaced the territory owners and took over the territory. The other outcome was for initiators to return to the same location, starting a gathering each time, over several successive days. They eventually established a small territory at this location, usually on territory boundaries. There were seven instances of territories being established in this way. Altogether, gatherings resulted in the establishment of ten territories, three by direct take-over following a single gathering and seven by aggressive squeezing-in following several gatherings. Gatherings were responsible for the establishment of about one-third of territories (Birkhead and Clarkson 1985a). These results show that gatherings clearly are associated with competition for space. They comprise dominant non-breeders attempting to obtain a territory, by force, early enough in the season to breed. It would be interesting to compare the quality of birds which obtain territories by gatherings and by 'squeezing in'. It seems likely that the former are the better quality birds. Their mode of acquisition is active and aggressive. In contrast, birds which acquire territories by squeezing in do so much more passively, and wait until most aggression has died down (see Chapter 3).

We have suggested that gatherings constitute 'territorial probing', that is, assessing the quality of the established birds, to see just how good they are at defending their territory. When the initiators fly directly into a territory their aim is probably to deliberately provoke the owners. If the owners' response is aggressive the gathering initiators will rapidly assess the situation and either leave or be rapidly evicted. On the other hand, if the owners' hold on their territory is marginal, as occurs among older birds or if the male is sick or injured, then the initiators will press home their attack and oust them. Sometimes the initiators are unable to remove the territory owners, but instead stake a claim on a small patch of land simply by choosing a location where territorial aggression is least and persistently returning to it. Once they have a small area which they can use as a base they are able to gradually expand their boundaries.

Why are birds other than the initiators and territory owners involved in gatherings? I think the answer to this is that there might be advantages for both other breeders and non-breeders in knowing about potential changes in territory ownership. Opportunities for other individuals to move to a better territory or increase their status might arise from a change in territory ownership.

Ceremonial gatherings apparently do not occur among either North American Black-billed or Yellow-billed Magpies (D. Buitron, pers. comm.; M. D. Reynolds, pers. comm.); Verbeek (1973) describes behaviours in Yellow-billed Magpies which resemble gatherings: groups of between two and seven first-year birds visited the breeding colony in the morning, mainly during the early breeding season in March and April. These birds often flew in single file,

visiting both old and new nests and being evicted by the territory owners. Such interactions were accompanied by much calling, but as far as I can tell from Verbeek's account, unlike gatherings, they did not involve more than one pair of territorial birds. While at Hastings I observed one of these 'invasions' by presumed non-breeding birds and the resulting behaviour was very like a European magpie gathering. However, I saw only one such incident during several hundred hours of field observation. The low frequency of this behaviour probably arises because flocks of non-breeding Yellow-bills do not live near the breeding birds, and because the pressure on breeding space is much less than in European magpies. Precisely how young Yellow-billed Magpies do become established as breeders would repay further investigation.

SUMMARY

Territoriality and the spatial distribution of nests are important aspects of magpie social organization. Most magpies in northern Europe defend large (5 ha) all-purpose territories. Breeding density can reach 30 pairs/km^2 and nests are regularly spaced. In southern Europe nests may be aggregated. In North America most populations show aggregated nest distributions: only a very small area around the nest is defended. As a result local breeding densities can be higher than in Europe. Yellow-billed Magpies breed in colonies (up to 30 pairs), show highly aggregated nest distributions, and defend very small territories. The differences in spacing patterns between the two magpie species, and between different populations, are a consequence of two ecological factors: food and nest sites. European magpies acquire territories in various ways and most dramatically through so-called 'ceremonial gatherings'.

CHAPTER 3

Social behaviour: breeding birds

It was apparent that in each pair [of Yellow-billed Magpies] one bird showed more concern than the other to keep with its mate.

Linsdale (1937)

An important aspect of any species' social organization is its mating system, the number of mates held by each partner. The most frequent mating system among birds is monogamy, where one male and one female work together to rear offspring. Other mating systems include polyandry, as occurs in Spotted Sandpipers where a female may have up to four male partners, and polygyny, where a single male may have several female partners, as in the Red-winged Blackbird. In some species more complicated mating systems exist consisting of a mixture of polyandry and polygyny, e.g. the Dunnock (Davies 1985).

Both species of magpie breed as pairs and are regarded as being monogamous. Although this sounds relatively unexciting compared with some of the other systems, it still leaves, as will become apparent, considerable scope for some interesting behaviours. Very occasionally male European magpies may be bigamous: in our study we recorded 2 instances out of 127 where a male had two female partners simultaneously. In one case the male's partner from the previous year was declining in health when a second female appeared in the territory. In the other case a second female simply attached herself to an existing pair. In both instances only a single, normal-sized and uniformly patterned clutch of eggs was laid and incubated.

Pair bonds may remain intact for several years. Indeed, Verbeek (1973) thought that Yellow-billed Magpies generally paired for life. The length of time that magpies in our study area remained paired was highly variable. Some pairs formed in the spring, but lasted for only a single breeding attempt. At the other extreme some pairs remained together for as long as both birds were alive which in our study was up to four years. Buitron (1988) also recorded several pairs of North American magpies remaining together for successive years. Baeyens (1981b) looked at pair bonds in her magpies and found that about one-third of all pairs changed partners between seasons. She also found that magpies often 'divorced' their partner in order to pair with a bird in a better quality territory. Baeyens was able to classify territories as either good or poor quality (see Chapter 10), and found that if one member of a pair occupying a good territory died, its place was often taken by a bird from a poor territory, divorcing its partner in order to do so.

DISPERSAL OF BREEDING BIRDS

In most areas breeding magpies are remarkably sedentary and no populations are known to undertake migration. Long-distance movements sometimes occur in response to cold weather in the northern USSR, and in Cyprus birds have been seen setting off over the sea towards Turkey (Flint & Stewart 1983).

Once they have acquired a territory magpies tend to re-use it in successive years, either remaining there continuously as in many European magpies, or returning each spring. In our study all magpies were highly sedentary, and the median distance moved between breeding attempts in successive years was just 25 metres. There was no difference between males and females. In terms of territories, 95% of birds moved less than one territory distance between years. Even over several years there was no tendency for dispersal distance to increase (Fig. 15). Buitron (1988) also found that individual magpies in North America tended to breed in the same area year after year and the mean distance moved between years was 280 m (range 0 to 790 m, $N = 20$). Although in absolute terms this was ten times greater than in our study area, in terms of territories it was almost exactly the same (see Chapter 2). Among Yellow-billed Magpies, breeding birds remain near their territories throughout the year and frequently re-use nests in the same territory in successive years (Verbeek 1973).

PAIR FORMATION

Pair formation in young European magpies usually takes place in the non-breeding flock (see Chapter 4). It is a subtle affair and consists mainly of

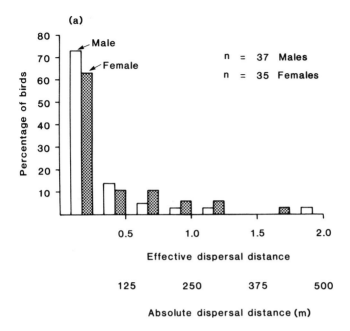

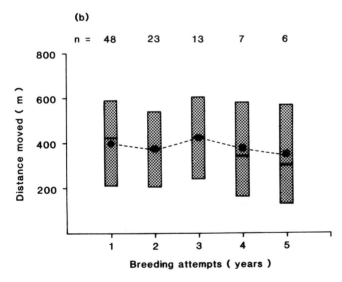

Fig. 15.   *Dispersal of breeding magpies in the Sheffield study in terms of number of territories moved (effective dispersal distance) and absolute distance moved. (a) Shows the distance moved between one breeding season and the next for 37 males (open bars) and 35 females (shaded). Although females move slightly further than males, the difference is not significant. (b) Distance between natal site and successive breeding sites (males and females combined). Dots: means; bars: median values; box: one SD. There is no tendency for the distance from the natal site to increase with successive breeding seasons. Redrawn from Eden (1987a).*

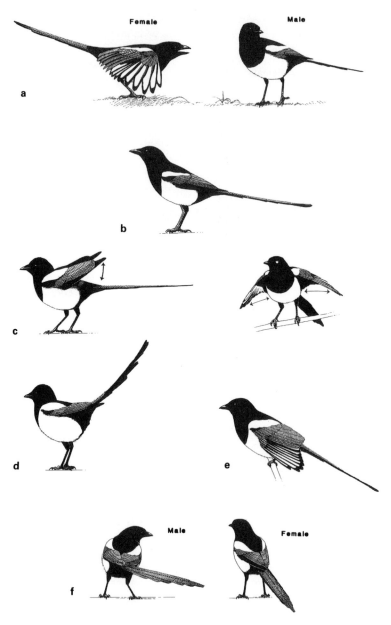

Fig. 16.   *Magpie displays and postures: (a) female (left) begging from reluctant male, (b) upright posture, (c) vertical wing flicking (left) and horizontal wing flicking and closed nictitating membrane, (d) tail flirting, the tail is flicked from its usual position into this upright position, (e) wing-flash, the wing is drooped exposing the primaries, (f) pre-copulatory display, the male (left) circles the female with his tail tilted towards her. Drawings by David Quinn.*

prospective partners spending more and more time in each other's presence, until they eventually remain together most of the time. There appear to be no displays specifically associated with the formation of a pair bond; nevertheless once the bond is formed pair members perform a number of displays not seen among unpaired individuals. Older birds that have already bred at least once also form new pair bonds, either because they have been divorced or because their partner has died. Again, there are no obvious displays associated with this. Males do not for example perform any advertising display, as occurs in some birds. The displays performed by established pairs include greeting by wing- and tail-flirting. They also engage in mutual preening, begging, court-ship and copulation (Fig. 16).

Pair formation in North American magpies in captivity has been studied by Komers and Dhindsa (1989) and Dhindsa *et al.* (1989a): their study showed that high-ranking males were more likely to form pair bonds than subordinate birds. Social status had no effect on a female's tendency to form a pair bond, but older females were more likely to do so than younger birds. Komers and Dhindsa suggest that females actively choose males, and do so by taking a more active role in courtship displays. These authors also found that when given a choice, females preferred adult to first-year males. This makes good sense since an adult male is likely to have had some breeding experience and may therefore be a better parent.

Among Yellow-billed Magpies Verbeek (1973) thought that young birds might form pair bonds from within the non-breeding flock. He also noted that the flock provided a focus for the activity of adult birds which had lost a mate, and may have helped them find a new partner. The repertoire of social signals shown by paired Yellow-billed Magpies includes all those observed in Black-bills (see Chapter 12), but in addition includes bill-nibbling and 'tugging'. Bill-nibbling may simply be an extended version of allopreening (where one bird preens another), and is accompanied by a soft warbling call. Tugging involves the male picking a small piece of vegetation – a leaf stalk or a twig – and presenting it to the female. The pair then tug at it until the female gets it, after which she drops it. This display is accompanied by soft vocalizations. Verbeek (1973) suggests that alloopreening, billing and tugging all serve to help maintain the pair bond, and often serve as preliminaries to courtship feeding and other 'courtship' behaviours (see below).

RELATIONSHIPS WITHIN THE PAIR

Among European magpies established pairs often occupy their territory throughout the year, but during the winter months do not obviously spend much time in close contact. As the days begin to lengthen, however, the pair start nest building and spend increasing amounts of time together. They choose a nest site and spend time at the site displaying to each other. Their calls (Table 5 and Fig. 17) are often relatively quiet, and the displays subtle and difficult to see. When pair members are choosing a nest site they come

TABLE 5: *A summary and classification of European magpie calls*

Call[1]	Performer (sex)	Context
Tweet	both	1–2-day-old chicks, grades into coo-call
Coo-call	both	Chicks, but also adults in agonistic situation, when bird is approached
Purr	both	Adult to stimulate nestlings to beg
Shrill note	female	Incubating female in response to male returning with food
Shriek	both	Agonistic interactions between adults
Squawk	both	Distress call, when held in hand or caught by predator
Chattering	both	Various situations: alarm, mobbing, conspecific interactions
Chatter call	both	Shortened version of chattering.
Dark call	both	Pair at nest; nest-site showing display; also by male during circling
Clear call	both	Various situations: given by female during begging, male during circling, when chasing territorial intruder; approaching bird gives clear call to conspecific
Babble singing	male	Fledgling of both sexes babble sing. Adult males: possibly equivalent to song in other passerines.
Soft singing	male	Courtship
Rhythmic singing	male	Courtship
Crunch	female	Uttered within pair bond, mainly by female
Chirp	male	Uttered within pair bond mainly by male

Notes: (1) Terminology from Enggist-Dublin (1988): information from P. Enggist-Dublin and personal observations.

together at the selected spot uttering the nasal, buzzing 'dark call' (Fig. 17), each bird simultaneously quivering its wings and tail while standing on its toes. Pairs also sit in close bodily contact and occasionally allopreen each other. Allopreening most often occurs after the pair have been involved in aggressive encounters, such as with a territory intruder (Fig. 16). One spring I recorded every instance of allopreening I saw among seven marked pairs. Of 26 occurrences, 22 (85%) were of the female allopreening the male; only 4 times did the male preen his mate. My interpretation of this behaviour is that it helps to maintain the pair bond, serving as a form of reassurance.

Male magpies also sing during the early part of the breeding season. Three different types of male song have been recognized: soft singing, rhythmic singing and babble singing. The first time I heard the latter 'song' I could hardly believe it was being uttered by a magpie since it is so unlike their other vocalizations. It consists of a series of soft, warbling notes interspersed with a number of higher pitched sounds (Fig. 17). Some individuals apparently incorporate the sounds of other birds or animals (e.g. crickets) into their

Male Yellow-billed Magpie singing to nearby mate. (Photos: T. R. Birkhead).

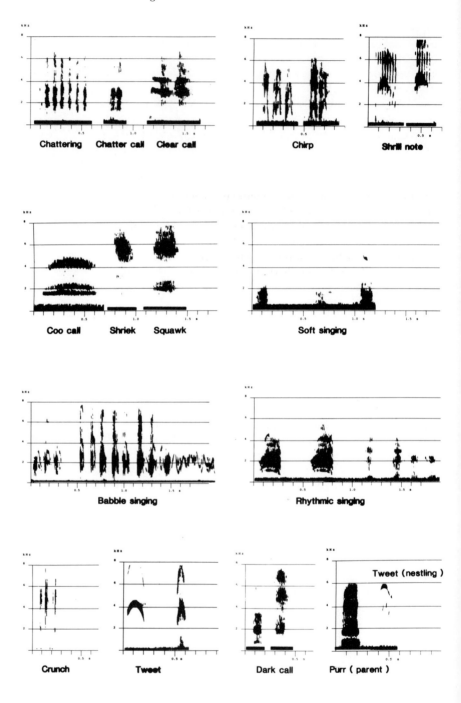

Fig. 17.   *Sonagrams of the main vocalizations of European magpies. (From Enggist-Dublin 1988; Copyright P. Enggist-Dublin.)*

babble song (Baeyens 1979). All three types of magpie song are relatively quiet and sound rather similar to the 'sub-song' that occurs in other passerine birds. One of the possible functions of magpie song is the stimulation of the female in the days prior to egg-laying. Among Yellow-billed Magpies I recorded singing only in males while they were with their partner, and it appeared to occur most frequently during the two weeks before laying. It is quite possible therefore that the Yellow-billed Magpie's song serves the same purpose as that in some other bird species in helping to bring the female into breeding condition.

Black-billed Magpies in both Europe and North America also sing in the company of their partner, but the occurrence of song in relation to the female's breeding cycle has not been investigated. However, it is known that North American magpies sing in other contexts. When Keith Clarkson and I visited Chuck Trost and Eric Stone's study area in Idaho, they told us that magpies sometimes sang at potential predators and suggested that it was a way of increasing their dominance status, rather like a school-boy cheeking a teacher in order to boost his standing among his peers! Magpies sing at stationary hawks and owls, and as we also witnessed, humans. As we set up our telescopes to start watching a group of magpies, one bird flew towards us and landed on a nearby fence. For several minutes it faced us and poured out its gentle, esoteric song! I have not observed European magpies singing at predators in this way. More field observations are necessary before any firm conclusions can be reached about differences between races in singing behaviour and the functions of song in magpies.

When nest building starts in earnest the pair spend increasing amounts of time together in the nest, and advertise the ownership of their territory by tree-topping (see Chapter 2). As daylength increases both sexes undergo physiological changes, consisting primarily of an enlargement of their gonads. This aspect of the life cycle was studied in detail by Erpino (1969) working with North American magpies. He found that the male's testes start to increase in size well before the beginning of nest building, and reached their maximum at the start of egg laying. Sperm production commenced during a relatively early stage of nest construction, about 14 to 21 days prior to the female laying (see Chapter 7). However, as soon as laying starts sperm production and testes size decrease (Erpino 1969). This might be a peculiarity of North American magpies, which produce replacement clutches relatively infrequently; it seems unlikely that the same pattern occurs among magpies in Europe where several replacement clutches can be produced (Chapter 7).

The female's oviduct and ovaries start to develop during nest building and, not surprisingly, reach their peak just before and during the laying period. During this time a further change takes place: the development and activation of the female's sperm storage tubules. These are minute, sausage-shaped tubules situated in the oviduct at the junction of the shell gland and the vagina, which serve to store sperm after the female has mated. These tubules probably occur in all birds, but as we shall see, they play a vital role in one of the most interesting aspects of the magpie's sex life.

Nest construction can take several weeks (see Chapter 7), but there is usually an interval of about eleven days between the completion of the nest and

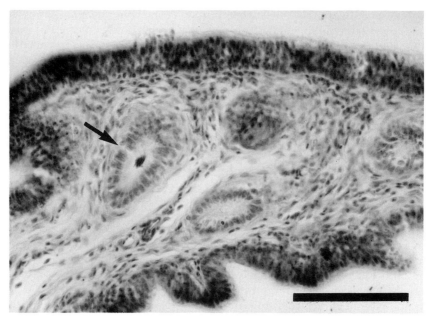

Sperm storage tubules (SSTs) of European Black-billed Magpie. Cross-sections of several SSTs are shown and one containing sperm (dark masses) is indicated by the arrow. Scale bar = 100 μm. (Photo: D. Hollingworth).

the start of egg laying (Erpino 1968b). It is during the last five days of this interval that most 'courtship' behaviours take place. Since most pair bonds have been formed by this stage of the breeding cycle the behaviours are not courtship in the strict sense of the word.

Among both species of North American magpie one of the most obvious activities of the female at this time is begging. Starting several days before her first egg is laid (Fig. 18) the female begs noisily and conspicuously from her partner. She crouches before him, flapping her wings and uttering a high-pitched, whining cry: the clear call (Fig. 17). He ignores her – at least initially – and starts to feed her only once she has started egg laying (Yellow-billed Magpie; pers. obs.) or commenced incubation (Buitron 1988). European magpies start food begging on the day they lay the first egg (after laying), but Yellow-bills and most North American Black-bills start two days before the first egg is laid. It is not clear why this difference should exist.

The main 'courtship' display is circling, in which the male approaches and starts to walk around his partner, usually about 0.5 m away. His white feathers are fluffed until he assumes an almost spherical appearance and he adopts an upright posture, tilting his tail towards the female. He approaches, softly uttering the dark call and babble singing, and performing wing-flirting and wing-quivering (Chapter 12). The display generally ends with the female walking or hopping away, usually with the male in pursuit. Courtship can occur on the ground or in trees. Circling displays occur most often during the

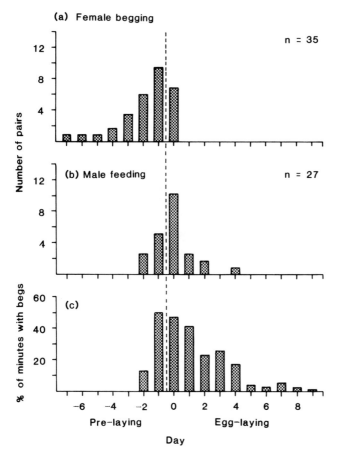

Fig. 18. *Temporal pattern of female begging and male feeding in North American Black-billed Magpies relative to egg laying. The first egg was laid on day 0. (a) The day on which the female first begged, (b) the day on which her partner first fed her, and (c) the mean rate of begging by females. From Buitron (1988).*

four or five days before the first egg is laid, although they do not appear to be particularly common.

I have watched several pairs of European magpies for a total of about three hundred hours during the pre-laying period and seen only nine copulations. I estimated that each pair of magpies probably mate only three times for each clutch of eggs they lay (Birkhead *et al.* 1987). All of the copulations that I observed occurred between four days before the onset of laying and the day the second egg was laid. Usually successful copulations are solicited by the female who flaps her wings as if begging, and when she squats and spreads her wings and tail the male steps onto her back (Clegg 1962). Cloacal contact lasts only one or two seconds. Copulation can occur either on the ground or on a low branch, and I once saw it take place on a wall.

In Yellow-billed Magpies copulation and the male's precopulatory circling
and babble singing are almost identical to that found in Black-billed Magpies
(Verbeek 1972b, 1973). I looked at this aspect of the Yellow-billed Magpie's
behaviour quite closely and, because the birds I watched were relatively tame,
I ended up with more detailed information on them than I had for European
magpies. Circling was always initiated by the male and tended to occur up to
two weeks before egg laying, and was more frequent after laying had started. I
never saw circling result in successful mounting. Copulation occurred over a
very restricted time period: mainly the fifth, fourth and third days before the
first egg was laid. It occurred mainly in the morning, either on the ground or in
a tree. All copulations were initiated by the female uttering a repetitive
growling call (audible only at close range) followed by her squatting on her
tarsi with her wings outspread and drooping. The male was always close by
when this occurred: he approached quickly and mounted for about two
seconds. Like European magpies, Yellow-bills probably copulate only three or
four times for each clutch.

MATE GUARDING AND EXTRA-PAIR COPULATION

In the Royal Palace at Sintra, Portugal the Magpie Room has no fewer than
136 magpies painted on its ceiling, each one bearing in its beak a rose,
inscribed with the words 'Por bem', or 'It's nothing'. These were apparently
the ingenuous words spoken by King João I when his wife caught him kissing
one of her ladies-in-waiting! To stop the chatter the king had as many magpies
as there were ladies at court painted on the ceiling. If King João knew as much
about the extramarital relationships of magpies as we do now he would
probably have chosen some other bird to decorate his ceiling!

To put the magpie's extramarital behaviour in perspective, let us start by
looking at the normal relationship between male and female members of a
pair. Among European magpies, the male starts to take special interest in his
partner from about four days before egg laying. He stays much closer to her
than previously, and follows her every move. In fact at this time he virtually
never lets the female out of his sight. If she flies off to feed in a new area, he
follows. If she hops behind a wall, he goes too. On the few occasions that he
does move away from his partner she does not follow him. In other words the
proximity of the two birds is maintained entirely by the male. Following
behaviour persists until midway through laying the clutch. Eggs are laid early
in the morning and while the first two or three eggs are being laid the male
follows the female to the nest and waits for her to lay, then as she leaves the nest
he resumes his following. After the third egg is laid the female spends long
periods in the nest and the male is much less likely to follow her when she
leaves the nest (Fig. 19) (Birkhead 1979, 1982).

Why should the male be so keen to remain so close to his female? The answer
is that without doing so he runs the risk that his female might be fertilized by
another male. Male magpies regularly sneak into their neighbours' territory at

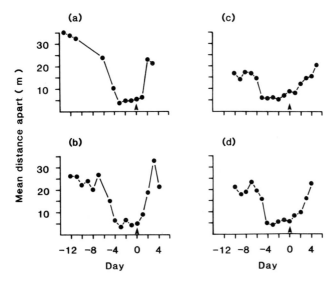

Fig. 19. *Mate guarding by European magpies. (a)–(d) represent four different pairs. The points show the mean distance between partners relative to the day the female laid her first egg (day 0). From Birkhead (1982).*

this stage of the breeding cycle and attempt to mate with the female. The benefit to a male from this behaviour is obvious: he fathers extra offspring without the effort of helping to rear them. The reason why such sneaky matings are worthwhile may be related to the fact that females store sperm prior to using it to fertilize their eggs. The length of time that female magpies can store sperm is not known, but in other birds it ranges from six days to ten weeks (Birkhead 1988). It therefore seems likely that in magpies a mating that takes place several days before egg laying can fertilize eggs. Male magpies capitalize on this and try to get extra-pair copulations whenever they can.

All the extra-pair mating attempts that I have seen have been made by paired magpies. Although unpaired males are capable of producing sperm (Erpino 1969) they rarely if ever participate in extra-pair copulations. Clearly it is not in a paired male's interest to allow his female to be mated by another male, and males looking for sneaky matings have to work hard to approach a guarded female. One case, observed by Sandy Goodburn, involved a fertile female foraging with her attendant partner amongst clumps of bracken. The male from an adjacent territory cautiously approached the female using the vegetation as cover. He succeeded in getting right up to the female and started to mount her before her partner noticed, came rushing over and chased him off.

The close following by the male of the female during her fertile period constitutes mate guarding: he is simply staying close enough to intercept other males. Paired males also use another tactic to protect their paternity – territorial aggression. The traditional explanation for why birds defend

Yellow-billed Magpies mate guarding, the male on the left. (Photo: T. R. Birkhead).

territories during the breeding season is that it ensures an exclusive food supply for themselves when their food requirements are greatest, that is, when they are feeding young. However, if this were true then we might expect territory defence to be most intense during the chick-rearing period. In the magpie's case this is certainly not true and so is unlikely to be the whole explanation. When I examined magpie territory defence relative to the female's fertile period, I noticed a marked decrease in activity as soon as the female had laid her clutch (Fig. 20). This suggests that one function of the magpie's territorial behaviour is to help protect the male's paternity. A subsequent review by Møller (1987a) has shown that in most species territoriality follows a similar pattern, supporting the idea that one function of territoriality is to reduce the risks of cuckoldry.

In North America Buitron (1983a) also looked at mate guarding and extra-pair mating attempts in magpies (Fig. 21). Her results and mine differ in several ways, but the differences are almost certainly due to the differences in nest spacing and social organization of our two magpie populations. In her study area magpie nests were well spaced out (see Chapter 2) and her birds did not defend territories in the same way as our Sheffield birds. Probably as a consequence of this she found that mate guarding occurred gradually over the few days before egg laying and not abruptly, as I found. Also, Buitron showed that male magpies usually waited until their own female was no longer fertile before going off to look for extra-pair matings (Fig. 21). Because nests were so well spaced, some birds had to fly a kilometre or more in their search. By

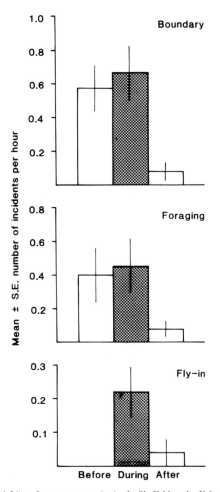

Fig. 20.   *Territorial intruders among magpies in the Sheffield study. Values are the mean number of intruders per hour (± SE), before, during and after the female's fertile period (see text), for three types of intruder: boundary, foraging and fly-in. From Birkhead (1979).*

contrast, in our study area territories were densely packed together with contiguous boundaries, and males seeking extra-pair matings simply walked or flew a few tens of metres across the territory boundary.

The importance of mate guarding for males was demonstrated by an incident in which a guarding male fell asleep. I was watching a pair in which the female had started to lay and was in the middle of her fertile period. She was foraging on the ground, with her partner sitting a few metres away on a wall. As I watched them I noticed the male's head drooping, and as he fell asleep his head fell below the level of the wall so that he could no longer see his partner (Fig. 22). Within seconds the male of the neighbouring pair, which

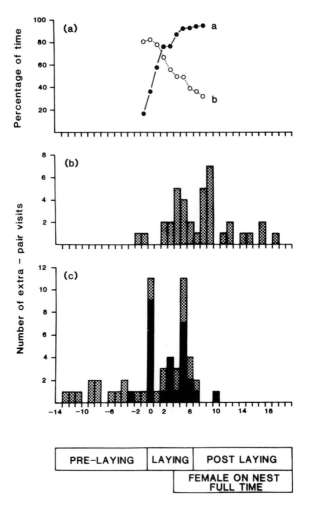

Fig. 21.   *Temporal pattern of pair and extra-pair activities of North American Black-billed Magpies. Day 0 is the day the first egg of the clutch is laid. (a) Line a shows the amount of time the female spent in the nest. Line b shows the amount of time the male partner had his partner in view. (b) Frequency of extra-pair visits by male magpies, relative to the stage in the breeding cycle of their mates. (c) Reproductive stage of females involved in extra-pair visits by males. Black bars indicate the female begged from, or was courted by the extra-pair male. Shaded areas: no interaction during the extra-pair visit. From Buitron (1983a).*

had been foraging together, flew over and mounted the female. As he did so she uttered a short cry. This woke her partner who swooped down off the wall and chased off the intruding male. During that commotion I assumed that the paired male's aggression was directed entirely at the intruding male, but in fact the intruder slipped quietly back to his own territory, while the paired male chased his partner towards the nest tree. This was not the end of the matter for the next day the male started to build a new nest in a tree a few

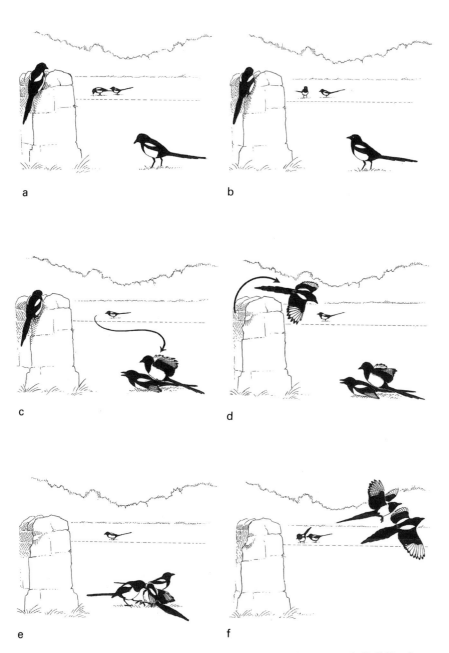

Fig. 22. *Sequence of events during an extra-pair copulation attempt by magpies in the Sheffield study. (a) Mate-guarding male on wall watching fertile female partner foraging, neighbouring pair in their territory (broken line = territory boundary). (b) Guarding male falls asleep with his head below wall. (c) Neighbouring male flies in and mounts female. (d) Guarding male wakes up and (e) attacks intruding male. (f) Guarding male chases his partner into nesting tree (see text).*

metres from the original one. The female continued to lay and completed her clutch in the original nest, but the eggs were abandoned. She then laid a second clutch in the new nest. I suspect that the male started a new breeding attempt to that he did not have to risk rearing offspring fathered by his next-door neighbour. The female probably had little choice in the matter because, as in almost all corvids, she is dependent upon her partner to feed her while she incubates.

During the mate-guarding period the female spends much of her time foraging. Her clutch of six eggs weighs about 60 g, or 26% of her body weight, so she probably has to accumulate substantial reserves to form the eggs. At the same time, however, the male appears to spend less time than usual foraging. Studies of several other birds have shown that guarding males lose weight during this period (Møller 1987b). The male of one of the pairs that I observed in detail had a novel solution to this problem. Shortly before he started mate guarding he hid a large piece of bread near the base of the nest tree. During the mate-guarding period, whenever his female went into the nest (where she was safe from other males), the male partner unearthed his piece of bread and fed for a few moments before caching the food again (food hoarding is dealt with in detail in Chapter 5).

Extra-pair copulation also occurs in the Yellow-billed Magpie, and Verbeek's (1973) observations as well as my own suggest that it might be even more frequent than in Black-billed Magpies. Interestingly, some female Yellow-bills appear to seek extra-pair matings, and (less frequently) some males attempt to obtain extra-pair copulations by force. Verbeek describes one instance where a female at the edge of her territory begged from a male neighbour. The male partner saw this happen and flew down first to chase the other male, and then to pursue his partner back to the nest. Two days later the same female approached and begged from the same extra-pair male, who attempted to mount her. The mating was disrupted by the male partner, who once again chased his female back into the territory. On another occasion, involving other birds, a pair had just copulated, when a strange male arrived and attempted to copulate forcibly with the female. She escaped and the extra-pair male flew off when the male partner approached. The colony that Verbeek watched in detail during one year contained six pairs and five of the males were involved in extra-pair copulation attempts. As in European magpies, male Yellow-bills attempted extra-pair copulations both before and after their own partners were fertile. Writing about this aspect of the Yellow-billed Magpie's behaviour Verbeek (1973) states that males actively defend their partners from other males seeking extra-pair copulations, but he does not mention whether males guard their partner by close following, as do Black-billed Magpies. However, Linsdale's (1937) observation, quoted at the beginning of this chapter, indicates that mate guarding does occur. The observations I made with Keith Clarkson confirmed that intense mate guarding does occur in the Yellow-billed Magpie.

Verbeek (1973) also noted that the time when Yellow-bills are most territorial coincides exactly with the period when females are most fertile, i.e.

just before and during the early part of egg laying. During this time the pair forage alone within their territory, a situation which contrasts directly with other periods, when all colony members feed together outside their territories. Our observations confirmed this pattern for which there are two explanations: either the territory contains abundant food supplies only at this time, or, the function of the territory is to help the male protect his paternity. Our data indicate that the relationship between territoriality and mate guarding might be an indirect one. Yellow-billed Magpies start to guard their partner once copulation starts, five days before the first egg, but guarding appears to end before the female has started laying. This is an unexpected pattern since the female is still capable of being fertilized at this time. The reason for the intensity of mate guarding is that the male is trying to do two things at once: guard his partner and feed her. Starting two days before she lays her first egg, the female begins her incessant, tedious food begging. By the time the female has laid one egg the male is providing quite a lot of her food, feeding her either at or in the nest. At this stage he forages exclusively in his territory. I suspect that by defending this area the male ensures an adequate food supply close to the nest and this enables him to forage *and* keep an eye on his female.

The one question that remains about extra-pair matings in both magpie species is whether they ever give rise to offspring. The recently developed technique of DNA fingerprinting, which has successfully revealed both extra pair paternity and intra-specific brood parasitism in a number of bird species, should eventually allow us to answer this question for magpies. There is, however, another possible way of examining this problem. Chuck Trost and Lisa Reed (pers. comm.) found that the pattern of black and white on the primaries and secondaries of juvenile North American Black-billed Magpies was very similar among brood members but differed markedly between broods. Occasionally they found a bird whose wing pattern differed from all other brood members, indicating that it might have been the result of either an extra-pair mating or a dumped egg (see Chapter 7). If this could be verified using DNA fingerprinting it would be an extremely useful and cheap way of determining parentage among magpies.

ROOSTING

Magpies roost either singly or communally. Throughout the year in our study area territorial birds roosted either singly or in pairs within their territory, while non-breeders, birds without territories (Chapter 4), most often roosted in groups of 10 to 20 individuals within their normal home range. However, during the winter months a large communal roost, containing up to 150 birds, formed about one kilometre from our study area. Despite extensive searches we never found any of our colour-marked birds at this roost, yet magpies must have travelled at least one kilometre to join it. In Sweden Gyllin and Kallander (1977) found that magpies flew a maximum of 4 kilometres to reach a roost.

Magpie communal roosts are often situated in 'safe' locations, such as in trees over water, in reed beds or in thorny bushes (Gyllin & Kallander 1977; Reebs 1986). At the large roost near our study area birds started to arrive in the vicinity two or three hours before darkness. They often arrived in small parties of three to six birds and congregated in fields near to the clumps of hawthorns which were used for roosting. They spent most of their time either foraging or sitting quietly in the trees or on walls. Flurries of activity sometimes occurred, with some or all of the birds flying and chasing each other for a few moments (Ward 1952). Pre-roost gatherings seem to be a consistent feature of communal magpie roosts in Europe, and some of the early references to 'ceremonial gatherings' involving a hundred or more birds (see Chapter 2) almost certainly refer to these aggregations.

The birds rarely entered the roost until it was too dark to see clearly, but as they did so it was often an impressive sight to see a hundred or so birds sitting like so many Christmas decorations in a single bush! The birds spent the night in the middle of dense hawthorn bushes. Møller (1985) found that magpies generally roost about half-way up their roost tree, using lower branches on cooler nights, and the leeward side during windy weather. In Reebs's (1987) study, magpies roosted in conifers and perched beside the trunk on the lowest leaf-bearing branches immediately below the canopy. While asleep magpies have their eyes closed and their bill tucked under the scapular and back feathers. Depending upon the temperature the body feathers are more or less fluffed up: on cold nights most of the head and the legs and feet are covered (Reebs 1986). It has been estimated that when night-time temperatures are around $-20\,°C$, magpies can save about 8% of their energy by roosting in dense conifers out of the wind (Mugaas & King 1981).

In Møller's (1985) study in Denmark he found that roosts occurred mainly during the winter months (Fig. 23) and varied in size from 3 to 130 birds. Adjacent roosts were separated by an average distance of 1.9 km. Birds arrived up to two hours before dark, although most arrived during the last 40 minutes of daylight. However, there were differences in the arrival times of different social categories. Birds in the best-quality territories (see Chapter 10) arrived later than other birds, and those from the poorest territories arrived earliest. In the morning most birds departed before sunrise, and the birds from the best-quality territories left first. As soon as pairs started nest building in the spring they stopped using the communal roost, and numbers declined.

Why do magpies in some areas roost communally? The reason why birds of many species roost together has puzzled ornithologists for a long time. There have been a number of suggestions, including protection from predators or from adverse weather conditions, or to enable birds to exchange information about the location of food. Møller (1985) suggests that magpies roost communally so that they can monitor the mating status of their territorial neighbours. I think this explanation is unlikely because it is probably just as relevant for the birds in my study population to do this, yet they did not roost together. A more likely explanation relates to the availability of food. In our study area magpies could probably obtain most of their food from within their territories

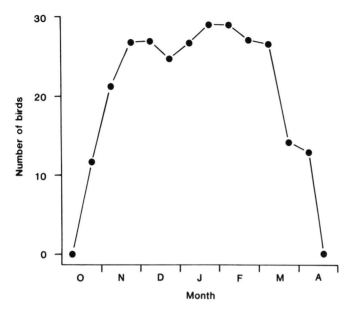

Fig. 23.   *Seasonal changes in the number of magpies using a roost in Denmark. From Møller (1985).*

and had no need to roost elsewhere. The birds in Møller's study may have left their territories to roost communally because food was more difficult to find. Møller (pers. comm.) has suggested that this might be true for birds from low-quality territories, but points out that it does not explain why birds left good-quality territories in order to roost with other magpies.

Yellow-billed Magpies also roost communally outside the breeding season (Verbeek 1973), and sometimes in groups of several hundred birds (E. Greene, pers. comm.). All colony members, and sometimes the birds from several colonies, roost together. Roost sites are generally located away from any breeding colony. Yellow-billed Magpies usually roost within the canopy of Live Oak trees and have not been recorded using their nests for roosting (except for females during the breeding season). In contrast, North American and Eurasian magpies in the colder parts of their range sometimes use their nests for roosting (Erpino 1968b; A. P. Møller, pers. comm.). A summary of the pattern of roosting among different social classes of Yellow-billed Magpies is shown in Fig. 24.

MOBBING GROUPS

Small groups of magpies sometimes occur as they mob a predator, such as an owl, raptor, fox, cat, or stoat. Indeed, gamekeepers sometimes use tame or model owls to attract magpies within shooting range (see Chapter 11). I have

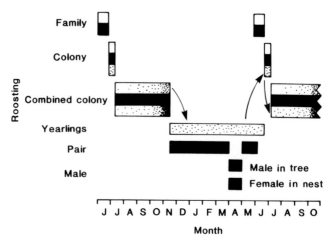

Fig. 24.   *Seasonal changes in the roosting behaviour of three categories of Yellow-billed Magpies at the Hastings Reservation. Juveniles (white), yearlings (stipple) and adults (black). From Verbeek (1973).*

seen parties of up to ten magpies taunting a fox or cat, calling loudly and rushing forward to tweak the predator's tail. The loud chatter calls uttered during mobbing (see Chapter 8) undoubtedly attract the attention of other magpies, and most birds in the area probably have a vested interest in driving the predator away. Although most of the animals that magpies mob are predators or potential predators, they sometimes appear to mob species which are unlikely to pose a threat, such as the European Kestrel.

An interesting behaviour shown by both species of magpie is the 'mobbing' of a dead magpie or even one or two isolated tail feathers. These 'funerals' have been discussed by a number of authors (e.g. Verbeek 1972b), but their function remains obscure.

SUMMARY

Both species of magpie are monogamous: male and female cooperate to rear young. Pairs sometimes remain together for several successive breeding seasons, but 'divorce' also occurs. Breeding magpies of both species are remarkably sedentary and rarely move more than one kilometre between years. Pairs are thought to form within the non-breeding flock. Studies of captive North American Black-billed Magpies indicate that females actively choose their mates and, when given a choice, prefer older males. Pair bonds are maintained by a variety of visual, vocal and tactile signals. Most copulation and associated displays occur during the eleven-day interval between the end of nest construction and egg laying. Pair copulations are infrequent in both species. Copulation attempts outside the pair bond however are frequent, and paired males protect their paternity by mate guarding. Breeding pairs tend to roost either alone or together within their territory during the breeding season. At other times both breeders and non-breeders roost communally, sometimes in large groups. Magpies also form groups to mob potential predators.

CHAPTER 4

Social behaviour: non-breeding birds

*One for sorrow, two for mirth, three for a wedding, four for a birth.
Five for rich, six for poor, seven for a bitch, eight for a whore. Nine for
a burying, ten for a dance, eleven for England, twelve for France.*

Anon.

In Black-billed and Yellow-billed Magpies the breeding birds form only part
of the population: the rest is made up of non-breeding birds. The non-breeding
individuals are those which are either too young to breed or are unable to
obtain a territory. The behaviour of individuals in the non-breeding segment
of any bird population is one of the 'neglected areas of avian field biology'
(Verner 1985). The Black-billed Magpie, however, is one of the few species in
which the social organization of non-breeding birds has been examined in
detail. Much of the information in this chapter comes from Simon Eden's
investigation of the non-breeders in our study population.

Life for a young magpie is difficult: once it has reached independence its
main priority is to survive. If it is lucky it may eventually become a breeder,
but relatively few birds get this far (Chapter 6). Predation and starvation
eliminate all but the fittest individuals. Natural selection has resulted in the
evolution of a number of behavioural strategies which increase the young
magpie's chances of becoming a breeder and making its own contribution to
subsequent generations.

Non-breeding birds can make up a substantial part of a magpie population. In our study area they represented between 26% and 56% of the total number of birds in different years. A similar range of values has been obtained in most other European studies: 20% in Baeyens's (1981a) study, and 60% in Högstedt's study (pers. comm.) (Birkhead *et al.* 1986). In Møller's study area there were relatively few non-breeders: less than 5% of the population (A. P. Møller, pers. comm.). Most non-breeding magpies are birds in either their first or second year (see Chapter 6). However, the large proportion of non-breeders in Högstedt's study occurred because the average age of first breeding was relatively high, with very few first-year birds breeding (G. Högstedt, pers. comm.). Of 227 non-breeders in our study area 81% were first-year birds, 17% were second-years and the rest (just four individuals) were older birds. These older individuals were birds that had once held territories and bred but had lost their territory during a take-over (see Chapter 2). Since we could sex magpies only once they started to breed we did not have detailed information on the sex ratio in non-breeding flocks. Of 227 birds recorded as part of a flock, 107 were subsequently sexed. This indicated that there was a slight (but non-significant) excess of males: 62 (58%) were males (42 first-years, 19 second-years and one older bird) and 45 (42%) were females (30 first-years, 12 second-years and three older birds).

There is little information on non-breeders among Black-billed Magpies in North America. Flocks of young birds certainly occur and Deborah Buitron (pers. comm.) estimated that about 40% of her study population consisted of non-breeders. In contrast to the situation in Europe, these non-breeders seemed to roam quite widely and were not amenable to study. As a result there are no details of the age or sex of non-breeders. It is interesting that in Reese and Kadlec's (1985) study, 40% of the breeding population consisted of first-year birds, and they did not record the presence of non-breeding birds in the breeding area. In Yellow-billed Magpies most birds do not breed until they are two years old, so flocks of non-breeders mainly comprised first- and second-year birds (Verbeek 1973).

DISPERSAL

After fledging, young magpies generally remain in their parents' territory for several weeks, after which they start to form a loose non-breeding flock. Eden (1989) found that in our study area these flocks formed around a few territories in which young had been produced, and shared a common home range of 30–50 ha. The average distance between a magpie's natal nest and the centre of its first-winter home range was 323 m or 1.2 territories ($N = 135$ birds; both sexes combined). The distance moved between a bird's first and second winters was also low, and while slightly greater, did not differ significantly from that of first-year birds (Fig. 25). For both first- and second-year birds the dispersal distances of females were slightly greater than those of males, but none of the differences was statistically significant. In terms of the

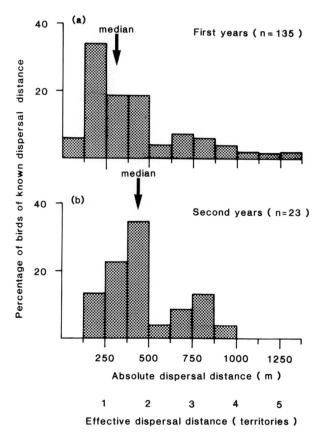

Fig. 25.   *Post-fledging dispersal of magpies in the Sheffield study. The distance is that between the natal nest and the centre of (a) the first-winter home range (in December, about 6 months after fledging), in terms of metres and numbers of territories crossed (= effective dispersal distance). (b) Second-year birds (sexes combined). Second-year birds moved significantly further than first-years on average ($\chi^2 = 6.5$, 1 d.f., p < 0.05). From Eden (1987a).*

number of territories moved, these distances were as follows: first-years, males: 1.1, females: 1.7; second-years, males: 1.6, females: 2.9. As a result of this low dispersal 50–60% of young birds had home ranges which overlapped their natal territory. This had important consequences for their survival since those which remained close to home survived significantly better than those moving further away. Of 50 young birds known to be alive in the September of their first year, and still living in part of their natal territory, 47 (94%) were still alive by the following April. But of 27 young birds which dispersed away from their natal territory, only 18 (67%) were still alive in April (Eden 1987a).

Most dispersal took place in September and October shortly after the young birds became independent of their parents. Although dispersal continued after this time it was much reduced, and most young magpies which survived to breed first did so close to where they spent their first winter. The median

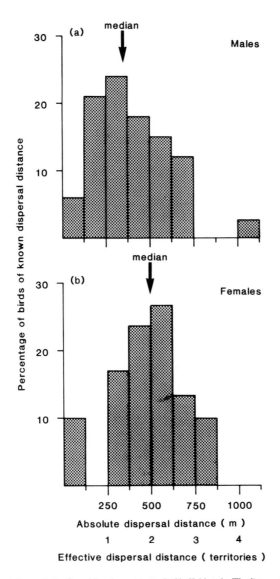

Fig. 26. *Natal dispersal of male and female magpies in the Sheffield study. The distance is that between the natal nest and the bird's own first breeding attempt. Other conventions are as in Fig. 25. Although females tend to disperse further than males, the difference is not significant (Mann-Whitney U test, z = 1.6, p = 0.11). From Eden (1987a).*

distance between a magpie's natal nest and its own first breeding attempt was 425 m (range 0–798 m), or about two territories away (N = 48 birds; both sexes combined). Again, females tended to move slightly further than males, but the difference was not significant (Fig. 26). Although related birds often bred close together we never recorded any incestuous pairings.

In Baeyens's (1979, 1981a, b) study females dispersed further than males, whereas G. Högstedt (pers. comm.), found that dispersal distances were similar for each sex: mean values were 760 m for males ($N = 34$) and 730 m for females ($N = 20$), and the medians were 600 m for both sexes.

The distances moved by young magpies in our study are among the lowest recorded for any passerine; only 12% (8 out of 66) of birds first bred more than three territories away from where they were reared. Analysis of ringing recoveries (e.g. Holyoak 1971) provides a similar picture. It is not clear why dispersal should be so low, but Eden's (1989) results suggest that staying near home is a better strategy than moving away. This was true despite the relatively small number of opportunities for young birds to obtain territories in our population.

For North American magpies there is relatively little information on dispersal distances. D. Buitron (pers. comm.) colour-ringed 176 fledgelings, but few of these were ever seen again. One first-year male was found dead 6 km away from its nest, another of unknown sex was recovered 9 km away, and one was found dead 200 km away! Millar (1964) also recorded two long-distance movements (over 500 km) of young North American magpies. Of Buitron's young birds, 3% (three males and two females) returned to nest within one kilometre of where they were fledged. Similar values were obtained by Kerry Reese (pers. comm.): of 223 nestlings or fledgelings ringed, only 12 (6%) subsequently bred in his study area. These data suggest that overall dispersal is probably considerably greater than in our study (see also Chapter 6). Verbeek (1973) indicates that for Yellow-billed Magpies some young birds move away from the colony during their first year, but the older birds which form the non-breeding flock generally breed in or near their natal colony.

FLOCKING

The non-breeding birds in our study area formed a loose flock. There was little evidence of much flock cohesion; rather, it appeared that a group of birds shared a common home range and as a result, sometimes spent time together. Flocks varied in size from 10 to 52 individuals, but only rarely did all members flock together at the same time. When this happened it was when food was highly localized, either when snow left only a few suitable feeding areas, or because a farmer 'muck-spread' a field. In both the Sheffield and Bristol studies (Vines 1981) the size of foraging groups of magpies peaked in midwinter (Fig. 27).

Within non-breeding flocks two types of social relationships developed: those concerned with dominance and those associated with pair formation. The former were the more obvious and usually manifested themselves during competition for food. The two types of social interaction were linked since a bird's dominance status also affected its subsequent chances of breeding (see Chapter 3).

It is not uncommon within feeding flocks of magpies to see one bird discover a food item only to have it stolen by another individual. Sometimes the bird

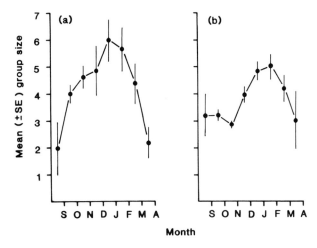

Fig. 27. *Seasonal changes in group size (mean ± SE) of non-breeding magpies in the Sheffield study, during (a) winter 1981–1982, and (b) 1982–1983. From Birkhead* et al. *(1986).*

will simply stand aside as the other approaches, and let it take the food item from the ground. At other times a tussle might ensue as the discoverer tried to hang on to its prize. Two displays also occurred during aggressive inter-actions, the 'head-up' and 'stretch' (Fig. 28). These displays, which may be different-intensity versions of the same signal, seem to occur when birds are evenly matched. If contestants are of very different size or status, then one simply defers to the other. Among more closely matched birds, both may perform head-up, but if neither bird retreats then both may perform the stretch display. This usually results in one bird retiring. The stretch may be a way that the birds assess each other's relative body size or height (Eden 1985a). These same displays are also performed by North American magpies, but Cheryl Webb (pers. comm.) found that they were given only by males.

Fig. 28. *Head-up (left) and stretch displays of the Black-billed Magpie, used in aggressive interactions. The stretch display is a more intense version of head-up.*

European magpies fighting on sheep carcass. (Photo: M. Wilkes).

Male Yellow-billed Magpie performing stretch display (central bird): an aggressive posture (see text). (Photo: T. R. Birkhead).

Stretch display (see text) by European Black-billed Magpie. Note the white nictitating membrane covering the eye of the displaying bird (see text). (Photo: M. Wilkes).

If the identity of the individuals involved in such interactions is recorded it soon becomes clear that some individuals are consistently dominant over others. 'Peck orders' are often thought of as being linear, with A dominant over all others, B dominant over all except A, C dominant over all except A and B, and so on. However, either this was not the case among our magpies or we did not collect sufficient data to detect it. We found it easier to categorize birds according to the proportion of encounters which they won, and to divide the birds into three dominance classes. The top birds won more than two-thirds of their encounters, middle-ranking birds won between one-third and two-thirds of interactions, and low-ranking birds won less than a third of their encounters. We calculated mean dominance ranks for males and females and for first- and second-year birds, scoring 1 for the highest dominance class, 2 for middle-ranking and 3 for low-ranking birds. Males were usually dominant over females, but there was no difference between first- and second-year birds (Table 6).

In addition to the behaviours described above, magpies may use other ways to signal their dominance status. Moholt and Trost (1989) found that the highest-ranking bird of a group of captive North American Black-billed Magpies spent the greatest amount of time near a predator, a wild Cooper's Hawk, perched on the outside of the aviary. It would be interesting to know whether the same behaviour occurs among wild magpies. Komers (1989) also looked at dominance relationships in several small groups of captive North

TABLE 6: *Dominance ranks for first- and second-year male and female non-breeding magpies*

Sex	First-year			Second-year		
	$\bar{x}$	SD	N	$\bar{x}$	SD	N
Males	1.5	0.72	24	1.4	0.54	5
Females	2.5	0.52	12	2.7	0.57	4
Unknown	1.9	0.80	27	—	—	—

Means are calculated from dominance ranks: 1 (high), 2 (middle) or 3 (low ranking). Males have significantly higher ranks than females ($p < 0.01$) for both age classes. There were no second-year birds of unknown sex, whose dominance ranks were measured. From Birkhead *et al.* (1986).

American magpies. He found that males were invariably dominant over females, and that males tended to form linear hierarchies, whereas females did not. Komers also found that among male magpies, first-year birds were usually dominant over adult birds. This is in striking contrast to the situation among European magpies, where territorial adults always dominate non-breeders. Chuck Trost also recorded this unexpected pattern of dominance among his wild birds in Idaho. He has suggested (unpublished) that the dominance of first-year birds may explain why adult magpies appear to mimic first-years during the autumn when the two age-classes forage together. First-year birds have pink mouths, grey eyes and a white-tipped bill, whereas adult breeders have a black mouth, dark brown eyes and a black bill tip. However, during the autumn adults assume the juvenile form in these features, presumably in an effort to minimize the effects of being dominated by first-year birds.

Eden (1987b) made a detailed study of the dominance relationships among young magpies, both in the wild and in captivity. He found that although there was a tendency for heavier birds to have higher rank (correlation between body weight and dominance rank: $r = 0.32$, 57 d.f., $p < 0.02$), this effect disappeared when each sex was considered separately. So although males were heavier and dominant over females, within each sex weight had no effect on status. Two other factors affected status: hatching date and dispersal distance. Older birds were generally dominant over younger ones, and non-dispersing birds were higher ranking than those which left their natal territory. In other words the amount of time a young bird had spent in an area, its familiarity with that area or the other birds within it, was the main factor which determined the outcome of a dispute. An early-hatched bird which remained in its natal territory during its first winter was likely to attain a high social rank. At the other extreme, a late-hatched bird which then left its natal territory was likely to have the lowest status. A bird which arrived in the non-breeding flock relatively late in the season was likely to achieve a lower rank than one which arrived earlier.

In order to determine the relative importance of arrival time in the flock and

Colour-ringed European Black-billed Magpie in the hand. (Photo: D. Hollingworth).

dispersal distance on status Eden (1987b) performed an ingenious experiment. With the help of several assistants he hand-reared 44 magpies and subsequently released them into the non-breeding flock. In performing this experiment we incurred the wrath of a local poultry farmer who was dismayed at the prospect of even more magpies! The young magpies were individually marked and on fledging released into a large aviary (5 × 20 × 4 m), where their dominance status was recorded. The birds were then divided into three groups of equal average status, and released one month apart in the centre of the wild non-breeding flock's home range. Their subsequent status in the wild was then recorded. The first group of magpies was released as the wild flock was forming, and their status remained similar to what it had been in captivity. The later-released groups, however, suffered marked reductions in dominance status (Fig. 29), suggesting that the length of time a bird has spent in the flock has important consequences for its status. This result suggests that if young magpies are going to leave home they should do so as soon as possible. However, their best chance of survival is to remain in or close to their natal territory (Eden 1987b), so why do they disperse at all? The answer seems to be that they often have no choice. Most young magpies probably attempt to remain at home, because this is the best option, but if food supplies within the natal territory decrease during the course of the winter the less dominant birds may be forced to disperse. The quality of magpie territories varies (Chapter 10) and so the likelihood of young birds being forced to leave due to food shortages will also vary. Some young birds are able to remain close to home throughout the winter, others may have to leave at various times thereafter.

European magpies fighting in snow. (Photo: M. Wilkes).

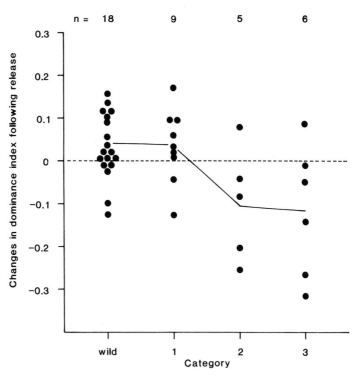

Fig. 29.   *Changes in dominance of wild and 'immigrant' young magpies in the Sheffield study following the immigrants' release from captivity. Birds in the later release groups 2 and 3 suffered the greatest decrease in status (p < 0.05) (see text). From Eden (1987b).*

HOME RANGES OF NON-BREEDING MAGPIES

During the autumn and winter the home range of individual, non-breeding magpies in our study area was about 18 ha, considerably larger than the adult's territories (see Chapter 2). The home ranges of individual flock members tended to be similar, but not identical, and overlapped the territory boundaries of the breeding birds (Fig. 30). This situation contrasts with that of Carrion Crows where, despite several similarities to magpie social organization, non-breeding birds occupy completely separate areas from the adults (Charles 1972; Loman 1985).

The location of the non-breeding flock's home ranges varied from year to year, and may depend partly on the presence of suitable food supplies. In the three winters between 1979 and 1982 the main flock in our study area occurred in a different location each winter. However, after 1982 a small poultry farm was established and the open-topped pens provided access to an abundant food supply for the magpies. In the following three winters the flock occurred in the same area, centred around the poultry farm (Fig. 31). Not all non-breeding magpies shared a common home range, since a small proportion (9%, 20 out of 227) lived solitarily on the parent's territories. Among flock birds those of different dominance status spent different amounts of time foraging with other members of the flock. The lowest dominance category spent more of their time foraging outside the main flock area and also tended to forage with fewer birds. Presumably by doing so they avoided the more dominant individuals and were able to forage in relative peace.

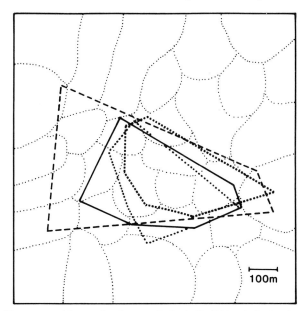

Fig. 30.   *Home ranges of four non-breeding magpies in the Sheffield study (various heavy lines), in relation to the territorial boundaries of breeding birds (dotted lines). Scale = 100 m. From Birkhead et al. (1986).*

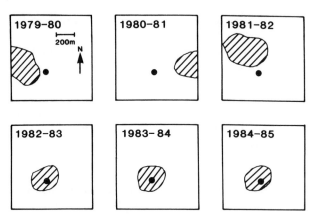

Fig. 31.   *Location of the collective home range of the non-breeding flock in the central (one kilometre) square of the Sheffield study area over six winters. From 1982/83 winter a poultry farm was established at the buildings indicated by the black circle; from then on this provided the focus for the flock. From Birkhead* et al. *(1986).*

Why do most non-breeding magpies forage in groups? Eden (1989) showed that the rate at which magpies found food increased with group size, up to about five or six individuals. This might suggest that flocking enhances feeding success, but a more likely explanation is that groups of magpies tend to form where food is abundant. If this is true then there is no advantage in feeding socially. It simply occurs as a consequence of the spatial distribution of food. However, there are two other potential benefits from group living: protection from predators and pair formation. In our study area predators such as the Goshawk were scarce, but the Carrion Crow was an important and aggressive competitor for food. Crows often displaced magpies from food, or chased them and stole it from them. On one occasion we even saw a crow catch and kill a magpie in flight following an encounter over food. By foraging in a flock magpies might be able to dilute the effects of crow interference (Bossema *et al.* 1986; Eden 1989). Vines (1981) found that magpies in larger groups continued to forage for longer in the presence of crows than did smaller groups. Competition between Carrion Crows and magpies is discussed further in Chapter 5. Pair formation may be facilitated by flocking, allowing birds to compare a range of prospective partners. Moreover we know that pairs can form from within the flock (Chapter 3).

RELATIVES WITHIN FLOCKS

Despite the low dispersal rates resulting in closely related birds living in great proximity we detected no kin-directed behaviour among our magpies. There was no evidence that members of the same brood specially associated together within the flock, nor that they avoided aggressive confrontations.

Similarly, we did not notice parents treating their offspring differently from other flock members.

SOCIAL ORGANIZATION OF NON-BREEDING MAGPIES

We can summarize the main features of the social organization of young magpies in our study area thus: most birds remain in or near their natal territory, living as part of a loose flock. Dispersal is similar for both males and females, although the latter showed a slight tendency to move further. This may have been partly due to the fact that some females acquire breeding status by pairing with 'widowed' males (see Chapter 3). Within the flock birds compete for dominance, and high rank greatly increases the chances of breeding. Most birds which survive to breed do so within one territory of where they were reared. It is clear from Chapter 2 that breeding opportunities in our population were extremely limited, and birds often had to compete vigorously for space. This raises some interesting questions, and invites comparison with other birds.

Several species, including corvids such as the Florida Scrub Jay, breed cooperatively. One or more young from previous seasons remain on their natal territory and assist their parents to breed. Because helping in this way appears 'altruistic', the way in which it has evolved has been the subject of a number of studies (Woolfenden & Fitzpatrick 1984; Brown 1987). One explanation is that in those situations where breeding opportunities are extremely limited, parents might do better to permit their offspring to remain on the territory with them, rather than forcing them to disperse. In return for being allowed to stay, the young birds help their parents to rear subsequent broods. Everyone

benefits from this system: the adults have to work less hard, and the helpers gain experience, and also help to rear further brothers and sisters. The extremely limited dispersal and shortage of breeding sites (territories) in magpies appears to make them prime candidates for cooperative breeding. Indeed, until the mid-1970s very little was known about the behaviour of magpies, other than that they were highly social and had low dispersal rates. Part of the reason for starting our study was the possibility that magpies might breed cooperatively. Why don't they? Our results indicate that after taking into account the survival rates of adults (Chapter 6), and the prospect of producing chicks, the likelihood of a magpie helper having younger siblings to help is lower than the chance of obtaining a territory. In other words, a young magpie's best option for increasing its genetic contribution to future generations is to breed rather than help. In addition, given the nature of breeding failures (see Chapter 9), the presence of one or more helpers might do little to enhance fledging success.

SUMMARY

Magpies first breed in their first, or more usually their second year. Before they breed young birds live in loose flocks and can sometimes make up over half of a magpie population. Most information is available for European magpies. Dispersal between the natal nest and the first breeding attempt is low: a few hundred metres, or about two territories. Females disperse slightly further than males. A dominance hierarchy exists within the non-breeding flock, and high-ranking birds are those most likely to breed. Males are usually dominant over females. Birds of different status adopt different strategies as non-breeders. An interesting difference between European and North American Black-billed magpies is that in the latter, first-year birds are dominant over adults outside the breeding season.

CHAPTER 5

Feeding and food hoarding

Beetles it eats in very large quantities, and also feeds upon worms,
snails and various similar creatures, so that the harm which it does to
the game and poultry is probably more than compensated by its good
offices in ridding gardens and cultivated ground of their varied foes.

Wood (*c.* 1880)

Magpies are generalists, living and feeding in a wide range of habitats and
utilizing a broad spectrum of food types. Both species forage almost exclusively on the ground, feeding mainly on animal prey during the summer months
and adopting a more vegetarian diet during the winter. Throughout the year
they exploit bird and mammal carcasses, such as road kills, but they also catch
small vertebrates for themselves. Their habit of hoarding any surplus food
during periods of food shortage may be a key adaptation that allows them to
survive in what might otherwise be unsuitable areas. Food hoarding may also
have played an important part in the magpie's expansion into urban and
suburban areas.

FEEDING METHODS AND HABITAT SELECTION

Both Black-billed and Yellow-billed Magpies obtain most of their food by picking up items from, or just below, the surface of the ground. They also take fruit from trees, overturn cow-pats in their search for food, and will catch and kill small reptiles, birds and mammals. Foraging occurs in a range of habitats but some are clearly preferred over others. In Denmark, Møller (1983a) found that magpies preferentially fed on grassland throughout the year, particularly around wind breaks, roadsides and in gardens. They rarely fed in long grass and usually avoided areas with crops. They also avoided bare soil, except in the period immediately following harrowing or ploughing. Bare soil is generally much less rewarding than grassland, except during ploughing and harrowing when ground invertebrates are exposed. The magpie's preference for feeding on grassland, particularly where domestic stock are grazing, was clear in our study and has been recorded by others, both in Europe (Holyoak 1974b) and in North America (Swenson 1980). The same is also true of Yellow-billed Magpies (Linsdale 1937; Verbeek 1973). In Britain, and presumably elsewhere, permanent grassland is particularly rich in invertebrates. For example, on grassland the biomass of earthworms, an important food for magpies in some areas, was five times higher (23 g/m^2) than on cereal stubble or ploughed land, and a similar pattern existed for other invertebrates (Tucker 1989).

Møller (1983a) also noticed that magpies fed extensively in areas near water and with high groundwater levels, such as meadows, where soil invertebrates occur near the surface. A sudden increase in the water level can result in large numbers of worms, snails and insects being driven to the surface, providing abundant food for magpies. Verbeek (1973) recorded a similar increase in food availability for Yellow-billed Magpies, following heavy rain.

The amount of time magpies spend foraging varies through the year, with summer being the most active time (Fig. 32). This is the period of peak food demands since it coincides with the late nestling and early fledging period. Most adults were therefore foraging not only for themselves but also for their young. The way in which birds searched for food also changed during the course of the year. During the summer birds took more steps and pecked less than at other times. Møller (1983a) suggested that this occurred because food was most abundant during the summer months and magpies were able to be more selective about what they took. Another seasonal change in feeding behaviour, noticed by several of those studying magpies, is the tendency for birds to forage in flocks in winter. However, as discussed in Chapter 4, flocking probably occurs in response to localized food supplies.

Verbeek (1973) examined the seasonal pattern of feeding and other behaviours in Yellow-billed Magpies: annual time budgets for each sex are shown in Fig. 33. The amount of time spent feeding varied throughout the year in relation to food abundance and daytime temperatures. Food was most abundant during April and May, and reached its lowest levels during the dry summer months in August and September. As with Black-billed Magpies, the

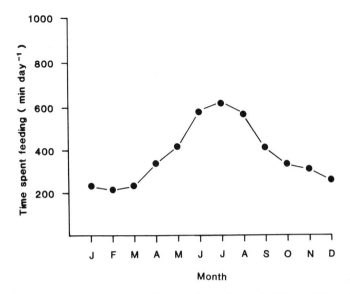

Fig. 32. *Seasonal changes in the amount of time spent foraging by magpies in Denmark. From Møller (1983a).*

maximum amount of time spent foraging occurred during the chick-rearing period (Fig. 33). During the summer, when temperatures could be as high as 30–40 °C, Yellow-bills fed mainly in the early morning, while it was cool and before the invertebrates disappeared to avoid the midday heat. In the winter the opposite occurred, and Yellow-billed Magpies fed mainly in the afternoon, presumably in anticipation of a relatively long winter night.

DIET

There have been a number of studies of the diet of Black-billed Magpies. Some of these were undertaken to determine whether magpies were harmful or beneficial to man (e.g. Kalmbach 1927; Collinge 1930). The magpie's reputation as a predator of the eggs and young song- and gamebirds is well known (see Chapter 11), but several studies indicate that these contentious items form only a small proportion of its diet.

Adult diet
Almost all studies that have examined the diet of adult magpies through the year have found that they feed mainly on plant material of various kinds during the winter, and animal material, mainly ground invertebrates during the summer (Csiki 1919; Kalmbach 1927; Holyoak 1968; Tatner 1983) (Fig. 34). Birds in suburban and urban areas supplement their diet throughout the year with food provided either deliberately or accidentally by man (Balança

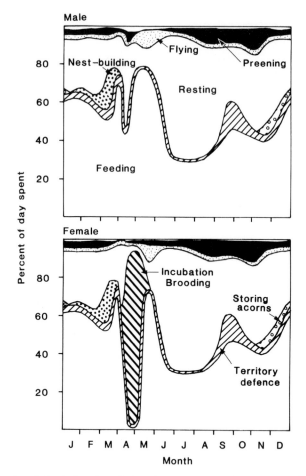

Fig. 33.   *Annual time budgets for male (upper) and female (lower) Yellow-billed Magpies at the Hastings Reservation, California. From Verbeek (1972a).*

1984a). Items such as bread and other household scraps in gardens or on city refuse tips are frequently eaten, and around farms magpies readily steal food provided for domestic stock.

Assessing the relative importance of different items in a species' diet is quite difficult, and a variety of techniques have been utilized to assess what magpies eat. Most studies have analysed the gizzard contents of shot birds (e.g. Kalmbach 1927; Holyoak 1968). It is, however, also possible to examine regurgitated pellets (Birkhead & Clarkson 1985b; Reebs & Boag 1987) and faecal material for food remains, and to use emetics in order to examine gizzard contents (Tatner 1983). The diet of nestling magpies can be determined relatively easily by placing soft wire collars around their necks to prevent them swallowing the food brought to them by their parents (Owen

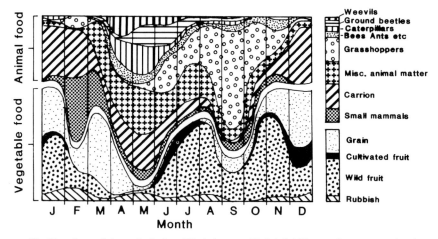

Fig. 34.   *Seasonal changes in the diet of North American Black-billed Magpies. Proportions are based on volume. Data derived from 313 Magpie stomachs. From Kalmbach (1927).*

1956). These different techniques all suffer from some sort of bias. Nevertheless they do provide a general picture of what Magpies eat.

In rural areas grain and fruit are important components of the diet during the autumn and winter (Holyoak 1968; Tatner 1983). In their study of birds and berries in southern England Snow and Snow (1988) found whitebeam to be the most important fruit taken by magpies. The same was true in our study, but we also noted magpies eating hawthorn and rowan berries. In addition, we regularly saw magpies pluck entire pears from a tree and fly off with them to eat elsewhere. Elsewhere, in northern Europe magpies have been seen feeding on the berries of elder, dogwood, mistletoe, spindle, dog rose, sea-buckthorn, and holly. In Spain magpies sometimes eat figs and grapes (Snow & Snow 1988).

Throughout the summer invertebrates form a substantial part of the diet. Tatner (1983) found, by using pitfall traps, that these organisms were most abundant between May and July, the time when many magpies are feeding young. Around Manchester, beetle larvae, adult beetles, ants and leatherjackets (the larvae of Tipulid flies) were the most important invertebrate components of the magpie's diet (Fig. 35). Holyoak (1968) obtained similar results from his study of magpies in lowland England and Wales.

Magpies also catch, kill and eat vertebrates from time to time. There are occasional records of them killing frogs, lizards, snakes, bats and moles, and they take small mammals such as rodents and small birds more frequently (Collinge 1930). Of 351 magpie gizzards collected in Hungary, 59 (17%) contained small mammal remains, 19 (5%) lizards and just 7 (2%) had bird remains (Csiki 1919). It is important to note that these values overestimate the numbers of vertebrates actually killed: some could have been eaten as carcasses. On one occasion I saw a magpie on the ground and running and jumping about in a highly erratic manner. My first thought was that the bird

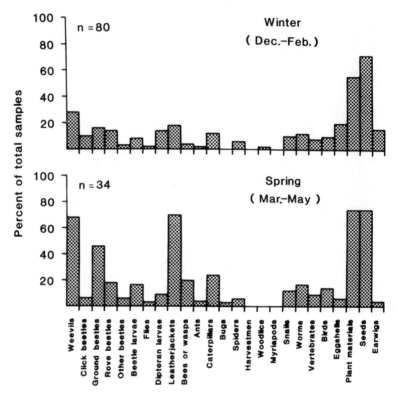

Fig. 35.   *Winter and spring diets of magpies in Manchester. Data show the percentage of all samples (pellets, gizzards and emetic samples) containing each food type. The increase in invertebrates in the spring samples is apparent. From Tatner (1983).*

was having an epileptic fit. Then, when I viewed the magpie in a telescope, I could see it was actually chasing a mouse or vole, which was frantically trying to escape by darting around in circles. They prey was eventually caught, held in the feet and killed by several hefty blows from the bill. The magpie continued to hold the prey and dismembered it by pulling pieces off with its beak.

Magpies are sometimes sufficiently agile to catch small birds. They occasionally catch sparrows in and around their roosts. I have seen magpies at dusk chasing and catching House Sparrows which were roosting in ivy on buildings. Rolfe (1965) describes how magpies caught roosting Tree Sparrows in a large reed bed in northern Spain. Up to 250 magpies and 1200 sparrows roosted in the area. About an hour before sunset, when the sparrows were in the reeds, groups of about six magpies plunged into the reeds after them. As they did so clouds of sparrows erupted from the marsh and occasionally a magpie caught one. On some evenings as many as 60 magpies were involved in this predatory activity.

European magpie beside dead sheep. (Photo: M. Wilkes).

Group of European magpies and a Buzzard scavenging on a dead sheep. (Photo: M. Wilkes).

Magpies occasionally attack larger prey. There are several records of them apparently killing half-grown and adult rabbits. In no instance has the actual method by which the magpie killed such large animals been recorded, but in most cases the magpie's first action after the prey is dead is to remove its eyes. They reputedly do this to injured or sickly sheep and lambs (see Chapter 11).

The diet of Yellow-billed Magpies has not been studied as thoroughly as that of Black-billed Magpies, but it appears to be broadly similar. The diet comprises a mixture of animal food, largely insects during the summer,

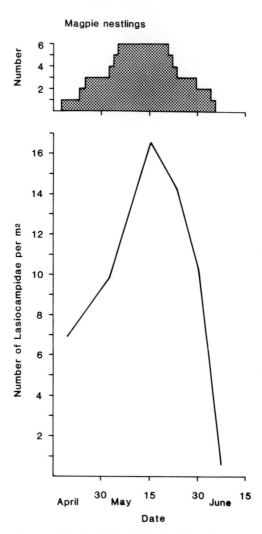

Fig. 36.   *Seasonal pattern of food availability for nestling Yellow-billed Magpies. The lower graph shows the changes in abundance of an important food item, the larvae of a moth in the family Lasiocampidae. The peak in abundance of this food coincides with the peak number of chicks in the population. From Verbeek (1973).*

supplemented by vegetable material, such as grain during the winter (Kalmbach 1927; Linsdale 1937). During the summer Yellow-billed Magpies feed extensively on grasshoppers and the larvae of butterflies and moths (Kalmbach 1927; Verbeek 1973). One mode of feeding they use which I have never seen among European magpies, is flycatching from the tops of tall trees. The food of the Yellow-billed Magpie appears to differ from that of Black-billed Magpies in two important respects. First, the main insect food for both adult and nestling Yellow-bills is highly aggregated and unpredictable in space and time. This is the main reason why this species breeds colonially (see Chapter 2). Although birds often tend to forage singly, once a food supply, such as a field of grasshoppers, has been located, it is exploited by all colony members. Verbeek (1973) describes how Yellow-billed Magpies quickly respond to the sight of a bird flying between a particular feeding site and the colony. Within a short time most colony members were foraging there together. The second interesting feature about this species' food is its seasonal pattern of abundance. Verbeek (1973) found that food abundance peaked in April and May, exactly the time when adults were feeding nestlings (Fig. 36). The sharpness of this peak, which is presumably determined by environmental conditions in California, indicates that the timing of breeding is probably much more critical for Yellow-billed Magpies than it is for Black-billed Magpies in Europe (Fig. 62).

Nestling diet
The food fed to young magpies in the nest has been looked at in a number of studies. For example, in the USSR (Eigelis 1964; Kekilova 1978), in North America (Kalmbach 1927), in southern Sweden (Högstedt 1980a), and in England in Wytham Wood near Oxford (Owen 1956) and the city of Manchester (Tatner 1983). In all these studies most of the food received by magpie chicks was ground-living invertebrates. However, in both Kalmbach's and Högstedt's studies rather more vertebrate material (27% and 20% by weight respectively) occurred than in the other two studies (12% in Manchester and none in Oxford).

In Tatner's study the main food items were leatherjackets, beetles, caterpillars and earthworms. The main difference between this study and Owen's was the larger proportion of defoliating caterpillars in the Oxford study. This is hardly surprising since the Oxford birds were foraging primarily in and around woodland. The diet of North American magpie nestlings included grasshoppers (17% of the diet), which were not recorded in the other studies. Leatherjackets and worms were not recorded in the diet of the North American magpie chicks. In Sweden nestling magpies were fed 25% earthworms, 20% rabbit carrion, 19% cereals and 12% weevils. The main differences between these four studies are illustrated in Fig. 37. On average the prey items fed to magpie chicks were about 7 mm long (Högstedt 1980a), and Tatner (1983) found that chicks younger than nine days old were given smaller items than older chicks. Young chicks received more flies, caterpillars and spiders, whereas older ones were fed more vertebrate material, worms, leatherjackets, hymenopterans and beetles.

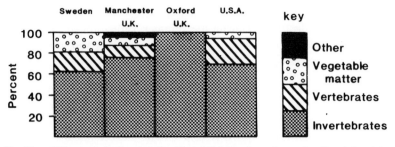

Fig. 37.   *Differences in the diet of nestling Black-billed Magpies in four studies. From left to right: Sweden (from Högstedt 1980a); Manchester, UK (Tatner 1983); Oxford, UK (Owen 1956), and Utah, Montana and British Columbia, North America (Kalmbach 1927). In the Swedish study most invertebrates were earthworms and weevils; vertebrate: rabbit carrion; and vegetable: cereals. In the Manchester study these were: weevils, beetles, caterpillars, small mammals and birds. In the Oxford study: caterpillars, flies and beetles. In the North American study: beetles, grasshoppers, flies, caterpillars and carrion.*

The studies described above show that invertebrates, especially beetles and caterpillars, are important components of magpie nestling diets. They also demonstrate that young magpies can be reared on a wide range of food types, and that adult magpies probably feed their young on whatever they can obtain most readily. The relatively small amount of vertebrate material in chick diets from some areas is somewhat unexpected, since, as Tatner (1983) points out, in terms of biomass one small mammal is equivalent to 54 leatherjackets or 3500 weevils! However, magpies must exploit carrion opportunistically, and live vertebrates may be difficult to locate and even more difficult to capture. The energetic costs of searching for and catching such prey may simply be excessive. In addition, by feeding their young on invertebrates magpies may be providing them with specific nutrients, not available in other food.

It is clear that Black-billed Magpies have a very varied diet. However, there are several important questions which remain unanswered. At present there is insufficient information to say to what extent the diets of urban and rural magpies differ, and simultaneous studies in adjacent areas need to be carried out. We also have relatively little information on the similarities and differences between adult and nestling diets: do adult magpies feed their chicks on exactly the same food as they themselves consume?

INTERSPECIFIC COMPETITION FOR FOOD

Over much of Europe the magpie shares its range with several other corvids (Goodwin 1986), and its diet is strikingly similar to that of two of them, the Carrion Crow and Jackdaw (Holyoak 1968). All three species forage extensively on grazing land and feed primarily on ground living invertebrates. It is not surprising therefore that these species compete with each other.

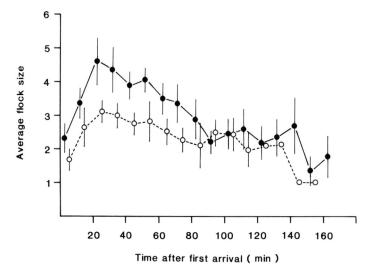

Fig. 38.   *Magpie flock size (±SE) with (open circle) and without (filled circle) Carrion Crows in the Sheffield study. The graph shows changes in flock size with time since the first birds arrived to the food provided. For the first 80 minutes Magpie numbers were higher in the absence of crows. From Eden (1987c).*

You don't have to watch European magpies for very long to realize that they and crows are arch enemies. Almost every study of magpies has commented on the aggressive interactions that occur between these two species (e.g. Högstedt 1980a; Baeyens 1981c; Vines 1981; Balança 1984b; Waite 1984). Because of their larger size (500 g versus 220 g), crows are usually dominant over magpies and Eden (1987c) has shown how they can disrupt the feeding behaviour of magpies. At feeding sites crows continually harassed magpies, lunging at them and chasing them. As a result the size of magpie feeding flocks was significantly smaller in the presence of crows (Fig. 38), and individual magpies fed for significantly shorter periods when crows were present (1.7 minutes) than when they were absent (2.1 minutes). It has been suggested that non-breeding magpies often forage in groups to gain some protection from crows (Bossema *et al.* 1976). Vines (1981) found that when crows were present at a feeding site the larger the group the magpies were in, the longer they were able to continue foraging. In the studies just described Carrion Crows and magpies bred in the same general area and often had overlapping territories. However, in northern Italy Fasola and Brichetti (1983) found that these species had a 'mosaic' pattern of non-overlapping territories. Such interspecific territoriality is a form of interspecific competition.

Ecologists define interspecific competition as occurring when two species have a negative effect on each other. Although the data from two of the studies described above hint that magpies suffer from the presence of crows, it is not clear whether the reverse is true. However, given that crows have to expend time and energy chasing magpies it seems likely that both species are disadvantaged by the other's presence. None the less, the relationship is far from even, and given the choice I would rather be a crow than a magpie. The type of competition that exists between magpies and crows is referred to as 'interference competition', since both species interfere directly with each other's foraging activity. However, the situation can be more extreme since crows sometimes kill adult magpies (see Chapter 4). They also disrupt breeding, by stealing nest material, causing magpies to desert, taking over the nest, or preying on their eggs and nestlings. Baeyens (1981c) observed crows ripping open the domes of magpie nests to steal eggs!

Magpies nesting close to Carrion Crow nests had very little chance of breeding successfully, and Baeyens (1981c) found that only 1 (4%) out of 23 magpie nests which had been disturbed by crows reared any chicks. In contrast about half of all nests not disturbed fledged young. Magpies reduce the effects of crows by several means. First, magpies are prepared to breed much closer to human habitation than crows. By doing so they can breed with relatively little interference because crows, more wary of man, are reluctant to use such areas (Balança 1984b). Second, magpies often site their nests in dense thorny bushes, or high up in trees on slender branches: both types of site restrict access by crows. The magpie's habit of roofing its nest (see Chapter 7) may also be an adaptation to minimize crow predation. These observations show that Carrion Crows and magpies are competitors. Although it is clear that magpies suffer from having crows in their territory, no one has tested the idea that magpies affect crows. This could be done by experimentally increasing or decreasing the density of magpies breeding within the territories of Carrion Crows.

Jackdaws and magpies also compete for food. Högstedt (1980a) found that the two species were morphologically and ecologically very similar. In January the body weight of magpies in his study area averaged 263 g, and Jackdaws 259 g (males only of each species). Beak sizes were also similar, the magpie's bill (38 mm) being about 10% longer than the Jackdaw's (34 mm). The two species spent 84% of their time feeding in the same habitats and the food fed to the nestlings of each species was also similar. Cereals, rabbit carrion, earthworms and a weevil, *Philopedon plagiatus*, made up 76% (by dry weight) of the magpie chick's diet. Cereals and the same species of weevil comprised 51% of the young Jackdaw's diet. The chicks of both species were fed on a large number of other invertebrates of a similar size. All these observations suggested that magpies and Jackdaws might compete for food during the breeding season and Högstedt (1980b) tested this idea by conducting an ingenious experiment. He compared the breeding success of magpies with and without Jackdaws feeding (and breeding) in their territories by placing Jackdaw nestboxes within magpie territories. The same pairs of magpies were compared with and without Jackdaws in two seasons, and their breeding success under these different conditions compared. The two groups started breeding at the same time and laid clutches of similar size. However, once the chicks hatched those magpies with Jackdaws in their territories

TABLE 7: *Interspecific competition between Jackdaws and magpies in southern Sweden. Comparison of magpie breeding performance with and without Jackdaws breeding in their territories*

	With Jackdaws		Without Jackdaws
Sample size (nests)	18		38
Laying date	20 April		21 April
Clutch size	6.5 ± 1.27		6.48 ± 1.11
Mean chick weight (g)[1]	182	***	208
Chicks fledged/pair	0.33 ± 0.85	***	1.68 ± 2.09
Chicks/successful pair	2.0 ± 2.46	***	4.0 ± 1.60
Percentage of pairs successful	17	***	42

Notes: From Högstedt (1980b).
Means are ±SD.
(1) At 21 to 25 days old.
*** = a significant difference.

experienced a marked loss of offspring, rearing an average of just 0.3 young per pair, compared with 1.68 young for the control birds (Table 7). This experiment clearly demonstrated that the presence of Jackdaws reduced the success of magpies, and this effect arose because the Jackdaws depleted the magpie's food supply, causing some magpie chicks to starve to death. As predicted, interspecific aggression between the two species was frequent during the magpie's chick-rearing period, with magpies attacking Jackdaws about three times each hour during foraging. Interestingly, Jackdaws did not suffer from the presence of magpies. Their breeding success, 2.3 chicks per pair, was similar to that recorded in other studies, suggesting that magpies had little effect on them. This result makes sense because, unlike magpies, Jackdaws are not tied to a territory and could forage over a wide area. Moreover, because they breed in cavities they are immune to predation by crows.

FOOD HOARDING

Food hoarding occurs in a wide range of mammals and birds, including several members of the crow family. This habit presumably evolved to allow animals to exploit food supplies which were temporarily abundant. Animals can eat only a limited quantity of food at any one time, and by hoarding the surplus they can reduce the chances of its being eaten by competitors. The success of food hoarding depends upon the hoarder being more likely to recover the hidden food than any other individual, and a number of mechanisms have evolved to enable birds to do this.

Of the corvids which hoard food, both Yellow-billed and Black-billed Magpies are short-term hoarders, caching and recovering food either the same day or at most a few days later. However, three species, the Jay, European

European magpie holding an acorn it is about to hide. (Photo: M. Wilkes).

Magpie in upright posture with food in bill. (Photo: M. Wilkes).

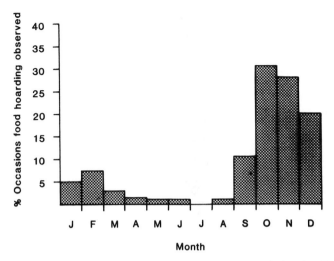

Fig. 39.   *Seasonal pattern of food hoarding by magpies in the Sheffield study. Based on 283 hoarding incidents. From Clarkson (1984).*

Nutcracker and Clark's Nutcracker, are long-term hoarders, using food which they have stored in the autumn to feed their young the following spring (Bossema 1979; Balda 1980; Tomback 1980).

Magpies have the reputation of stealing and hiding bright objects such as money or jewellery, and in Britain the magpie has been used by the police to symbolize the thief. In fact, there is no evidence whatsoever that wild magpies ever steal or hide anything other than food.

Although it has long been known that magpies hoard surplus food, most of the information has been qualitative and anecdotal, for both Black-billed Magpies (Hayman 1958; Turcek & Kelso 1968; Simmons 1970; Butlin 1971; Henty 1975; Waite 1985) and Yellow-bills (Linsdale 1937; Verbeek 1972b). There has been no detailed study of food hoarding in the latter species, and the following account is based largely on Keith Clarkson's investigation conducted in our study area.

Hoarding was recorded throughout the year, except in July (when few observations were made), but was most frequent during the autumn and early winter, when fruit and seed crops are most abundant (Fig. 39). At artificial feeding stations, where grain was provided for magpies (on 109 separate occasions: for methods see Chapter 1), they hoarded food on every occasion (except one) between September and January. In contrast, the incidence of hoarding fell to 70% in February and to 50% in March. The one exception occurred during December 1981 when the entire study area was covered in 0.5 m of snow. No magpies attempted to hoard on this day, but instead dominant birds attempted to guard the food we provided. Subordinate birds

TABLE 8: *Food items hoarded by magpies in the Sheffield area*

Type of food hoarded	N	%
Domestic refuse (bread, cakes, bacon rind, vegetables, etc.)	135	44.3
Dog faeces and kennel waste	50	16.4
Farmers' spillage: grain,	10	3.3
animal feeds	30	9.8
Acorns	34	11.1
Hawthorn berries	18	5.9
Whitebeam berries	13	4.3
Vertebrate carrion*	9	3.0
Pears	3	1.0
Cherries	1	0.3
Tomatoes	1	0.3
Elderberries	1	0.3

Note: * Includes Common Shrews, Wood Mice, Rabbit and a Blackbird. (From Clarkson 1984).

(see Chapter 4) collected food when they could, filled their gular pouch and flew off to eat the food elsewhere.

Clarkson recorded food hoarding away from artificial feeding stations on 305 different occasions over a three-year period. Only 23% of these involved the hiding of naturally occurring food items, such as acorns. The rest involved food provided directly or indirectly by man, and included household scraps, farmers' spillage and dog faeces (Table 8). Waite (1985) also recorded magpies hoarding acorns and bread in central England. In North America Buitron and Nuechterlein (1985) found that the main food which magpies cached was meat from prairie-dogs killed on the road. Interestingly, almost all food items that magpies cache are perishable, which is consistent with the fact that they are short-term hoarders.

Virtually all food caches were situated in the ground. Of 3184 caches observed by Clarkson, 3130 (98%) were made in areas of relatively short grass, 38 (1%) were made among leaves, and 15 (0.5%) in bare soil. A single cache was placed in a crevice in a drystone wall when the study area was covered in snow. In suburban and urban areas magpies also hoard food on rooftops (see Chapter 11). Yellow-billed Magpies also cache most food on the ground, but on several occasions I saw them hide meat from a dead ground squirrel and dog biscuits among clumps of lace lichen in oak trees.

We found that while hoarding magpies could carry up to 120 soaked wheat grains in their gular pouch and bill, combined. A total of 120 grains weigh 7.5 g; equivalent to 5.7 ml in volume. When caching magpies carry food both in their bill and their gular pouch, an extension of the mouth below the tongue (Eigelis & Nekrasov 1967). They then walk or fly to the caching area, keeping a lookout for other corvids, such as Carrion Crows, Rooks, or Jackdaws, which might steal the hidden food. Prior to hiding food a magpie often spends a few moments selecting what is presumably the most suitable area. Then, before making the cache the bird usually tilts its head on one side and looks at the

European magpies at a rabbit carcass. The bird at the back has filled its gular pouch with food. (Photo: M. Wilkes).

prospective cache site. This behaviour may allow the bird to identify the site and probably plays a crucial role in allowing the bird to recover the hidden food later. To make the cache the bill is pushed or hammered into the ground or grass, to form a small hole. The bill and pouch contents are then regurgitated into this and the beak is removed from the hole. The cache is then covered with a small tuft of grass, a stone, twig, or leaf. On average cache formation takes about ten seconds.

Caches are invisible to the human eye. On several occasions Keith Clarkson and I watched magpies hoarding food, one of us then walked to the precise spot where the food had been hidden, but was quite unable to see where the food was hidden. Only by digging up the turf could we find the caches. How then do magpies relocate their hidden food? The answer is that we do not really know, but it seems very likely that they simply remember where they put it. Clarkson examined this in an ingenious way: on certain days he provided dyed bread for magpies to hoard, using different coloured dyes on different days. Birds were later seen recovering coloured bread, usually the same day or at most after a few days, and when they did so they flew directly to the cache site and recovered the hidden food, usually without any hesitation. Hayman (1958) made similar observations. While this indicates that magpies can remember where they have hidden food, such observations may be biased in that the birds might fly directly to those caches whose location they *can* remember! However, it is quite likely that magpies are able to remember where they have hidden food: experimental studies with European Jays and Nutcrackers have shown that they are capable of memorizing the location of hundreds or thousands of caches for months (Swanberg 1951; Vander Wall & Balda 1977; Bossema 1979).

Magpies may also relocate their caches by smell. Buitron and Nuechterlein (1985) compared the ability of North American magpies to find artificial caches which they had made, consisting of raisins or suet, with or without a drop of cod liver oil. Of 30 'scented' caches (i.e. with oil) magpies found 15 within fifteen hours, but they found only 3 of those without cod liver oil – a highly significant difference. They also saw magpies walk directly past unscented caches, but approach scented ones directly. It is clear from these experiments that magpies, like several other bird species have a well-developed sense of smell. What is surprising is that the olfactory bulbs in the magpie's brain are relatively small compared with those species, such as the Brown Kiwi and Turkey Vulture, renowned for their olfactory sense. What is not known is whether magpies routinely use their sense of smell to relocate their own caches. Buitron and Nuechterlein (1985) suggest that magpies might use this ability to detect other magpies' caches. Early observers also suspected magpies of having a well-developed sense of smell. During the 19th century it was often noticed that whenever there was someone ill in a house, magpies would visit it, drawn apparently by the peculiar odour which 'was inseparable from a sick room' (Briggs 1849)! This may seem far-fetched, but it might be worth testing, or at least seeing if magpies can locate carcasses by smell.

KEEPING HIDDEN FOOD SAFE

During Clarkson's study he recorded a number of cache predators: Carrion Crows, Wood Pigeons, Rabbits, Wood Mice and slugs *Arion* spp. However, the most important cache predators were conspecifics, and magpies were very sensitive about hoarding food in the presence of others. If a magpie was approached while it was making a cache, the hoarding bird would usually try to recover its food and fly off to cache elsewhere. Robbery of caches took two forms, one where the cache was raided immediately after it was made, and the other where it occurred sometime later. Immediate cache robbery usually took the form of a dominant bird stealing food that a subordinate had just hidden. Only occasionally did non-hoarding individuals exploit the caches of hoarding birds. However, one of our colour-marked birds, an adult male, specialized in this method of foraging. He rarely hoarded any food himself, but regularly stole food from subordinate non-breeders hoarding food in his territory. To avoid longer-term cache robbery, magpies spread their caches about within their home range or territory, and are therefore referred to as 'scatter hoarders'. In contrast, certain squirrels and the Acorn Woodpecker store food in a single, central 'larder' or granary (Stapanian & Smith 1978; Koenig & Mumme, 1987).

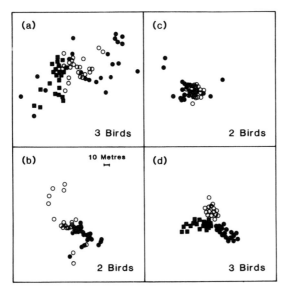

Fig. 40. *Spatial distribution of food caches for birds sharing a territory. (a) a male and two females (see text), (b) and (c) two pairs, and (d) a pair and one of their offspring which remained in the territory over the first winter. It is clear that within a territory individuals had largely non-overlapping caching ranges. Scale is identical in a, b, c and d. From Clarkson (1984).*

When magpies were hiding food they did so within a discrete area, so caches made on particular days tended to be spatially clumped. When both members of a pair were engaged in caching food they used different parts of the territory to do so. The same was true for a bigamous male and his two females which shared a territory (Fig. 40). The main advantage of using discrete areas for caching is that it allows birds to regulate the density of caches, which in turn determines their chances of recovering the hidden food (see below). Overall, magpies made their caches about 13 metres apart. However, one of the most interesting results obtained by Clarkson (1984) was that the spacing of caches differed markedly between different social categories of birds. Territorial birds made their caches closer together and nearer to the food source than non-breeding birds. The caches made by adults were 28 m from the source, and about 8 m apart. Non-breeders on the other hand often flew up to 65 m to hide food, and placed their caches about 18 m apart (Fig. 41). New territory owners adopted an intermediate strategy, travelling shorter distances than non-breeders but caching at similar densities to them (Fig. 41).

Many different animals hoard surplus food, and while 'larder' hoarders actively defend their hidden food, scatter hoarders, like the magpie, generally rely on the spacing of their caches to reduce the likelihood of their caches being robbed. Even within a species, variation in cache spacing may occur because the risks of cache robbery differ. Clarkson's detailed study revealed that the different spacing of caches between territorial and non-territorial magpies reflected the different risks of robbery.

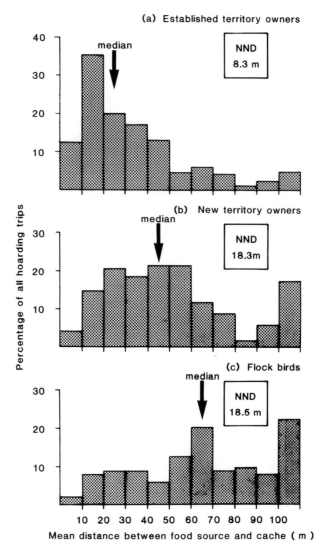

Fig. 41. *Frequency distribution of the distance travelled between a food source and the cache site for three categories of magpies in the Sheffield study: (a) established territory owners, (b) new territory owners, and (c) non-breeding, flock birds. Arrows indicate median distances. The box indicates the average nearest-neighbour distance for food caches, and is a measure of the proximity of adjacent caches. New territory owners are more similar to non-breeders than established territory owners (see text). From Clarkson (1984).*

Since other magpies were the main predators of cached food, those birds with *exclusive* use of a territory throughout the winter had a relatively low risk of losing cached food. On the other hand, birds whose territories also had to be shared with part of the non-breeding flock during the winter (see Chapter 4), had a much greater likelihood of having their stored food stolen. Non-territorial birds probably had the greatest risk of losing cached food, because of the way in which flock birds foraged. Once one magpie in a flock found a food item, or uncovered a cache, others came rushing over to see what it had found. They then started searching and feeding in the immediate vicinity. It seems very likely that if non-breeding magpies placed their caches close together they would lose a high proportion of them to others.

Clarkson *et al.* (1986) conducted an experiment to test this idea more rigorously. They selected nine territories: three where the occupying pair had exclusive use of the area, three where a small number (2 to 5) of other magpies

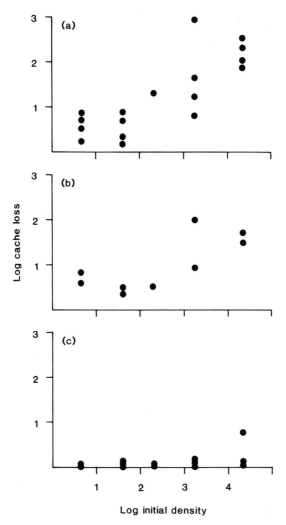

Fig. 42.   *The relationship between the length of time that artificial caches survived (log cache loss: high values indicate shorter survival time) and the density at which they were initially made, for three situations: (a) with many territorial intrusions, (b) intermediate, (c) very few territorial intrusions. It is clear that cache loss is highest when there are many intruders (a) and when the initial cache density was high. From Clarkson* et al. *(1986).*

foraged regularly, and three where a large non-breeding flock occurred in addition to the breeding pair. In each territory a series of artificial caches were made by the observers. This involved placing 7.5 g of wheat about 1 cm below the soil surface, mimicking naturally made caches. These artificial caches were laid out in grids ten metres square, and several grids of different density were made in each of the territories. So that the magpies had no visual clues to their location the caches were made at night. Under each cache a 2p coin was placed so that the cache could be relocated by using a metal detector! The grids were re-examined repeatedly over a four-week period to examine the rate that caches were lost. The aim of this part of the study was to assess how cache robbery differed in the three types of territory. The second part of the study looked at the way that territorial pairs in the three types of territory spaced their caches. It was expected that in those territories with many foraging magpies the territory owners would space their caches more widely than those which had exclusive access to their territory.

In territories with many magpies a high proportion of caches were lost, whereas in territories used only by the owners far fewer caches were lost (Fig. 42). Within the two types of territory with extra magpies, the highest density grids suffered the greatest predation. In other words, caches spaced close together were much more likely to be discovered than those spaced far apart. Natural caches were spaced appropriately. In those territories with many foraging magpies, the territory owners spaced their caches further apart than

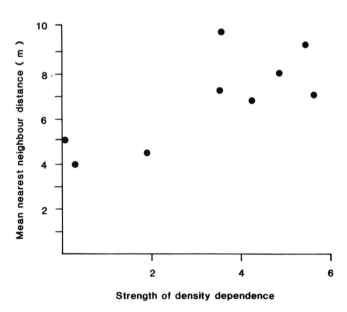

Fig. 43.   *Relationship between the spacing (mean nearest neighbour distance) of caches and the likelihood of cache loss (strength of density dependence) within individual territories (due to the number of other magpies using that area). The greater the number of birds using an area the further apart are caches spaced by territory owners. From Clarkson et al. (1986).*

TABLE 9: *Food-hoarding behaviour of birds occupying territories for different periods. Values are mean nearest-neighbour distances of caches (metres)*

	Mean nearest-neighbour distance	
Bird	*Territory occupied one year or less*	*Territory occupied three or more years*
Y YG	19.5	7.3
Y WB	22.5	9.3
R OY	12.6	4.7
R RW	20.6	7.2

Note: From Clarkson (1984). All comparisons based on a sample of 25 caches. All differences between time periods are significant ($p < 0.001$).

those having exclusive occupancy of a territory (Fig. 43). These results clearly demonstrate that magpies do not hide food at random, but instead are able to assess the risk of losing cached food to other magpies, and distribute their caches in such a way as to maximize their chances of recovering the hidden food. The apparently anomalous observation that new territory owners spaced their caches at a similar density to flock birds (Fig. 41), was not due to differences in the risk of cache robbery since the rate of intrusion by flock birds into these territories was identical to that for established territories (0.09 intruders per hour). Clarkson was able to look at the cache spacing of these same individuals three years later and found that all of them then spaced their caches in the typical 'territorial' manner (Table 9). The most likely expla-

nation for this 'lag' is that new territory owners continue to space their caches widely in order to assess the level of cache robbery in their new territory (Clarkson 1984).

SUMMARY

Both species of magpies are omnivores, feeding on a wide range of food types, mainly invertebrates during the summer and vegetable matter during the winter. Most foraging occurs in areas of short grass. In Europe magpies and Carrion Crows compete for food: interference competition between these two species is intense and uneven, with crows having a marked negative effect on magpie breeding success. Magpies also compete with Jackdaws, whose presence can also reduce magpie success. Both magpie species hoard surplus food, mainly in autumn and winter. They are 'scatter hoarders', making numerous small caches of food in the ground. Territorial magpies place their caches close together, and partners use non-overlapping areas during a hoarding session. Non-breeding magpies space their caches more widely. Experiments show that these patterns of cache spacing maximize the magpie's recovery rate of hidden food.

CHAPTER 6

Magpie populations

Previous to the year 1859 large flocks of magpies were frequently observed in the neighbourhood of Stocksmoor, near Huddersfield, when the weather was severe; sometimes they numbered thirty or even forty in a flock. But since that time the gamekeepers have nearly exterminated the species in that neighbourhood, and where formerly you could see scores you cannot see one now.

Gibson (1862)

Since the above was written things have changed considerably, and during the past thirty years magpie numbers in Europe have increased markedly. Magpies are not everyone's favourite bird and gamekeepers in particular have always regarded them as vermin. The expansion of magpies into suburban and urban areas is thought to place songbirds at risk and some city councils in Britain have even contemplated magpie culls. In Danish towns culling occurs regularly (A. P. Møller, pers. comm.) (see Chapter 11). In order to control a pest species efficiently, or to harvest a gamebird, or conserve a rare one, we need to understand something of its population biology. Three pieces of information are required to do this: (i) adult survival, the proportion of breeding birds surviving from one year to the next, (ii) survival to breeding age, the proportion of young which survive to become breeders, and (iii) reproductive output, the average number of young fledged per pair. With this information we can begin to predict how numbers might change over time. While this sounds straightforward, in practice it rarely is since obtaining accurate measurements of these parameters is often difficult. We also need to know something about the species' life-style in order to be able to identify the factors which are likely to limit its numbers. In other words, as well as knowing that magpie populations can increase at a particular rate, we also want to know what factors might set a ceiling on their numbers.

POPULATION TRENDS

The available evidence indicates that Black-billed Magpie numbers in North America have remained relatively stable or have declined slightly between 1966 and 1979 (Fig. 44). The decreases occurred in Montana and Alberta. Yellow-billed Magpies have apparently maintained their numbers over the same period (Robbins *et al.* 1986). In Europe magpie numbers have increased since about 1960; information on changes in numbers is available for

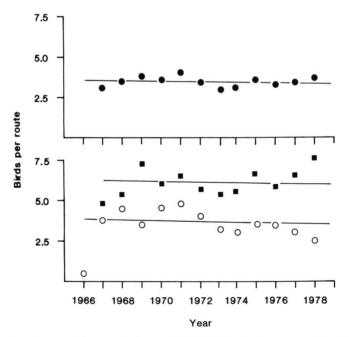

Fig. 44.   *Estimates of the population density of Black-billed Magpies in three parts of North America between 1968 and 1979. Open circle: central; square: western; filled circle: continental data. From* Robbins *et al. (1986).*

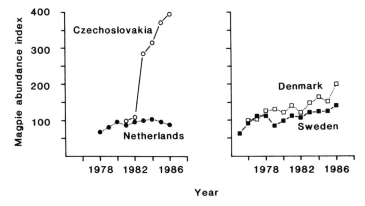

Fig. 45. *Changes in the abundance of magpies in four European countries. From Hustings (1988).*

Britain and for four other European countries (Fig. 45). All of these, with the exception of the Netherlands, show marked increases – the expansion in Czechoslovakia has been particularly dramatic.

In the British Isles magpie numbers have probably been increasing since the 1940s, and they continue to do so. Prior to this, numbers had been reduced as a result of extensive shooting and trapping by those interested in preserving game. During the 19th century, the heyday of gamekeeping, marked reductions in magpie numbers were recorded in several parts of Britain, especially in Scotland, and at the beginning of the present century their numbers may have been at their lowest level. However, the first signs of an increase were noted just after the First World War, in 1918, and were probably attributable to two factors: a decline in keepering during the war years and the ban, in 1911, of poisoned baits (Parslow 1967). Further increases were noticed in the late 1940s, after the Second World War. In Britain the number of gamekeepers has declined markedly during the present century (Fig. 46), and

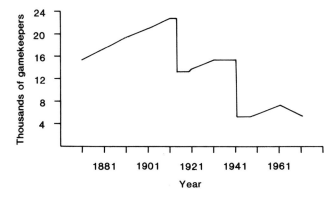

Fig. 46. *Changes in the number of gamekeepers in Britain between 1871 and 1971. From Newton (1986).*

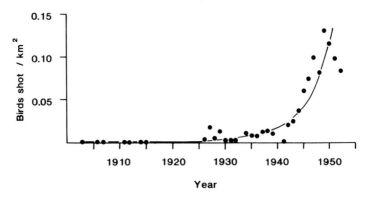

Fig. 47.   *Numbers of magpies shot per year on a single estate in Suffolk, England between 1903 and 1952, as an index of magpie population size (from data in Turner 1954). Line fitted by eye.*

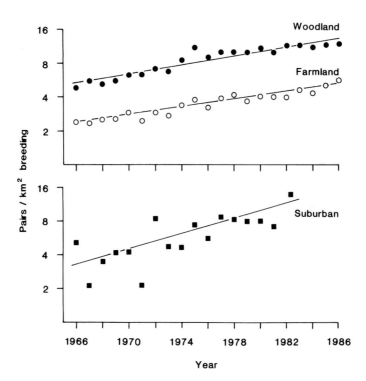

Fig. 48.   *Changes in the density of magpies in three habitats in England, based on the British Trust for Ornithology's Common Birds Census. Note that the density is presented on a log scale: this allows rates of change to be compared. It is clear that magpies on farmland and woodland have increased at a similar rate, whereas those in suburban areas have increased more rapidly (see text). From Gooch et al. (1991).*

the decline is considered by many people to be responsible, in part at least, for the growth in magpie numbers (e.g. Parslow 1973). Records of the numbers of 'vermin' shot by gamekeepers can also provide an index of the changes in magpie population (see below). A remarkable set of data which comprise a detailed record of all vermin shot on a single estate in Suffolk, eastern England, over the fifty-year period 1903–52, provide a clear picture (Fig. 47) of the changes in magpie numbers (Turner 1954).

Since the 1960s magpies, along with other species have been monitored by means of the Common Birds Census (CBC) index, which involves the estimation using standardized techniques of bird numbers on study plots distributed throughout the UK. The study plots cover two main habitats: farmland and woodland. As Fig. 48 shows, increases in these two habitats have been broadly similar, but the rate of change in suburban plots has been much higher (see also Chapter 11). The number of magpies shot continues to provide an index of their abundance (Fig. 49), and these data closely match the results from the CBC (see Gooch *et al.* 1991). In addition, the information on shot birds also illustrates regional changes in population increases (Fig. 49).

The status of the magpie in Ireland deserves special mention. Although fossil remains indicate that the magpie occurred in Ireland several million years ago during the Pleistocene, it was absent in early historical times. However, recolonization occurred in Co. Wexford in 1676 (Yarrell 1843;

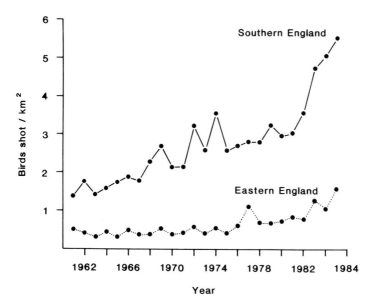

Fig. 49. *Differences in density and changes in density (arithmetic scale) based on numbers of magpies shot in southern and eastern England. From S. Tapper, A. Clements & M. Rands (unpublished).*

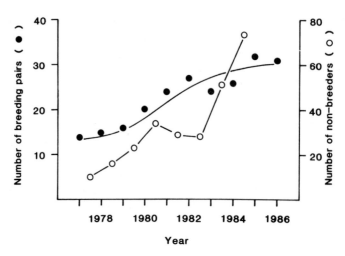

Fig. 50. *Changes in magpie numbers in the central square of the Sheffield study area between 1977 and 1986. Note that the number of breeding pairs (filled circles) levelled off at about 30 per square kilometre, whereas non-breeders (open circles) continued to increase.*

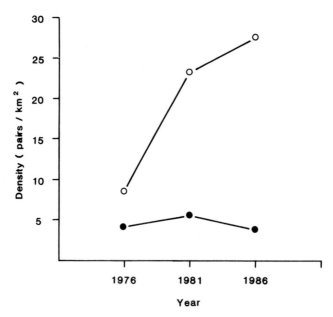

Fig. 51. *Changes in magpie numbers in two rural parts of the Sheffield area, with and without shooting. The area without shooting (open circles) includes the Sheffield study area. Data from the Sheffield Bird Study Group Magpie censuses. From Clarkson & Birkhead (1987).*

Armstrong 1940), and following this numbers must have increased dramatically for by the mid-1700s there was a reward for their destruction (Armstrong 1940). The first national survey in the late 1960s showed that they then bred in every county (Sharrock 1976). The density of breeding magpies in Dublin, at 16 pairs/km², is now among the highest recorded anywhere (see Chapter 11).

The number of magpies in our rural study area also increased over the period 1977–86 (Fig. 50), with the breeding population increasing at a rate of 12% per annum. This rate of increase was twice the national average in woodland (see Fig. 48) and may have occurred because we discouraged shooting and nest robbing. Indeed, as indicated above, a reduction in shooting pressure may well be one factor responsible for the overall increase in numbers. As part of a survey of magpie numbers in the Sheffield area (conducted by the Sheffield Bird Study Group), Keith Clarkson and I compared the changes in magpie numbers in two areas, in three censuses made at five-year intervals between 1976 and 1986. The first included our study area, while the second was a comparable rural area 10 km away on the south-east of Sheffield, but where shooting by gamekeepers occurred. The difference was dramatic and showed that shooting can maintain numbers at a lower level (Fig. 51). The results from our study (Fig. 50) show that the rate of increase in the last five years was lower than previously and that the breeding population levelled out at about 30 pairs per square kilometre. This suggests that magpie populations are indeed regulated by something, albeit at a higher level than many gamekeepers would like!

SURVIVAL RATES OF ADULTS

The first step towards understanding how these population increases have come about involves the construction of a 'life table'. This is a summary of the reproductive output and survival in relation to age (Perrins & Birkhead 1983).

The oldest known wild magpie is one bird ringed by Göran Högstedt in Sweden, and found dead in its sixteenth year. The oldest bird recorded in the British ringing scheme was 15 years old (BTO, pers. comm.). In our study area our oldest bird was in its ninth year when it died. The maximum recorded lifespan of a wild Black-billed Magpie derived from North American ringing returns was eight years (data from U.S. Banding Office); the oldest known Yellow-billed Magpie was still alive nine years after it was ringed as a nestling (W. D. Koenig, pers. comm.). Although these records are interesting, they do not provide the information we require. What we really need is a measure of the magpie's *average* life expectancy.

The magpie's lifespan can be obtained in two ways, either from the recoveries of ringed birds, or by following a population of individually marked birds over several years. The calculation of mean life expectancy from ringing recoveries makes a number of assumptions about the data which may or may not be fulfilled. As a result they may not be particularly reliable (Lakhani &

Newton 1983). On the other hand the sedentary nature of the magpie over much of its range makes it ideal for population studies based on observations of colour-ringed individuals.

Holyoak (1971) used ringing recoveries to examine mortality patterns in magpies and other corvids. He estimated, from a combination of British and Finnish recoveries, that about 60% of adult magpies died between one year and the next. From mortality rates like this we can estimate the average life expectancy, using the following formula:

$$\text{Mean life expectancy} = \frac{2 - m}{2m}$$

where m is the mortality rate expressed as a proportion. In this instance therefore, with mortality at 0.60, the expectation of further life is $(2 - 0.60)/(2 \times 0.60) = 1.2$ years. With hindsight and comparison with other species, it is now clear that such a mortality rate would be exceptionally high for a bird like the magpie (Perrins & Birkhead 1983). Tatner (1986) also calculated the mortality rates of magpies from a rather small sample of 15 recoveries, from birds he had ringed as chicks in urban Manchester. The mortality rate he obtained was considerably lower, just 33%, which gives a mean life expectancy of 2.5 years – more than twice that estimated by Holyoak (1971). Using Danish ringing recoveries Møller (1982b) found the mortality rate of adult magpies to be 26% – equivalent to a further expectation of life of 3.3 years.

Using colour-marked individuals Högstedt (1981a) found that the mortality rate of breeding magpies in his study area was 35%, giving a mean life expectancy of 2.4 years. Our colour-marked population yielded similar results. Based on 178 bird-years, mortality was 31%, and life expectancy 2.75 years. We also found some indication that males lived longer than females. Average mortality for males (based on 97 bird-years) was 25%, and for females (based on 81 bird-years) was 40%. Life expectancies were therefore 3.5 years for males and 2.0 years for females. This difference between the sexes was not statistically significant however.

Unfortunately no data exist for the survival rates of adult (or juvenile) Black-billed Magpies in North America. Verbeek (1973) found that 85% of his adult Yellow-billed Magpies survived between years. While this survival estimate is higher than that recorded for Black-bills in Europe, and indicates a life expectancy of 6 years, Verbeek's samples were extremely small (<10). However, Koenig and Reynolds (1987), working in the same area some years later, confirmed that the annual adult survival rate of Yellow-bills is about 80%. We clearly need more information on the population biology of both North American species, but particularly of Black-billed Magpies.

The recoveries of ringed magpies also provide information on the time of year when birds are most likely to die. Data from Britain and Finland (Holyoak 1971) and Denmark (Møller 1982b) indicate that the highest mortality rate of adult birds occurs during April, in the early part of the breeding season (Fig. 52). However, it is difficult to assess how accurately

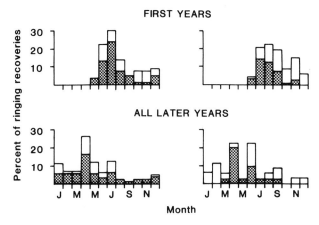

Fig. 52. *Seasonal pattern of ringing recoveries for magpies ringed in Britain (left) and Finland (right). Data are for birds during their first calendar year after fledging (top) and all older birds. Note that for birds in their first calendar year no recoveries can occur before May, since this is when the first young fledge. Shaded: birds shot, open: all others. From Holyoak (1971).*

ringing recoveries reflect the seasonal pattern of mortality since in our study and Högstedt's (1981a), both involving colour-ringed birds, no such pattern was apparent. Högstedt found that most birds died during the winter months, and in our study mortality was spread fairly evenly throughout the year (Clarkson 1984). It is not easy to determine why birds die, and in this respect ringing recoveries are unlikely to provide very useful results. For example, a ringed magpie which has been killed by man, either through shooting or being hit by a car, is much more likely to be reported, than is one which is killed and eaten by a predator. The fact that considerable mortality appears to occur during the early part of the breeding season suggests that mortality may be associated with the stress of obtaining or maintaining a territory (see Chapter 2). Predation by Goshawks was a major mortality factor in Högstedt's (1981a) study, but in our study it was impossible to identify any single factor as being important. We got the impression that food shortage was unlikely to be a significant mortality factor. Even during the weeks of freezing temperatures and extensive snow cover in the harsh winter of 1981/82, none of our colour-marked birds died. Of course the rigours of such a winter may have their effect later, but there was no evidence for this.

SURVIVAL RATES OF YOUNG BIRDS

As with most passerines, young magpies suffer high mortality after leaving the nest. This is reflected by the seasonal pattern of ringing recoveries (Fig. 52) and by our data from colour-ringed birds (Fig. 53). We found that only one-third of all chicks ringed in the nest survived the first four months of life.

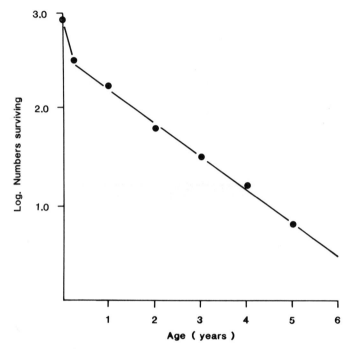

Fig. 53. *Survivorship curve for magpies ringed as chicks in the Sheffield study. Data are plotted as the log of the number still alive at different time periods. This shows that apart from high juvenile mortality in the first few months after fledging, the chances of a magpie dying remain remarkably constant over time (as reflected by the straight line).*

Undoubtedly some of these died before fledging, so this figure may overesti-mate mortality to some extent, but it still indicates that a fledgeling magpie has a relatively poor chance of survival. This period of high mortality coincides with the time when young magpies are becoming independent. It seems likely that their lack of experience and wariness makes them especially vulnerable to predators (Dhindsa & Boag 1989) and temporary food shortages. However, once they have survived the first four months their prospects improve, with the mortality rate remaining almost constant thereafter (Fig. 53). About 22% of chicks which fledged (119 out of 551), survived until the following April, the end of their first year (Eden 1985a). By this stage some of these birds had started to breed, while others were still in the non-breeding flock and did not breed until the following year (see Chapter 4). Eden (1985a) found that the two factors which had most influence on the survival of young magpies during the first few months of life were hatching date and body weight. Chicks hatched very late in the season had less than 20% chance of surviving, compared with 40% for those hatched earlier (Fig. 54a). There was also a tendency for late-hatched chicks to be lower in weight (on day 14) than chicks hatched earlier ($r = -0.260$, 164 d.f., $p < 0.001$). Overall, controlling for hatching date, the heaviest chicks had the greatest chance of survival (Fig.

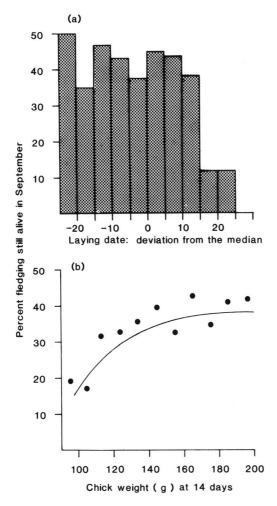

Fig. 54. *Survival of young magpies in the Sheffield study. (a) in relation to laying date, i.e. for the egg from which they hatched. Data are pooled over years and laying date is expressed as a deviation from the annual median laying date (see text): chicks from eggs laid very late in the season have the lowest chances of surviving. (b) Survival in relation to weight at 14 days old: the lightest chicks have the lowest survival chances. From Eden (1985a).*

54b). In terms of trying to understand the magpie's population dynamics, the most important measure of juvenile survival is the proportion of chicks which survive to breed. Overall, of the 720 chicks we ringed between 1977 and 1984, we subsequently found 96 (13.3%) breeding. Of these, 41 (43%) were females and 55 (57%) were males. Almost equal number of birds bred in their first and second year. Of 26 males 11 (42%) bred at one, 14 (54%) at two and 1 (4%), at three. Of 21 females 12 (57%) bred at one, and 9 (43%) at two. The difference between the sexes was not significant.

THE LIFE TABLE

With one further piece of information, on reproductive output, we can start to construct a life table for the magpie. Breeding success is discussed in detail in Chapter 9; here I use some of the information from our study to build the life table. A life table is a summary of the vital statistics of a population and it can be used to examine how a population maintains its numbers, or is expanding or declining.

Let us assume we are dealing with a population of 100 breeding pairs, 200 individuals. With 31% mortality, 62 adults will die each year. As shown in Chapter 9 the average breeding success in our study was 2.15 chicks per pair, so the total number of magpie chicks fledged is 215. I assume here that once magpies have started to breed they do so each year thereafter. Our study showed that with a very few exceptions this was true. Of the 215 fledged young, 62 or 29% would need to survive to breeding age simply to maintain a stable population. In our study the proportion of young birds which survived to breed varied between years, but was always below 29% (it varied from 5% to 17%). Clearly, the production of offspring was insufficient to replace the annual loss of adults. The most plausible interpretation of these results is that the growth of our study population occurred largely through immigration. However, before discussing immigration, it is probably worth considering how accurately we measured the other components of the life table.

The dispersal of adult breeding magpies was low, and very few adults were ever seen or found dead by members of the public outside the study area; this suggests that our estimate of adult survival might be reasonably accurate. Nevertheless, because we were dealing with relatively small numbers of birds the movement of just a few individuals out of the study area each year could result in our underestimating adult survival.

There are several potential sources of bias in our estimates of breeding success. First, our success at finding repeat nests varied from year to year; by failing to find every repeat nest we may have underestimated productivity. However, since repeat nesting attempts formed a fairly small proportion of the total and because they had a relatively low chance of fledging young (Chapter 9), this is unlikely to have had a marked effect on our estimate of reproductive output. Second, one of the main causes of breeding failure in our study (and in several others: Chapter 9) was desertion. In retrospect I suspect that visiting magpie nests reduces breeding success. Nest checks during the laying period are especially likely to result in desertion. We tried to keep nest checks to a minimum, visiting each nest only four times on average. None the less this might still have been sufficient to affect our results. It would be possible for someone to look at the likelihood of magpies rearing young, or the brood size of fledged young, for a sample of disturbed and undisturbed nests to check this.

The third and most likely stage where we might have underestimated success is in the proportion of young birds surviving to breed. More males than females survived to breed in our study area (although not statistically different from fifty-fifty), and suggests a bias in our estimation of survival. As I have shown in Chapter 4, the dispersal of young magpies in our study was very limited and most young birds remained in or close to the area to breed. However, there was a tendency for females to disperse further than males (see Fig. 26), and the fact that we had fewer young females than males breeding strongly suggests that some females dispersed away from the study area. We were aware of this problem at the outset and took two precautions to minimize it. We colour-marked all nestlings in a zone 0.5 km wide around the entire study area to see if there was movement into it, and we routinely searched this surrounding area for colour-ringed birds which might have moved out of the study area. As indicated above, we found very few movements in either direction. The only plausible explanation is that birds moved into the study area from further afield.

Immigration obviously cannot explain the widespread increase in magpie numbers over much of Europe. These increases could occur as a result of higher values of the three parameters, either singly or in combination. The two most likely factors responsible for the increase are higher adult or juvenile survival rates. If the annual adult survival rate was 80% instead of 69%, and breeding success and survival to breed were 2.15 chicks per pair and 24%, respectively, the population would increase at 6% per annum. Alternatively, the same rate of population growth would occur with 69% adult survival, breeding success at 2.15 chicks per pair, and 34% of chicks surviving to breed.

WHAT LIMITS NUMBERS?

Although magpies are increasing in many areas, their numbers are unlikely to expand unchecked for long. Sooner or later a point will be reached where one or more factors will start to reduce the rate of increase and numbers will then level out. What this level will be is not known, but it is clear that magpies can sometimes breed at relatively high densities, up to 30 pairs per square kilometre.

In our study area the number of breeding pairs increased initially and then appeared to stabilize (Fig. 50). Two factors were responsible for this levelling out: increased mortality of young birds and lack of breeding space. During the first five years of our study, when numbers were increasing most rapidly, the mortality of young magpies over their first winter (September to April) was negatively correlated with the size (density) of the breeding population (Clarkson 1984). This trend did not continue, but the situation is complicated by the fact that conditions changed during this time. In particular, the establishment of a poultry farm (see Chapter 4) probably increased the number of young magpies that the study area could support.

We obtained good evidence that a lack of breeding space limited numbers. Over our entire study area the breeding density varied from about 30 pairs/km^2 in the central area, to less than 5 pairs/km^2 on the valley tops (Fig. 8). The most notable difference between the low- and high-density areas was the lack of trees suitable for nesting on the valley tops. This suggests that in some areas breeding density may be determined by the availability of nest sites. We examined this idea further by dividing the entire area into forty 6.25 ha squares and looking at the relationship between the number of nests per square and the amount of tree cover. This analysis was performed on data for each of five years and in each case there was a positive correlation between the two variables. In three of the five years the correlations were significant. This supports the idea that the availability of nest sites plays a part in limiting breeding numbers. An appropriate experiment, such as that carried out by Charles (1972) to test the same idea for Carrion Crows, would have been to provide extra nesting trees. If trees were limiting then by providing extra ones we would have increased the size of the breeding population, just as it did in Charles's study.

The possession of a territory with both suitable nesting sites and food supplies is essential if magpies are to breed. This suggests that in the absence of other factors, such as predation (by natural predators or man), magpie numbers may be limited by territoriality. This was once a controversial area of population ecology, because it had been suggested (Wynne-Edwards 1962)

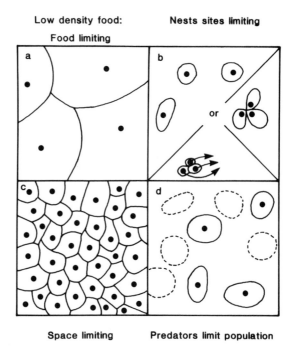

Fig. 55.   *Scheme to show the expected territorial system among magpies whose populations are limited in various ways. Filled circles: nest sites. (a) Food very sparse and limiting: magpies have very large territories. (b) Nest sites limiting; this can express itself in several ways: all available nest sites used and regular nest spacing, or aggregated nest spacing where in the available habitat'birds have either non-overlapping territories or very small territories that they leave to feed. (c) Space limiting: all breeding space occupied by territories. (d) Predators (including Man) limit the population, keeping it below the 'carrying capacity' so suitable territories remain unoccupied (filled circles).*

that territorial behaviour had evolved specifically to regulate populations. We now know that this is not true, but we do know that the regulation of numbers can occur as a consequence of territoriality. In other words, birds defend territories because by doing so they increase the quality or quantity of particular resources (Chapter 10), and a side-effect of this is that it sets an upper limit on the numbers that can breed in a particular area. This occurs because birds must defend a territory of a minimum size in order to obtain sufficient food. In the European magpie's case the minimum territory seems to be about four or five hectares.

A mechanism for how territoriality might regulate numbers was proposed by Brown (1969). He suggested that a species' habitat might range in quality from good to poor. The best areas were suitable for breeding, but the poorest areas would not provide enough resources to allow breeding. Initially, on moving into a new area the birds would occupy the best areas first; once these were occupied no further breeding opportunities would exist. However, birds could survive in the area as 'floaters', that is, as non-breeders. This situation is similar to that which occurred in our magpie population: as the breeding population levelled off, the number of non-breeders continued to increase (Fig. 50). The test of Brown's idea involves the experimental removal of breeding birds to see whether floaters take their place. Although we never removed birds, there were sufficient natural removals and replacements from the non-breeding flock to show that this is exactly what occurred (see Chapter 2). A summary of the factors which could limit magpie numbers is shown in Fig. 55.

SUMMARY

   Numbers of both magpie species in North America are stable. In middle latitudes of Europe, including Britain, magpie numbers are currently increasing. The reason for the increase is unknown, but may be related to the reduction in persecution by gamekeepers. A life table for the European magpie is constructed. Adult survival, based on colour-ringed birds, is about 70% (in Yellow-billed Magpies it is about 80%). Ringing returns show that most mortality of adult birds occurs in the spring. The mortality of young magpies is highest in the first three months after fledging, but remains constant after the first year. It is not known what sets a limit on magpie numbers, but space and nest sites are probably important.

CHAPTER 7

The breeding cycle: nests, eggs and incubation

Magpies . . . many absurd tales are told of this bird, which at the present day would only create a smile. It is said that if a person happens to espy her nest, and the bird observe him, that she will transport her eggs to some other place.

Hunt (1815)

The aim of this chapter and the next two is to provide an overview of the breeding biology of both species of magpie. For all organisms the single most important aspect of their lives is to reproduce, for if they leave no descendants they are evolutionary failures. On the other hand those individuals which are successful in reproduction are the ones whose characteristics will be passed on to subsequent generations. Effectively natural selection has ensured that all organisms will strive to produce the maximum number of offspring (Dawkins 1976), and a wide range of adaptations exist to enable them to do this.

NESTS

Magpie nests are large, distinctive and extremely durable. They can also be very conspicuous, particularly outside the breeding season when deciduous trees are without leaves. Usually a new nest is built for each nesting attempt, but sometimes an old nest is renovated.

The first sign that a pair are going to build at a particular location is that they place twigs or mud in a fork of a tree. These initial efforts are often accompanied by quiet vocalizations and a lot of wing-flirting between the pair – behaviours which may indicate a decision about the nest location. Erpino (1968b) looked at nest building among North American magpies in some detail and found that it proceeds in four phases. The first consists of the construction of a mud anchor. The birds collect mud or clay in their bill and place it at the site. Once sufficient mud is present, twigs and sticks are added to it. This marks the start of the second phase, which consists of building a stick framework. If the nest is roofed the overall shape is almost spherical. When the framework is nearing completion the birds start to collect mud again to begin the third phase, the construction of a mud bowl, which is usually built onto the mud anchor and eventually forms a deep cup about 15 cm wide and 10 cm deep. The fourth and final phase consists of lining the bowl with fibrous roots, hair and grass (Fig. 56). Nest building follows a similar pattern in European magpies, except that they usually appear to manage without a mud anchor. Both species of magpie build similar nests. A Yellow-billed Magpie's nest that Verbeek (1973) dismantled consisted of 1573 sticks and weighed 11 kg, some

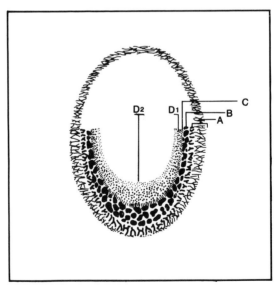

Fig. 56.   *Schematic diagram of a longitudinal section through a typical European magpie nest: A. external layer of sticks, B. clay or mud layer, C. inner twig and root layer, D1 inner lining, and D2 outer lining. Redrawn from Kulczycki (1973).*

70 times the weight of the bird. The only comparable information available for Black-billed Magpies comes from a single nest examined by Anders Møller (pers. comm.) in Denmark. This nest consisted of 598 sticks, weighed 4.6 kg, and measured 44 × 38 × 70 cm high.

Nest building takes about 40 days: three weeks for phases 1 and 2 combined, two weeks to build the mud bowl, and just three or four days to line the nest. The final phase is followed by a period during which the cup is shaped by the birds and no further material is added. A further eleven days (and up to three weeks) may elapse between nest completion and the start of egg laying (Erpino 1968b). The length of time taken by both species to construct a nest varies considerably, from three months to less than a week! In our study pairs which took a long time over building their nest were those which remained on their territory throughout the winter. These birds often started nest building as early as January, three months before egg laying, and appeared to build at a leisurely pace, producing well-constructed nests (Fig. 57). In contrast, birds which obtained a territory only in the current season spent less time building and usually produced much poorer nests.

Nest building occurs mainly in the first few hours of daylight. After midday there is little building activity as the afternoon is usually spent foraging. Both members of the pair participate in nest building, but each has a slightly different role. Males generally collect more sticks than females who in turn spend more time at the nest placing material brought by the male. In North America Buitron (1988) observed nest building in fourteen pairs of magpies building sixteen nests, and found that males made more trips to collect mud and large twigs, while females were more likely to collect grass. Overall, significantly more trips (63%) were made by males for nest material than females, and some made over three times as many trips as their mates. However, females spent much of their time inside the nest rearranging the material brought by the male, so on average each sex spent about the same amount of

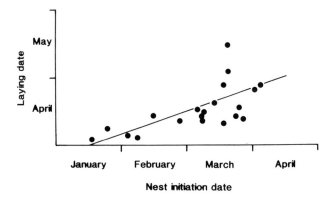

Fig. 57.   *Relationship between the start of nest building and the start of egg laying for magpies in the Sheffield study: birds which started nest building early also laid early in the season (r = 0.62, 19 d.f., p < 0.01). From Clarkson (1984).*

time building. The proportion of trips made by each sex, however, differed markedly (and significantly) between pairs and some of these differences were consistent between years. One female, for example, made the smallest proportion of trips (20% and 28%) of any female in both years of the study.

Among European magpies most nest material is collected within the territory, often close to the nest, but birds may sometimes fly beyond their territory boundary to find mud. The framework may be made from dead or live twigs, collected from the ground, from old magpie nests, or ripped from nearby trees. Thorny twigs, such as hawthorn or blackthorn in Europe, are often incorporated into the roof, and these probably help to deter predators (see below). In nests with a well-constructed roof there is usually a single entrance, but in poorly built nests the roof may be minimal, with no specific entrance. Magpie nests are generally thought of as being domed, but not all nests are roofed. In our study area and in the Netherlands about 20% of nests were open, though open nests appear to be rare among North American magpies (Table 10). D. Boag (pers. comm.) found that in Jilian Province, northern China, most magpie nests had either a very flimsy dome or were open. Baeyens (1981c) suggested that inexperienced magpies within her study population were more likely to build an open nest than experienced birds. Our data support this: pooling data for all years we found that 35% of nests built by first-year magpies ($N = 26$) were undomed, compared with 10% of 137 nests built by older birds.

New nesting attempts, either at the beginning of a season, or for a replacement clutch within a season, most often involve a new nest. In our study area the proportion of old nests that were renovated varied between 0 and 45% in different years. Overall, combining data for all years, 24% of 460 nests used for breeding had been used in a previous year. We found no tendency for magpies which had failed to rear young in one year to build a new nest the following year. Magpies may re-use nests, however, if nest sites or nest

TABLE 10: *Proportion of domed and open nests in different Black-billed Magpie populations*

Location	Total nests	Open (%)	Reference
UK, Sheffield	503	91 (18.1)	This study
UK, Sheffield (urban)	35	9 (25.7)	Eden (1985b)
UK, Manchester	136	1 (0.7)	Tatner (1982a)
Netherlands	79	18 (22.8)	Baeyens (1981c)
Poland	100	32 (32.0)	L. Jerzak, pers. comm.
Denmark	170	2 (1.2)	Henriksen (1989)
Morocco	9	0 (0)	T. R. Birkhead & D. Gosney, unpublished
Saudi Arabia	11	0 (0)	J. Gasperetti, pers. comm.
USA, South Dakota	56	1 (1.7)	Buitron (1988)
USA, Wyoming	63	0 (0)	Erpino (1968b)
USA, Idaho	100+	— (<1.0)	C. H. Trost & C. L. Webb, pers. comm.
Canada, Alberta	350	1 (0.3)	D. A. Boag & W. M. Hochachka, pers. comm.

materials are in short supply. There was some evidence for this in our study. As shown earlier, magpies breeding at higher altitudes almost certainly had a more limited choice of breeding site because trees were few and far between. As a result they may also have had difficulty finding suitable material to build nests. Combining data from six breeding seasons, we found that at altitudes greater than 200 m, 37% of nests were re-used each year, whereas only 19% were re-used at lower altitudes. Considering individual breeding seasons the same effect was apparent: in four out of the six years, pairs breeding at high altitudes were significantly more likely to refurbish an old nest.

In a study of urban magpies, Tatner (1982a) found that 36% of pairs (34 out of 94) re-used old nests, and he suggested that this habit may be peculiar to magpies breeding in towns. However, the value he recorded is similar to that from the high-altitude part of our rural population. It is possible that magpies in Tatner's study area may have been limited by the availability of nest sites or nest material. In Denmark, Henriksen (1989) found that 23–27% of nests were re-used each year. Among magpies breeding in North America there is relatively little information on the re-use of nests. Erpino (1968b), in two years recorded 2 out of 40 and 5 out of 40 (5% and 12.5%, respectively) of birds re-using nests, and Brown (1957) states that about 50% of nests were re-used, but provides no details.

Where nest sites are limiting magpies sometimes build new nests either on top of or close to existing nests. As a result several nests of different ages regularly occur in close proximity. This, together with the fact that magpies regularly visit old nests to collect nest material for their current nest, has led some people to believe that magpies build several nests in a season. The putative spare nests have been referred to as 'false' nests, and are supposed to fool potential predators (see references in Linsdale 1937). While this is an attractive idea, there is not the slightest evidence that it occurs!

Nest building by Yellow-billed Magpies follows a very similar pattern to that of Black-bills: nests are always domed, and may be constructed over two or three months before egg laying. A new nest is usually built each year, although Verbeek (1973) recorded one pair re-using nests in four consecutive seasons. Both sexes participate in building, but the task is divided as in Black-billed Magpies.

NEST SITES

Magpies usually nest in trees, although if none are available they will nest in low bushes or even on the ground. Holyoak (1967) refers to European magpies nesting in the following unusual sites: a hole in a building, a rock hole in a cliff, and even on an open cliff-ledge. In urban areas with few trees magpies sometimes nest on man-made structures (see Chapter 11).

A wide range of tree species is used for nesting. In our study area magpies used at least 21 different species, but appeared to show a preference for either low thorny bushes such as hawthorn or holly, or very tall trees, neither of

Multiple magpie nests in Sweden. (Photo: C. Magnhagen).

which made our nest inspections all that easy! Several studies have made statistical comparisons between the species of tree used for nesting with what was available. All of these show that magpies actively select particular types of trees and avoid others (e.g. Doo-Pyo & Koo 1986; May 1989). Around Edmonton in Canada, magpies nested in conifers twelve times more often than expected from their availability (Dhindsa *et al.* 1989c). In urban Manchester, magpies preferentially nested in hawthorn, Manchester poplar, Lombardy poplar, Jersey elm, holly and alder, and avoided lime, silver birch and sycamore (Tatner 1982b). In this study preferred tree species did not come into leaf earlier than non-preferred trees, but they did form denser canopies. Tatner suggested that this helped reduce the likelihood of predation in two ways: a close-knit canopy helped to prevent nest predators, like Carrion Crows, reaching the nest; it also allowed birds to build a roof on their nest. I tested the latter idea using data from seven years of our study by comparing the proportion of roofed and open nests in hawthorn and other tree species, but found no significant effects (see below).

Typical, domed Black-billed Magpie nest in the Rivelin Valley study area. (Photo: T. R. Birkhead).

Several observers have noticed the tendency for European magpies in rural areas to nest near houses. Møller (1978) has shown that this is an active preference and is probably another way that magpies avoid Carrion Crows. The latter species is more wary of man, and tends to avoid breeding near buildings (this is discussed further in Chapter 9).

Nests may be built near the top of the tree or bush, or part-way up. The height of the nest above the ground will largely be determined by the height of the tree or bush. On treeless Skomer Island, Wales, all magpies nest in or under bramble bushes less than 1 m above the ground. In Manchester the average height of 375 nests found by Tatner (1982a) was 13.8 m $\pm$ 0.2 SE. In our study area the average nest height was about 8 m, and in Denmark the average height of 300 nests was 4 m (Hansen 1950). Three-quarters of magpie nests in Wyoming, USA, were built less than 6.3 m above the ground (Erpino 1968b). The variation in nest height between studies is almost certainly due to the fact that tree species and their heights also vary.

The types of places used by Yellow-billed Magpies for their nests differ in two respects from Black-billed Magpies. First, Yellow-bills frequently build their nest within a clump of mistletoe: at Hastings over one-third of all nests were built like this (M. D. Reynolds, pers. comm.). Second, Yellow-bills almost always build at the very top of a tall tree. The average height recorded by Verbeek (1973) was 52 feet (16.9 m), and some were over 90 feet (30 m), and he suggested that this was to avoid predators. Not only are Yellow-billed Magpie nests a long way up (as anyone who has climbed to them will know),

Large nest of a Black-billed Magpie, just a few centimetres off the ground in a bramble bush on (virtually) treeless Skomer Island, Wales. (Photo: T. R. Birkhead).

Yellow-billed Magpie nests in a Valley Oak. There are three nests in this tree, the two right-hand ones were both used by different pairs in one year. (Photo: T. R. Birkhead).

they also tend to be sited at the end of either vertical or horizontal branches devoid of side limbs. In fact, the most likely explanation for the type of site used by Yellow-billed Magpies is to avoid predation by snakes. Several species, and especially the gopher snake, are expert tree-climbers and regularly take eggs and nestlings. Linsdale (unpublished) saw a king snake raid a low Yellow-billed Magpie nest.

TIMING OF BREEDING

Most birds are thought to time their breeding so that their chicks are being reared when food is most abundant (Lack 1954). In the following, the laying date for a particular pair of magpies is the day on which the first egg of the clutch is laid, and the overall population laying date refers to first clutches only, and is expressed as either the mean (= average) or the median (the date by which 50% of clutches were started).

Throughout Europe and North America most magpies start to breed some time in April (Table 11). In Burma and southern China laying occurs in

March, while in Tibet most clutches are started in May. Within Europe the geographic variation in the timing of breeding is small, with only a weak latitudinal trend for later laying at higher latitudes ($r = 0.584$, 12 d.f., $p < 0.05$). Holyoak (1967), using BTO records, found no latitudinal pattern in magpie laying dates within Britain. However, in Finland, von Haartman (1969) found that laying occurred significantly later around 64°N compared with 62°N (correlation with latitude: $r = 0.355$, 97 d.f., $p < 0.001$). Within North America most clutches were started in the second half of April but there was insufficient information to detect any geographic patterns. However, Kalmbach (1927) states that in the southern parts of the range, in Colorado, Utah and California, laying occurs in early April; further north, in Montana and Washington, laying occurs in mid-April, and in the extreme north, in Alaska, laying does not start before June.

In Europe the earliest recorded mean laying date was 8 April in Dublin (Kavanagh 1986), and the latest 18 May in northern Finland (von Haartman 1969). Since different studies were conducted in different years some of the variation between localities must be due to year effects. For example, in studies spanning three years at the same locality annual mean laying dates varied by 2 days (Dublin: Kavanagh 1986), 5 days (Anglesey: Seel 1983) and 6 days (Manchester: Tatner 1982a). In our study the median laying date varied by twelve days (12 to 24 April) over the eight years 1979–86. The greater variation in our study may have been due to the longer run of years, increasing

TABLE 11: *Timing of breeding in Black-billed Magpie populations*

Location	Egg laying[1]	Reference
UK, Sheffield	15 April	This study
UK, Sheffield, urban	10 April	Eden (1985b)
UK, Anglesey	12 April	Seel (1983)
UK, Manchester, urban	8–13 April	Tatner (1982a)
UK South-east	8 April	Connor (1965)
Ireland, Dublin	8 April	Kavanagh (1986)
Sweden, Revinge	22 April	Högstedt (1981b)
Norway, Trondheim	21 April	T. Slagsvold, pers. comm.
Poland	late March–early April	Klejnostowski (1971)
Netherlands	15 April	Baeyens & Koning (1982)
Finland	2–18 May	von Haartman (1969)
Spain, central	20 May	Valverde (1956)
Spain, Coto Doñana	20 April	Alvarez & Arias de Reyna (1974)
Spain, Caceres	20 April	Redondo & Carranza (1989)
Spain, Cordoba	20 April	Arias de Reyna *et al.* (1984);
		T. Redondo, pers. comm.
Saudi Arabia	April	J. Gasperetti, pers. comm.
USA, Wyoming	late April	Erpino (1968b)
USA, South Dakota	26 April	Buitron (1988)
USA, Utah	14 April	Reese & Kadlec (1985)
USA, Idaho	5–15 April	C. Trost and C. Webb, pers. comm.
Canada, Alberta	late April	W. Hochachka, pers. comm.

Note: (1) Values are mean or median lay dates (where a date is given) for first clutches.

TABLE 12: *Timing of breeding and spread of egg laying in Black-billed Magpies in the Sheffield study*

Year	Median laying date	(N)	Spread of laying[1]	No. of days
1979	23 April	(16)	15 April–20 May	35
1980	18 April	(35)	7 April–29 May	52
1981	16 April	(74)	31 March–2 June	63
1982	14 April	(72)	23 March–5 June	75
1983	17 April	(68)	23 March–4 June	74
1984	18 April	(82)	29 March–11 May	43
1985	12 April	(44)	25 March–13 May	49
1986	24 April	(36)	28 March–29 May	62

Notes: (1) Spread of laying is date of the first and last clutches (including repeats). Median laying dates are for first clutches only. Difference between median laying dates between years: $p < 0.001$.

the chances of hitting a particularly early or, more likely, a late season (Table 12).

Within any particular area climatic conditions can influence the timing of breeding. Our results show that if spring temperatures are low, breeding tends to be late (Fig. 58). High rainfall levels during the pre-laying period also appear to delay the onset of breeding. However, once the effect of temperature

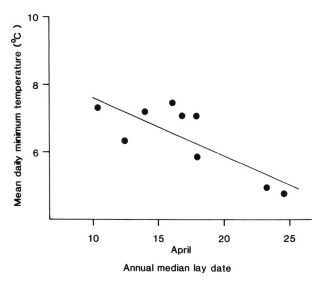

Fig. 58.   *Relationship between the annual median laying date in each of nine years of the Sheffield study and the temperature during the period mid-February to end of March. Breeding was later in cooler springs: laying date = 3.59 × temperature − 32.88, r = −0.75, 7 d.f., p < 0.02). From Goodburn (1987).*

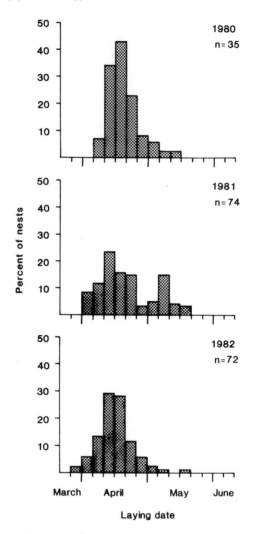

Fig. 59.   *Temporal pattern of egg laying in three years of the Sheffield study, 1980 and 1982 were typical years in which there was a single peak of egg laying, but in 1981 low temperatures and snow disrupted laying and resulted in two peaks (see text). Intervals are five days. From Clarkson (1984).*

is removed (using a partial correlation) the relationship between rainfall and laying date is no longer significant. On the other hand, the correlation between laying date and temperature is still significant after the effect of rainfall is removed. This means that cold springs rather than wet ones result in later breeding.

Within a season low temperatures associated with snow cover also retard laying. In most years of our study egg laying peaked some time in April. In 1981 however, laying showed two distinct peaks (Fig. 59). This occurred

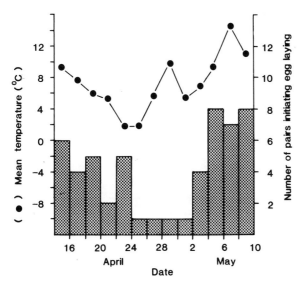

Fig. 60. *Pattern of egg laying in the Sheffield study during the spring of 1981 during a period of extremely cold weather (see text and also Fig. 59). Intervals are two days. From Clarkson (1984).*

because an exceptionally heavy fall of snow virtually stopped egg laying between 24 April and 3 May. During this time the study area was under about 1 m of snow and only five magpies started laying, but in the following ten days 15 clutches were started. Interestingly, the effect of low temperatures on clutch initiation was most pronounced five or six days after the start of the cold spell. Moreover, egg laying did not resume until five or six days after the temperature had started to increase (Fig. 60). This time lag may be the length of time it takes a magpie to form an egg.

Since temperature decreases with altitude, it is not unexpected to find that laying also tends to occur later among magpies breeding on high ground. Sheffield is notoriously hilly, and combining data from our study area with information collected from surrounding hills, we found a significant correlation between altitude and laying date (Fig. 61). For every 100 m increase in altitude laying was delayed by three days on average.

The mean or median provides a useful measure of the average timing of breeding, but does not tell us anything about the spread of laying. In the Sheffield study first clutches were initiated over 17 to 57 days in different years (Table 12). The earliest clutches were started on 23 March in 1982 and 1983, and the latest (first clutches) on 19 May (1978). In nearby Manchester the earliest and latest clutches recorded by Tatner (1982a) were on 21 March (1978) and 9 May (1979). In Dublin laying was particularly early, the first clutches being laid on 7 March, the latest on 30 April. Since magpies will lay replacement clutches if earlier breeding attempts fail, active nests can be found over a prolonged period. In our study area some replacement clutches were laid as late as the first week of June, and the maximum spread of laying for any

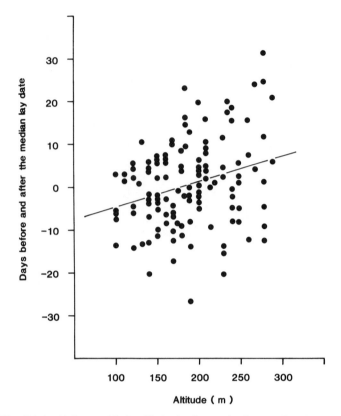

Fig. 61.   *Relationship between altitude and laying date (expressed as deviations from the annual median laying date) for magpies in the Sheffield study. Laying date = 0.056 × altitude − 9.96; r = 0.29, 120 d.f., p < 0.02. From Goodburn (1987).*

one year was 75 days (annual mean: 57 days ± 14; data for 8 years). Similar results were obtained by Holyoak (1967) from an analysis of BTO Nest Record Cards, and his study showed that the magpie has the longest breeding season of any British crow species. Since Black-billed Magpies in North America produce repeat clutches relatively rarely the same is unlikely to be true for them. The Yellow-billed Magpie seems to have an even more restricted breeding season (Chapter 5).

These results indicate that for magpies in Britain sufficient food for rearing chicks is available over a relatively long period of time during the late spring and summer. There has been no detailed study to see how closely the timing of the magpie's chick-rearing period coincides with food availability. However, it is possible to use some of the data collected by Tatner (1983) to look at this. As Chapter 5 showed, magpie nestlings are fed a mixed diet consisting largely of invertebrates. Tatner studied nestling diet in detail and in the same area he also undertook pitfall trapping of invertebrates throughout the year. By combining the information for his 27 categories of invertebrates we can

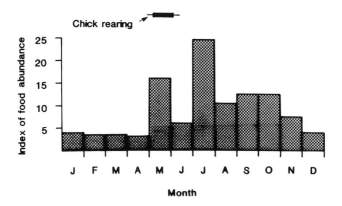

Fig. 62.   *Temporal pattern of food abundance in Tatner's (1983) Manchester study area. The food abundance index is the mean of all percentage categories of invertebrates. The mean (heavy bar), ± one standard deviation (lighter bar) for the chick-rearing period is indicated.*

produce an index of the seasonal abundance of these prey animals (Fig. 62). The main effect that this shows is a sudden increase in food availability during the magpie's chick-rearing period in May, and relatively high levels through-out the summer until November. Assuming that the relatively low value during June is an artefact of the data, it appears that magpies time their breeding so that their chicks hatch to coincide with a surge of invertebrate abundance during May. An even closer match between food abundance and chick rearing occurs in the Yellow-billed Magpie (see Fig. 36).

Black-billed Magpies lay replacement clutches about two weeks after the loss of the previous clutch. In North America the mean interval between loss of the first clutch and the start of the replacement was 16 days ($N = 9$; Reese & Kadlec 1985), 14 days ($N = 2$; Buitron 1988) and 13 days ($N = 7$; Erpino 1968b). In Britain the mean interval was 17 days in Manchester ($N = 34$; Tatner 1982a) and just 11 days in our study area ($N = 41$; Clarkson 1984). Clarkson also found that the replacement interval increased significantly through the season. For early breeders the interval averaged 10 days, and for late breeders, 13 days. This trend may reflect differences in bird or territory quality (Chapter 10).

Magpies in urban Sheffield breed earlier than those in rural areas. Tatner (1982a) first suggested that urban magpies might breed relatively early, based on a comparison of laying dates for his magpies in Manchester with those for the north of England derived from the BTO's Nest Record Card scheme (Holyoak 1967). Eden (1985b) was able to confirm this pattern by comparing the laying dates of magpies in our study area with those in urban Sheffield, just 5 km away, in the same season (1983). The mean laying date of 31 pairs of magpies in Sheffield was 10 April, 5 days earlier than those in the rural area. The mean altitude of nests in the city of Sheffield was lower than in our study area, but a comparison of 13 pairs of nests at the same altitude in the two areas also showed that urban birds laid earlier. Klejnotowski (1971) apparently found that magpies in urban areas of Poland started breeding two weeks earlier than those in rural areas. A number of other bird species breed earlier in towns than they do in rural areas (e.g. Perrins 1965). Advanced laying in urban areas may be due to the so-called 'heat island effect', that is, the heat generated by the city. Indeed, after taking into account differences in altitude, the mean temperature during the early part of the breeding season (March and April) was significantly warmer (11.8 °C) in Sheffield than in our rural study area (10.3 °C) (Eden 1985b). The slightly higher mean temperature in the city may have made natural food more available early in the season and allowed magpies to start breeding earlier. Kavanagh (1986) also suggested that relatively early laying of magpies in the city of Dublin may also have been due to warmer temperatures there.

Most of the information on the timing of breeding in magpies, particularly (i) earlier breeding in warmer springs, (ii) earlier breeding at lower altitudes, and (iii) earlier breeding in urban areas, all reflect a strong effect of temperature. A similar pattern has been found in several other bird species, including the European Blackbird (Snow 1958) and Sparrowhawk (Newton 1986). Later laying when temperatures are relatively low suggests that while magpies might attempt to breed at a particular time they may be unable to do so because low spring temperatures make food harder to find. In the magpie's case cold spring weather may make invertebrates less active and therefore less accessible. In addition, when temperatures are low birds may have to channel more of the food they do find into maintaining their body temperature rather than into breeding activities like egg formation.

The fact that food supplies can influence the timing of breeding in magpies has been demonstrated by some elegant field experiments by Högstedt (1981b) in Sweden. Magpies provided with extra food during the pre-laying period started laying 3.5 days earlier and started breeding over fewer days than control pairs. Högstedt's experimental design involved using the same pairs of magpies as experimentals (i.e. fed) and controls (unfed) in different years. Comparing the same females with and without extra food showed conclusively that those birds provided with extra food laid earlier. Three other studies, all in North America, have looked at the effect of providing magpies with extra food prior to breeding. In all cases the onset of laying was advanced relative to unfed pairs: by up to eight days (Hochachka & Boag 1987), seven days (Dhindsa & Boag 1990) and by four days (Knight 1988). Since these studies advanced laying by a maximum of eight days, food availability must be one of several factors which determine the timing of magpie breeding.

There is relatively little information on the timing of breeding in Yellow-billed Magpies. Although nests were inaccessible in Verbeek's (1973) study, he was able to assess when egg laying, hatching and fledging occurred by watching the behaviour of the parent birds. Verbeek's data are based on a small sample of nests in a single colony over four years. Average laying dates varied between 7 and 15 April, and the spread of laying averaged 19 days. There was a marked tendency for laying to be most synchronous when laying was early. In 1971 the mean laying date was 7 April, and all birds laid over just 9 days. At the other extreme, in 1968, laying occurred over 35 days with a mean of 15 April.

CLUTCH SIZE

Magpies usually lay about 6 eggs, although individual clutches can contain as few as 3, or as many as 9 or 10 eggs. In Britain the average size of first clutches varied between 5.5 and 6.7 eggs (Table 13). North American magpies are determinate layers, laying a fixed number of eggs regardless of the experimental removal or addition of eggs to their nests during laying (Davis 1955). As mentioned earlier, the number of eggs that magpies lay in clutch is relatively large. This can be seen most easily by comparing the average clutch size of magpies (5.6) with that of six other European corvid species: Carrion Crow, 3.9; Raven, 5.2; Rook, 4.3; Jackdaw, 4.3; European Jay 4.5; and Chough, 4.1. (All data are from BTO Nest Record Card scheme from southern England, except for Raven and Chough, which are from the rest of Britain; Holyoak 1967.)

For European magpies there is a weak positive correlation between latitude and clutch size, but this was not significant ($r = +0.361$, 14 d.f., NS). In many other passerines there is a strong tendency for clutch size to increase with latitude (see Perrins & Birkhead 1983). The weak relationship in the magpie

Clutch of European magpie eggs (Photo: T. R. Birkhead).

TABLE 13: *Clutch size of Black-billed Magpies*

Location	Clutch size[1]			Reference
	Mean	*SD*	*N*	*Reference*
UK, Sheffield	6.00	1.13	(367)	This study
UK, Sheffield, urban	5.79	1.32	(35)	Eden (1985a)
UK, Anglesey	5.76	1.06	(267)	Seel (1983)
UK, Manchester, urban	5.56	1.44	(86)	Tatner (1982a)
UK, South-east	5.87	1.32	(37)	Connor (1965)
UK, Scotland	6.70	1.20	(15)	Love & Summers (1973)
Ireland, Dublin	5.70	0.96	(71)	Kavanagh (1986)
France, Paris Basin	5.68	—	(40)	Balanca (1984b)
Finland	6.4	—	—	von Haartman (1969)
Netherlands	5.3–6.2	—	—	Baeyens (1981c)
Denmark	6.46	1.27	(104)	A. P. Møller, pers. comm.
Sweden, Revinge	6.21	0.95	(28)	Högstedt (1981b)
Norway, Trondheim	6.64	1.31	(118)	T. Slagsvold, pers. comm.
Poland	6.00	1.11	(22)	Jerzak (1987)
Spain, Coto Doñana	6.10	0.90	(108)	Alvarez & Arias de Reyna (1974)
Spain, Caceres	6.15	1.40	(34)	Redondo & Carranza (1989)
Spain, Cordoba I	6.23	0.97	(111)	Arias de Reyna et al. (1984); T. Redondo, pers. comm.
Spain, Cordoba II	6.26	1.02	(76)	T. Redondo, pers. comm.
USA, Wyoming	6.12	1.60	(34)	Erpino (1968b)
USA, South Dakota	6.20	1.10	(31)	Buitron (1988)
USA, Utah	6.50	1.10	(184)	Reese & Kadlec (1985)
Canada, Alberta	6.47	1.07	(55)	Hochachka (1988)

Note: (1) First clutches only.
Cordoba I = Espiel, Cordoba II = Cardeña: two separate study areas.

data arises from the relatively large clutch size (6.2 eggs) of birds breeding at the most southerly locations in southern Spain (37°N). Interestingly, the clutch size of North American magpies was generally larger than those in Europe, by about half an egg on average (Table 13), but there was no indication of any latitudinal pattern. This is discussed further in Chapter 12.

In our study area the average size of first clutches varied significantly between years, from 5.53 ± 1.07 ($N = 17$) in 1978 to 6.31 ± 1.25 ($N = 64$) in 1984. Two factors appeared to account for this variation: climatic conditions and the timing of breeding. Clutches were smaller in years when the pre-laying period was wet and when laying was late (Fig. 63). Although laying occurred later in cooler springs, clutch size was not significantly affected by pre-laying temperatures and partial correlations showed that laying date and rainfall affected clutch size independently. The size of first clutches also varied within a season, with birds breeding early producing the largest clutches. In eight out of nine years for which we had information, clutch size declined through the season, but in only two years (1981 and 1984) was the decline significant. This might have been due to the relatively small sample sizes obtained in single years. We checked this by combining data for all years, but using data for individual females only once (selected at random). This showed conclusively

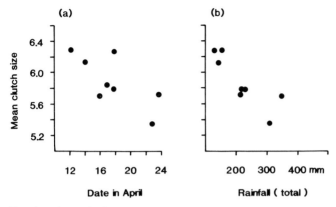

Fig. 63.   *Annual mean clutch size of magpies in the Sheffield study in relation to (a) annual median laying date, and (b) the total amount of rainfall during February and March. Clutch size is smaller on average in years when breeding is late, although the trend is not quite significant (r = −0.698, 6 d.f., p = 0.07). Clutch size was significantly smaller in years with heavy spring rain (r = −0.860, 6 d.f., p < 0.01). From Goodburn (1987).*

that clutch size decreased with laying date (Fig. 64: $r = -0.513$, 177 d.f., $p < 0.002$). However, this result also suggests that only a quarter of the variation in clutch size could be accounted for by laying date. Other workers have also reported seasonal declines in clutch size (Tatner 1982a; Seel 1983; Reese & Kadlec 1985; Kavanagh 1986), but the rate of the decline varies between studies. In most cases it is rather weak, and at most amounts to a reduction of about one egg over the season. The most likely explanation for this

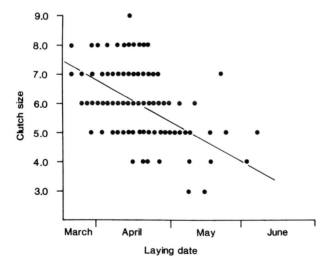

Fig. 64.   *Relationship between clutch size and laying date (first clutches only) in the Sheffield study, for individual pairs (but using each pair only once), (r = −0.513, 177 d.f., p < 0.002). Note that many points overlapped and these are not shown here.*

TABLE 14: *Number of eggs in first and repeat clutches for magpies in the Sheffield study*

Year	First clutches			Repeat clutches		
	Mean	SD	(N)	Mean	SD	(N)
1979	5.53	1.06	(18)	5.50	0.70	(2)
1980	5.83	1.06	(47)	5.66	0.57	(6)
1981	5.73	1.06	(83)	5.30	1.84	(30)
1982	6.15	0.94	(77)	5.76	1.03	(42)
1983	5.87	1.17	(72)	5.33	0.81	(6)
1984	6.31	1.25	(81)	5.69	0.85	(13)
1985	6.29	1.20	(56)	5.50	1.16	(12)
1986	5.77	1.20	(52)	5.50	1.16	(12)

Notes: The difference between first and replacement clutches was significant only in 1982 and 1984 ($p < 0.05$). However, in all 8 years replacement clutches were smaller than the first clutches and this difference is significant (binomial test, $p < 0.002$).

decline is that it is caused by young magpies which tend to breed late in the season and lay relatively small clutches (see Chapter 9).

Replacement clutches probably contributed very little to the seasonal decline in clutch size. Although replacement clutches tended to be laid relatively late in the season, on average they were not significantly smaller than original clutches (Table 14). A comparison of the size of 14 original clutches (6.14 ± 0.86 SD) and first repeats (6.29 ± 0.61) from our study showed no significant difference in size. However, second repeat clutches, laid after the initial repeat clutches were removed, were significantly smaller (5.36 ± 1.28) than earlier ones (Fig. 65).

Altitude had only a small effect on clutch size. Magpies breeding at altitudes of more than 200 m adjacent to our study area had a mean clutch size of 5.76 eggs $\pm$ 0.99 SD ($N = 51$), not significantly different from those below 200 m (5.90 ± 1.02 ($N = 71$)).

The average size of 70 Yellow-billed Magpie clutches was 6.5 eggs $\pm$ 0.93 (Linsdale 1937). At Hastings Reservation Reynolds (1990) recorded a mean clutch size of 5.70 ± 1.28 eggs ($N = 140$) during the 1981 to 1985 breeding seasons; the most frequent clutch was six eggs.

BROOD PARASITISM

It might seem rather odd to discuss parasitism here, but the number of eggs in a magpie's nest may be affected either by other magpies (intra-specific brood parasitism), or by interspecific brood parasites, such as the Great Spotted Cuckoo.

The possibility that Black-billed Magpies are intra-specific brood parasites was discovered by Chuck Trost and Cheryl Webb (1986) in Idaho, USA.

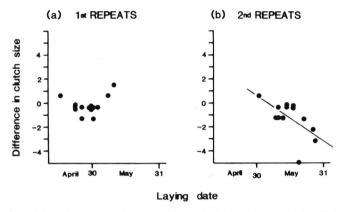

Fig. 65. *Relationship between laying date and changes in clutch size between (a) the initial clutch and the first repeat, and (b) between the first and second repeats. Each point is data for two clutches laid by the same pair. In (a) there is no change in clutch size with laying date, but in (b), later-laid second repeat clutches become progressively smaller through the season (r = −0.59, 12 d.f., p < 0.05). Data from the Sheffield study. From Clarkson (1984).*

Intra-specific brood parasitism is known to occur in a number of bird species, such as the Moorhen and the European Starling (Rowher & Freeman 1989). However, these species parasitize conspecifics simply by laying one or more eggs in their nests. What apparently happens in the magpie's case is remarkable: the birds lay in their own nest and then transfer eggs to nests of other magpies. Trost and Webb marked each egg with a unique number as it was laid. On subsequent nest checks they discovered that some numbered eggs had been transferred between nests. Overall, of 39 nests examined 15 (38%) lost between one and three eggs during incubation and 3 (8%) had eggs added. When I first read their account I was rather sceptical. Had they misread the egg numbers, or miscounted the eggs? However, subsequently it has been shown that Cliff Swallows regularly parasitize conspecifics both by laying in other birds' nests and by transferring eggs between nests (Brown & Brown 1988). In magpies also, egg moving may be a form of parasitism, but we need more information to demonstrate this. In our study we numbered eggs within each nest (but not with nest numbers), and although we noted eggs disappearing during incubation we never suspected eggs of being added to other nests. However, it is all too easy to overlook something like this, especially as our nest checks were kept to a minimum. In Trost and Webb's study magpie nests were relatively close together, with groups of three to six nests within 50 m of each other and this may have facilitated egg transfer (see also Chapter 2). Another possible explanation, suggested to me by Anders Møller, is that Trost and Webb's frequent nest checks, to number eggs as they were laid, may have been a factor causing birds to move eggs.

In India the magpie (race *sericea*) is parasitized by the Koel, and in Spain and southern France the magpie plays host to the Great Spotted Cuckoo. This cuckoo parasitizes several crow species, but in Europe the magpie is the main host. The cuckoo usually lays during the magpie's laying period and in order to ensure that laying occurs at the correct time female cuckoos secretly watch magpies near their nest during the pre-laying period. When the time comes for the cuckoo to lay, the male distracts the magpies by flying noisily towards the nest, allowing the female cuckoo to slip in and lay. Like the better-known European Cuckoo, Great Spotted Cuckoos can lay extremely rapidly, in just 3 seconds.

The eggs of the Great Spotted Cuckoo mimic those of the magpie. During the famous Coto Doñana expeditions (Mountfort 1958), parasitized magpie nests were overlooked initially because this mimicry was so good. The eggs of the two species are almost identical in colour, shape and size. Magpie eggs in southern Spain measured 33.7×23.7 mm (volume index (length $\times$ breadth^2) = 18.9), while Great Spotted Cuckoo eggs measured 32.0×24.0 (VI = 18.4). The close match bertween the two species' eggs has evolved because magpies are very good at discriminating between their own eggs and those of other species. Indeed, despite their excellent mimicry, about one-quarter of all Great Spotted Cuckoo eggs laid in magpie nests are ejected.

Great Spotted Cuckoos sometimes lay their egg from the rim of the magpie's nest. This may speed up laying and minimize the risk of detection, but it also results in one or more of the host's eggs being dented. The cuckoo's own eggs are protected from damage by their relatively thick shell, which is 1.2 to 1.5 times heavier than that of the magpie's. The damage to the magpie's eggs is of little consequence to the cuckoo, and may actually be advantageous since damaged eggs are removed by the host. Soler (1990) found that 81% (17 out of 21) parasitized magpie nests contained at least one damaged egg, compared with none in unparasitized nests. The damage was caused either by crushing (as the egg was laid) or by pecking (by the cuckoo), with about equal numbers of each type of damage. In no case were Great Spotted Cuckoos ever seen to remove magpie eggs. However, magpies removed damaged eggs from their nests, so the average clutch size of parasitized clutches (5.0 ± 1.3 ($N = 22$)) was less than that for those unparasitized (6.1 ± 1.1 ($N = 33$), $p < 0.005$).

The eggs of the Great Spotted Cuckoo hatch after an average of 12.8 days' incubation, significantly less than the magpie's 18–24-day incubation period (see below). With a head start and a rapid growth rate, the young cuckoos usually crush the young magpies (Arias de Reyna *et al.* 1982). If not, they invariably end up getting more food and effectively starving their nest mates to death. The young cuckoos do not eject host eggs or young as the European Cuckoo does. If the cuckoos hatch 3 or 4 days before the young magpies, none of the latter survive. Similarly, if two cuckoo eggs are laid in the same magpie nest, their chances of survival are determined by their hatching order. Normally Great Spotted Cuckoos lay only a single egg in each magpie nest, but two, or sometimes three cuckoos may use the same nest. Cuckoos can greatly decrease the reproductive output of magpies: Alvarez *et al.* (1976) found only

11% of parasitized nests produced magpie chicks, compared with 69% for unparasitized nests. The corresponding figures in Soler's (1990) study were 19% and 78%, respectively, and the average number of magpie chicks fledging from parasitized nests was 0.31 compared with 2.56 for unparasitized nests ($p < 0.001$).

Magpies are not indifferent to having Great Spotted Cuckoos laying in their nests and in some cases retaliate by ejecting the parasite's egg(s). However, the extent to which they do this depends upon how long the two species have occurred in the same geographical area. Where magpies and Great Spotted Cuckoos have coexisted for a long time, such as at Santa Fe, southern Spain, natural selection has favoured magpies which eject parasitic eggs, and as a consequence the breeding success of cuckoos is low; only 11% of cuckoo eggs result in fledged young. In contrast, at Gaudix, also southern Spain, but an area colonized by cuckoos only since the 1960s, magpies have not had time to evolve the ejection response to the same extent and relatively few cuckoo eggs are thrown out. The breeding success of cuckoos is, as one might expect, much higher, at 44% (Soler & Møller 1990).

INCUBATION

There has been some confusion over the duration of the magpie's incubation period, and this has arisen because magpies delay the start of incubation until part-way through laying the clutch. A bird's incubation period is generally considered to be the interval between laying and hatching of the last egg of the clutch. It has apparently not been possible to obtain this information for magpies. In fact, the commonly quoted incubation period of 18 days for both species (Verbeek 1973; Goodwin 1986) refers to the interval between laying of the last egg and hatching of the first chick. Tatner (1982a) found that the interval between laying and hatching for the *first* egg was 24 days (mean = 23.7 days $\pm$ 1.5 ($N = 52$)). Since incubation starts several days after the first egg is laid the true incubation period must lie between 18 and 24 days, probably being 21 or 22 days. The incubation period of North American and European Black-billed Magpies and of Yellow-billed Magpies appears to be the same.

As in most members of the crow family, incubation is undertaken entirely by the female. If she dies during incubation the male does not attempt to incubate and the breeding attempt is abandoned. The amount of time spent on the nest increases through egg laying, and once the clutch is complete female magpies spend 90–95% of their time on the nest (Fig. 66). A similar pattern was recorded for Yellow-billed Magpies by Verbeek (1973). Buitron (1988) found that even when females came off the nest, to stretch, preen and defecate, they rarely fed. This is because they are fed by their partner on the nest, on average 1.6 times each hour (Buitron 1988). Among Yellow-billed Magpies the male fed his partner 2.5 times each hour (Verbeek 1973).

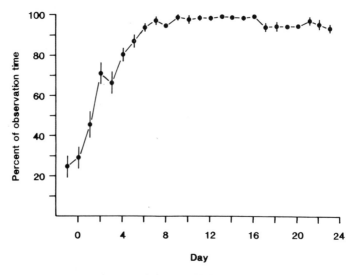

Fig. 66.   *Amount of time female North American Black-billed Magpies spend in the nest in relation to the start of egg laying. Day 0 is the day on which the first egg of the clutch is laid. By the time females have completed the clutch and are incubating they spend 80–90% of their time in the nest. From Buitron (1988).*

EGGS

Both species of magpie generally lay their eggs in the morning. Our observations of European magpies indicate that laying generally occurred in the first three or four hours of daylight. Trost and Webb (1986) and Verbeek (1973) made similar observations for Black-billed and Yellow-billed Magpies, respectively, in North America. One egg is usually laid each day, although there may sometimes be a gap of one or two days between eggs. Information on this point is difficult to obtain since we found that magpies very readily deserted their nest if we made daily nest checks during this stage of the cycle.

The eggs of both species are similar in size, shape and colour. They are pale greenish blue, heavily spotted with olive brown. There is quite a lot of variation in egg colour both between and within magpie clutches. This variation is less in Yellow-bills than it is in Black-billed Magpies (A. P. Møller, pers. comm.). The differences in egg colour between females can sometimes be dramatic, and several of our marked females laid distinctively coloured eggs over several seasons.

Magpie eggs vary in size both between populations and within populations. The average dimensions of 100 British magpies' eggs was 32.9×23 mm (Witherby 1920). A simple way of comparing the egg size of different populations is to calculate an egg volume index from length $\times$ breadth^2. This index is strongly correlated with fresh egg weight ($r = 0.96$, 61 d.f., $p < 0.001$. Egg weight $= 1.765 \times$ volume index $+ 1.212$; Clarkson 1984). Newly laid

European magpie eggs from three different clutches to show the variation in colour and markings (courtesy of Sheffield City Museum). (Photo: by T. R. Birkhead).

eggs in our study area averaged 9.9 g in weight or about 4.2% of female body weight. For Yellow-billed Magpies the mean fresh weight of eggs in a single clutch was 8.3 g or 5.7% of female weight (Table 15), with average dimensions of 30.8 × 22.4 mm (Linsdale 1937). The size of eggs differs between magpie populations and, not unexpectedly, is related to the size of the birds. The largest eggs are those laid by the race *bottanensis*, averaging 38.6 × 26.5 mm,

TABLE 15: *Weight of magpie eggs expressed as a percentage of female body weight*

Location	Adult female weight (g)	Egg weight (g)	Egg weight as % of female weight	Reference
Black-billed Magpie				
UK, Sheffield	233.0	9.9	4.2	This study
Norway, Trondheim	213.5	10.1	4.7	T. Slagsvold, pers. comm.
Sweden, Revinge	204.4	10.1	4.9	Högstedt (1981), pers. comm.
Netherlands	208.8	10.2	4.9	Baeyens 1979; J. Walters, pers. comm.
USA, Utah	163.2	9.5	5.8	Reese & Kadlec (1985)
Canada, Alberta	181.4	9.1	5.0	W. Hochachka & D. A. Boag, pers. comm.
Yellow-billed Magpie	145.5	8.3	5.7	Verbeek (1973)

with a volume index of 27.1. The smallest are those from *hudsonia*, 32.5 × 22.9 mm index: 17.0. Using data on egg dimensions for eight races of *P. pica* and the Yellow-billed Magpie (from Linsdale 1937) and wing length (as an index of body size), from Fig. 95, there was a significant correlation between volume index and wing length ($r = 0.749$, 7 d.f., $p < 0.05$).

Compared with other passerine birds of similar size, magpies lay small eggs. The relationship between body weight and egg weight for passerines (Rhan *et al.* 1985) shows that a bird the size of a European magpie should lay an egg weighing about 14 g, some 40% more than they actually do. The magpie's relatively small egg is undoubtedly related to the number of eggs in the clutch, which as we have seen, is relatively large.

Within a population a number of factors can affect egg size. The two main ones are female characteristics and food availability. Female body size in magpies may determine egg size to some extent. Clarkson (1984) found a significant positive correlation between wing length and egg volume index for five female magpies, but clearly more data are needed to verify this pattern. However, egg size is highly consistent within females, both for different clutches within the same season, and between years. This effect was sometimes quite obvious in the field. Some territories in our study area were occupied by unmarked females but we suspected that the same individuals were involved because the eggs were so similar in size, shape and colour between years. This size consistency could be due to either attributes of the female, or the territory she is breeding in (see Chapter 10).

Female age also affects egg size, with the youngest females producing the smallest eggs (see Chapter 9; Fig. 79). This effect may be associated with body size since we know that first-year females in Europe at least tend to be smaller than older females (see Chapter 1). Another explanation for the age effect is that as they get older and more experienced, females become more efficient at foraging and are therefore able to produce bigger eggs. An age effect may also explain why egg size tends to decrease, albeit slightly, through the season. Young females tended to lay late in the season (see above) and produce relatively small eggs. In our study egg size was negatively correlated with laying date in all eight years, although in only one year was this trend statistically significant.

Egg size was not related to clutch size, except in a single instance. In one season Clarkson (1984) looked at egg size in repeat nests in relation to whether the repeat clutch was the same size or smaller than the original clutch. Of 15 pairs whose repeat clutch was smaller than the original, 11 (73%) laid eggs which were larger than those in the original. In contrast, of 21 pairs that kept their clutch size the same between attempts, only 8 (38%) increased their egg size. This result suggests that, for repeat nests, a trade-off between clutch size and egg size might exist.

Because of the difficulty of checking nests during laying we do not have any information on egg size in relation to the laying sequence. However, we have examined the variation in egg size within clutches. The size of eggs was measured as their volume index (VI). This is a convenient measure of size

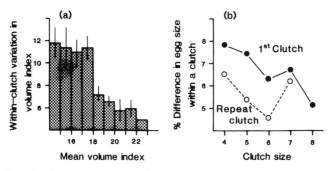

Fig. 67. *Variation in magpie egg size within a clutch in relation to (a) the average size of eggs in that clutch, and (b) the number of eggs in the clutch. Variation in egg size is as described in the text. (a) Shows that most variation occurred in clutches comprising the smallest eggs (r = 0.93, 7 d.f., p < 0.01). (b) Shows that egg size variation also tends to decrease with clutch size, for first (filled circles) and repeat nesting attempts (open circles) (first: r = −0.814, 3 d.f., p < 0.1; repeats: r = −0.760, 2 d.f., NS). From Clarkson (1984).*

since it can be made at any time, unlike weight which decreases as the egg loses moisture during incubation. The variation in egg size within clutches (expressed as ((mean VI − VI of the smallest egg)/mean VI) × 100) was 6.7%. Two trends were clear: when eggs and clutches were large, variation within the clutch was small (Fig. 67). Both these results may be associated with bird or territory quality. For example a poor-quality female or one in a poor-quality territory may experience an irregular food supply and as a consequence lay a small clutch of variably sized eggs. On the other hand the variation in egg size within the clutch under such circumstances may be adaptive and be part of a brood reduction strategy (Slagsvold *et al.* 1984). The idea is that if food is short during chick-rearing small chicks hatching from small eggs (see below) will be the first to die, thereby increasing the survival chances of the rest of the brood. Although we know that brood reduction occurs in Black-billed Magpies (see Chapter 8), the role of egg-size variation has not been investigated.

Further evidence that egg size reflects female quality comes from the strong correlation between egg size and breeding success (Fig. 68). At first sight this relationship suggests that egg size determines breeding success, but it is unlikely that this is a causal relationship. It is much more probable that both breeding success and egg size are correlated with one or more other factors, such as female quality or territory quality. This is not to say that egg size has no effect on breeding success. For example, last-laid magpie eggs which hatched were significantly larger than those that failed to hatch (Slagsvold *et al.* 1984).

In addition to these female effects there is also evidence that food availability can affect egg size. Indirect evidence for this was obtained by Clarkson (1984); he found that eggs laid during a period of extensive snow cover were significantly smaller (VI = 16.17 ± 1.49, *N* = 11 clutches), than those laid either before (18.66 ± 1.61, *N* = 34) or after (18.57 ± 1.61, *N* = 30) the snow. Direct evidence for the effect of food on egg size comes from three studies in

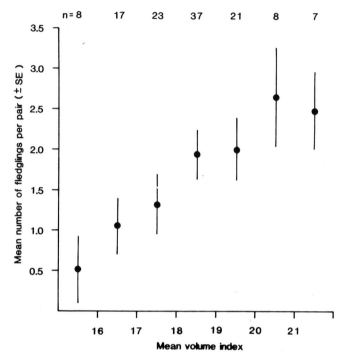

Fig. 68.   *Relationship between mean egg size (volume index – see text) and the number of chicks fledged per pair ($r_s = 0.34$, N = 121, p < 0.001). This graph suggests a causal relationship: that bigger eggs result in higher breeding success, but see text. From Clarkson (1984).*

which magpies were provided with additional food. In each case the fed birds produced larger eggs (Table 16).

We eat chicken eggs rather than those of passerines like the magpie because chicken eggs are more nutritious and taste better. They do so because they contain proportionately twice as much yolk as passerine eggs. The relative amount of yolk in birds' eggs is related to the mode of development of the emerging chick. Chickens have precocial young which are capable of running around, feeding themselves, and maintaining their own body temperature shortly after hatching. In contrast, young magpies are altricial: they hatch blind and helpless and must be brooded (by their mother) almost continuously for the first 5–10 days of life. The difference in egg composition between altricial and precocial species is most easily seen by comparing the relative amounts of yolk and albumen, the yolk : albumen ratio. In the magpie this is 0.23, and it is similar in other passerines (all altricial): Great Tit 0.29, Pied Flycatcher 0.33 and Starling 0.24. The ratio is much higher in species with precocial or semi-precocial young: Herring Gull 0.41, Common Guillemot (= Murre) 0.59, chicken 0.52, Mallard 0.78.

In our study area magpie eggs weighed 9.9 g on average. Of this 7.3 g (74%) was albumen, 1.7 g (17%) yolk and 0.8 g (8%) shell. The albumen is 90%

TABLE 16: *Size of Black-billed Magpie eggs for experimentally fed and control birds*

Location	Fed			Unfed			Reference
	Mean VI	SD	N	Mean VI	SD	N	
UK, Sheffield[1]	19.68	0.91	11	18.89	0.93	11	Clarkson (1984)
Sweden, Revinge[2]	20.56	0.98	20	19.09	0.91	29	Högstedt (1981b)
Canada, Alberta[3]	17.35	1.20	21	16.89	1.41	32	Hochachka (1988)

Notes: Values are volume indices of eggs (see text).
(1) Data are for first and repeat clutches by the same females ($p < 0.001$).
(2) Data for different females. Original data expressed as fresh egg weight, but converted to volume index for comparative purposes ($p < 0.02$).
(3) Data for different females ($p < 0.1$).

water and 10% protein, and the yolk is 57% water, 28% lipid (fat) and 15% non-lipid dry matter. Yolk formation is energetically costly and time-consuming for the female. It probably takes 5–10 days of intensive foraging to accumulate sufficient material to form a clutch. Also, because yolk contains most of the nutrients required by the developing embryo, one might expect the yolk to be the single most important component of the egg. It seems likely therefore that the size of the yolk will be influenced by the amount and quality of food the female can obtain during the pre-laying period. Supplementary feeding experiments support this idea: magpies provided with extra food tended to lay relatively large eggs (Table 16). Moreover, as we have seen there is some evidence that large eggs might be more successful than small ones. Indeed, chicks hatching from large eggs were heavier and structurally larger than those from smaller eggs (see Chapter 8). However, when Clarkson (1984) examined the composition of the eggs from magpies given extra food compared with 'unfed' birds the results were surprising. There was no difference in the size of yolk, and in fact most of the increase in size was due to an increased water content (in yolk and albumen). Hochachka (1988) performed the same experiment with magpies in North America and obtained essentially the same result. These results are difficult to interpret, and indicate that we still have a lot to learn about egg formation and what constitutes a good egg in magpies.

REPEAT NESTING

As already indicated, Black-billed Magpies in mid- and northern latitudes of Europe may make several nesting attempts in a season. The maximum number we recorded by a single pair was four: the original plus three repeats. In our study of 155 first nesting attempts that failed, over the entire study period, 10 (6.5%) relaid in the original nest and the rest re-nested elsewhere. Of those that used a different nest 129 (89%) built a new nest and 16 (11%) re-used an old magpie nest. Tatner (1982a) obtained similar results, except that a significantly ($p < 0.05$) higher proportion of pairs (6 out of 29, or 21%) in his study re-used the original nest.

The proportion of pairs that made one or more repeat nesting attempts was difficult to determine accurately. This was because by the time repeats were being made most trees were in leaf and the magpies were difficult to watch and new nests extremely difficult to find. The proportion of pairs which repeated after initial failure varied from 17% (6 out of 36) in 1984 to 72% (44 out of 61) in 1981. Part of this variation undoubtedly occurred because the amount of time we spent looking for repeat nests differed between years. In addition, the extent of failure through natural losses also varied between years. For example, the high number of repeat nesting attempts in 1981 occurred because a heavy snowfall during the peak laying period caused many pairs to fail and we spent a lot of time searching for repeat nests. In 1982 clutches were removed (under licence) as part of an experiment, and virtually all repeat nests were located: in that year 74% (52 of 70 failed first attempts) produced replacement clutches.

I suspect that the difficulty of finding repeat nests must be common to most magpie studies. Indeed, Seel (1983), working in North Wales, explicitly states that most of his information is from first nests. This makes it difficult to compare the incidence of repeat nesting between studies. The only difference I can detect is the apparent scarcity of repeat nesting among North American magpies. This can be examined by comparing proportions of pairs which failed that re-laid. Unfortunately few studies provide sufficient information to allow us to do this. Combining data for all years of our study (but excluding 1982, the year in which clutches were experimentally removed), 229 initial failures were followed by a repeat nesting attempt in 103 (45%) of cases. Tatner (1982a) followed 117 original attempts and of those that failed, 49% re-nested. In contrast, in southern Spain, re-nesting was very rare. Redondo and Carranza (1989) suggested that this was because the hot, dry Mediterranean summer curtailed the period over which food was available for feeding nestlings.

In North America Brown (1957) and Reese and Kadlec (1985) also found re-nesting to be rare, with only 16% and 10%, respectively, of failures being followed by repeat attempts. Information from other studies also suggests that re-nesting is relatively infrequent among North American magpies (Hochachka & Boag 1987). Only single re-nesting attempts have been recorded in North America (Erpino 1968b; Reese & Kadlec 1985). In our study, and in Tatner's (1982a) some birds laid two or three repeat clutches. In addition, in North America repeat nesting occurred only after the loss of eggs, never after the loss of chicks. Tatner (1982a) working in Manchester, recorded 6 (27%) out of 22 pairs which lost chicks producing replacement clutches. We never recorded repeat nesting after the loss of chicks in the Sheffield study.

In conclusion, it looks as though environmental conditions have a marked effect on the duration of the magpie's breeding season. The low incidence of repeat nesting in southern Europe and North America indicates that the hot, dry summers in these areas result in a relatively short period when conditions are suitable for rearing young. It is rarely worthwhile therefore replacing a lost clutch. Repeat nesting is also rare in the Yellow-billed Magpie (Verbeek 1973), which also breeds in an area with very dry summers. There is additional evidence to support this idea. In Utah clutch size and breeding success declined markedly through the season (Reese & Kadlec 1985), indicating that optimum conditions for breeding occurred over a shorter period of time than in mid- and northern latitudes in Europe, where clutch size and breeding success showed either no significant decline or only weak trends.

SUMMARY

Magpies build large, stick nests. In North America most nests are roofed, but in Europe up to 30% may be open. Nests are built in bushes or trees, more rarely on man-made structures or on the ground. Yellow-billed Magpies consistently build at the top of tall trees. Both sexes build, and nest construction takes about 40 days. Nests may be re-used in subsequent years. There is no evidence that magpies build 'false' nests. Egg laying usually occurs in April. Within each region, laying is earlier in warmer springs. The breeding season is relatively long in mid- and northern latitudes in Europe and shorter in areas with dry summers, such as southern Europe and North America. Both species lay about six eggs. For Black-billed Magpies clutch size is about half an egg larger on average in North America compared with Europe. Within a season clutch size decreases with later laying. In southern Europe magpies are parasitized by Great Spotted Cuckoos, which can greatly reduce magpie breeding success. In North America magpies sometimes parasitize each others' nests. Incubation is by the female alone and lasts 24 days (from laying to hatching of the first egg). Eggs weigh about 10 g or 4–5% of adult female weight. Individual females lay eggs of similar size and colour in successive years.

CHAPTER 8

The breeding cycle: chicks and their care

When the nest of the Magpie is approached, should it only contain fresh eggs, the bird slips quietly off them; should she, however, be sitting, it often requires repeated blows on the trunk of the tree to dislodge her; and when the young birds are hatched, both parents will fly around the tree at some considerable elevation uttering cries of alarm.

Seebohm (1883)

The chicks of both magpie species hatch 18 to 19 days after the last egg is laid and, within a clutch, hatching occurs over two or three days. On emerging from the egg the chick is blind and covered by just a few wisps of down. In both species only females brood the young and, during hatching, they sit tightly and are very reluctant to leave the nest. Females sometimes continued to brood as we climbed the nest tree, leaving only when someone's head appeared over the side of the nest.

Buitron (1988) found that in North America females brooded young nestlings for over 80% of the time initially, but as they got older they were brooded less and less (Fig. 69). By the time the chicks were 15 days old they

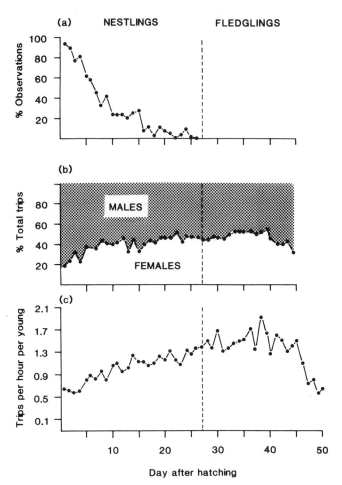

Fig. 69.   *Brooding and feeding of North American Black-billed Magpie chicks in relation to time after hatching and fledging. (a) Shows the percentage of time females brooded young in the nest; (b) shows the relative feeding effort by male and female parents, and (c) shows the rate at which chicks were fed by both parents (expressed as feeds per chick per hour). Data based on 21 different pairs of birds and 1457 hours of observation. From Buitron (1988).*

were brooded for less than 10% of the time. However, during cold or wet weather the female sometimes brooded very large chicks. Since the female performs all the brooding, her contribution to feeding the young was less than that of the male. In the first 12 days after hatching females fed chicks at a rate of 1.4 feeds/hour, whereas males provided 3.1 feeds/h; a total of 4.5 feeds/h. During the last half of the nestling period females fed chicks at a higher rate than earlier (2.6 feeds/h) and males also increased their feeding rate to 3.5 feeds/h: 6.1 feeds/h in total. The difference in feeding rate between the sexes persisted even after the young had left the nest, although it was less marked

Magpie breeding habitat in southern Spain in T. Redondo's study area. The nesting trees are Holm Oaks and the shrub layer has been removed to create pasture land. This habitat, referred to as 'dehesa' is typical of southern Spain (cf photo on p 37 of habitat in the Coto Doñana). (Photo: L. M. Arias de Reyna).

than previously. The rate at which chicks were fed, by both parents, increased through the nestling period and the first part of the fledging period. Thereafter it decreased as the young became independent (Fig. 69). As a result of the male's greater effort in feeding the chicks, and his care for the female during incubation, his overall energy expenditure during the breeding season, exceeded that of the female by about 30% (Fig. 70) (Mugaas & King 1981). Given the male's contribution, it is not surprising that his help is essential if breeding is to be successful. In a series of experiments in which male North American Black-billed Magpies were removed during incubation or early chick-rearing, females consistently failed to rear any young alone (Dunn & Hannon 1989).

Parent magpies defend their nestlings by calling and mobbing potential nest predators, including ecologists. The extent of parental concern is positively correlated with the age and hence the 'value' of the chicks to the parents. With increasing age, a nestling's chances of survival increase, and so the parents correspondingly put more into their defence (Redondo & Carranza 1989).

Among Yellow-billed Magpies the pattern of chick brooding and feeding is broadly similar to that described for Black-bills: female brooding decreases with increasing age of the chicks, and initially males feed chicks more frequently than females. Up until the time the chicks were about 15 days old they were fed about four or five times an hour by the male, and two or three times an hour by the female. Thereafter both parents fed the chicks two or

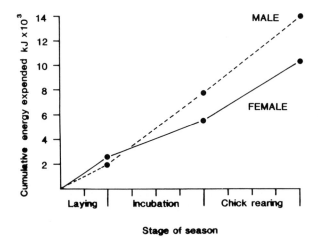

Fig. 70.   *Cumulative energy expenditure of male and female North American Black-billed Magpies through the breeding cycle. Males expend 30% more effort overall than females in breeding. (Redrawn from Mugaas & King 1981.)*

three times each hour. Verbeek (1973) found that during the early stages of incubation the male obtained most of his food and that for his partner from within the territory. As incubation proceeded he obtained an increasing amount from outside the territory, until the female started to feed the young. The male then fed mainly in the territory while the female fed outside it. Verbeek offers two explanations for this sex difference in feeding. It may have occurred because the larger male was better able to protect the nestlings. Alternatively, it may have been a way in which males reduced their energy expenditure. During incubation and the first half of the chick-rearing period the male spends a considerable amount of time ferrying food back to the nest for his partner and their young, flying as much as 25 km each day. Since males start their moult ahead of females, the female might be in better condition while feeding nestlings. The estimates for the amount of energy expended in breeding indicate a similar difference between the sexes as in Black-billed Magpies (Mugaas & King 1981). Verbeek's results also indicate that Yellow-billed Magpies might expend more energy overall because they have so much more flying to do than Black-bills.

Interestingly, neither species of magpie has been seen carrying faecal sacs of their young away from the nest, and it is presumed that they eat them. Later, as they grow, the chicks simply defecate on the edge of the nest.

It is difficult to estimate how much food young magpies received during each feed since the food is carried in the throat pouch (but see Chapter 5). Buitron (1988) thought that females might contribute slightly smaller feeds than males because of their smaller body size and, therefore, smaller throat pouches.

A magpie which loses its partner during incubation or the nestling stage is

European magpie about to feed young in the nest: note the distended pouch beneath the bill. (Photo: M. Wilkes).

unable to rear the young alone (Dunn & Hannon 1989). For example, Buitron (1988) reports two cases where females lost their mates during the chick-rearing period and then lost all their chicks within five days. If the young have fledged, however, a single partner seems to be able to cope. A male which lost his partner two days after the young fledged increased his feeding rate from 4.8 feeds/h to 6.7, and six of the seven fledglings survived to independence. In another case, a female had to rear her five offspring alone after her partner was killed by a falcon. This bird also stepped up its feeding rate, and four of the five young survived to at least 60 days old. In both these cases, a single parent was unable to provide as much food as two parents, despite the increased feeding rate. In the first instance each chick received 1.7 feeds/h with two parents, but only 1.1 with one. Similarly, in the second case, the values were 1.4 feeds/h with two and 0.9 with a single parent (Buitron 1988).

Buitron's (1988) detailed observations of individually marked birds also showed, rather unexpectedly, that North American magpies will sometimes adopt and help to rear unrelated chicks. This behaviour is not what we expect from individuals which are selfishly trying to maximize their own reproductive success, and therefore it is of some interest. A female that lost her partner during incubation, soldiered on alone contrary to expectation, but spent about 20% less time incubating than normal. One week after her mate had disappeared, another male came on the scene, and the pair occasionally engaged in courtship, although the new male did not feed the female (see Chapter 3). When the eggs hatched, some ten days later, he started to bring the female food and also started to feed the chicks. At first, his feeding rate was

European magpie feeding young in the nest. (Photo: M. Wilkes).

low (about 1 feed/h on average), and hers was relatively high (3.2 feeds/h), but over the next three weeks they became more similar (male: 1.4 feeds/h, female: 1.6 feeds/h) and two of the four young eventually fledged. Another case involved a male that lost his partner the day after their young fledged. Five days later a new female was associating with the male and being courted by him, between his feeding of the young. After a few days this female also started to help feed the young. These acts of adoption may not be as altruistic as they first appear, and may represent just one of several ways of obtaining a mate and a territory (see Chapter 2). By providing a relatively small amount of help with rearing another bird's offspring, a magpie may be able to form a pair bond and obtain a territory for the following season.

NESTLING DEVELOPMENT

The weight of the chick at hatching is, as one might expect, closely correlated with the size of the egg it hatches from. Chicks from larger eggs tend to be both structurally larger and heavier (mainly due to the amount of water they contain, rather than the amount of yolk), than those from smaller eggs (Clarkson 1984).

During the first two days following hatching the chicks beg in response to either parent returning to the nest and uttering the 'purr' call. This call, which is rather like a soft cough, stimulates chicks to reach up and utter the 'tweet' begging call. As the chick grows this is gradually replaced by a rather different begging call, the 'coo call' (see Fig. 17) (Enggist-Dublin 1988). The first feathers, on the body, start to appear about eight days after hatching, and the first primaries break through the feather sheaths on about day 10. The tail feathers appear a little later, on day 13 or 14. The eyes open on the seventh or eighth day after hatching. Linsdale (1937) shows a series of photographs of young North American Black-billed Magpies at different stages of development. At hatching young European magpies weigh in the order of 7 g, and their weight increases rapidly until at around 18 days of age the weight levels off at about 179 g, or 84% of adult weight (Fig. 71). Eigelis (1964) found that during the first 20 days of life each magpie chick consumes 550 g of food, so with an increase in body weight of 172 g during this time the chicks' conversion efficiency is about 30%.

The pattern of tarsus growth follows a similar pattern to weight (Fig. 71), but is less variable at a given age. This is because it continues to increase even

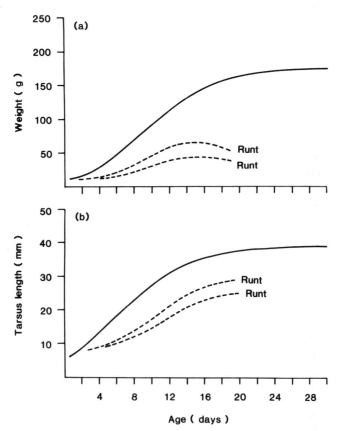

Fig. 71.   *Growth of nestling European magpies in terms of (a) weight, and (b) tarsus length. Results for two 'runt' chicks, which did not fledge, are shown separately as dotted lines. The growth curves are derived from six broods of chicks and eight measurements for each two-day period. From Tatner (1984).*

if food is in short supply. Tarsus length can therefore be used to predict the age of young magpies with a reasonable degree of accuracy. When fledging occurs at around 27 days old the flight feathers still have 20% of their growth left to complete, and the tail rather more. The flight muscles are still relatively small, and this undoubtedly helps to account for the relatively weak flight of fledglings (Tatner 1984).

The nestlings of birds with different life-styles tend to develop in different ways. For example, the young of aerial feeders such as swallows, must channel rather more of their resources into wing and feather growth before leaving the nest than those of ground feeders (Ricklefs 1968). Ground feeders like the magpie must be able to walk well by the time they fledge, and therefore their legs and feet grow rather more rapidly than some other parts of the body. Thus it is not surprising to find that magpies have achieved over 90% of their tarsus growth by the time they are 16 days old. Well-developed legs may also be advantageous to magpie nestlings before they leave the nest, by helping them to reach up and beg for food and to avoid predators. In addition, young magpies clamber around the nest and surrounding branches for several days before they actually leave the nest. Unlike the legs, the flight muscles and wing feathers have completed only 42% and 80% of their growth, respectively, by the time the chicks fledge.

The young magpie's response to nest predators changes as it becomes older. When Redondo and Carranza (1989) visited nests with chicks younger than 13 days, the young birds simply begged at them. Between the ages of 13 and 18 days the young crouched in the nest, clutching the lining of the nest with their

A brood of 14-day-old European Black-billed Magpie chicks just after being ringed. (Photo: J. Pellatt).

feet. From 18 days onwards young birds were likely to leave the nest as an observer approached it. The young magpies climbed along branches, away from the nest to escape from the 'predator', but once the danger had passed they went back to the nest.

We did not weigh chicks on a regular basis in our study, but instead weighed the entire brood, dealing with each chick separately, 14 days after the first chick hatched. Since hatching is asynchronous, some chicks will obviously have been slightly younger than 14 days. Using the growth curve shown in Fig. 71, chicks at 14 days are, on average, about 20% below their fledging weight. We used the mean weight of chicks within a brood as an index of their body condition in order to make comparisons between years. Mean weights varied significantly between years (Appendix 5), ranging from 141.7 g in 1980 to 166.3 g in 1983. The weight of a chick at or close to fledging is often taken as a measure of breeding success, since several studies (e.g. Perrins 1965) have shown that post-fledging survival is positively correlated with fledging weight. Differences in mean fledging weights between years may reflect the suitability of conditions for breeding. However, despite a 15% variation between years we could find no environmental factor that correlated with chick weight between years (Goodburn 1987). Nevertheless, combining data over several years indicated that the heaviest chicks were the ones most likely to survive (see Fig. 54).

Differences in body weights of nestlings (at the same age) between areas may also reflect feeding conditions. Such comparisons are not straightforward, however, since the adult birds may also differ in size in different areas (Chapter 1). To correct for this, one can express the nestling weight as a percentage of the adult body weight. Even this is not perfect since adult weights may differ throughout the year. The general conclusion from Table 17 is that magpies fledge at about 180–200 g, or 75–100% of adult weight. The

TABLE 17: *Fledging weight of Black-billed Magpie chicks*

Location	Chick weight (g)	As % adult weight	Reference
UK, Manchester	179	75	Tatner (1984)
UK, Scotland	185	77	Love & Summers (1973)
UK, Anglesey	200	83	Seel (1983)[1]
Netherlands	180	79	Baeyens 1979; Walters (1988)
Sweden, Revinge	189–208	86–94	Högstedt (1980a; 1981b)
Norway, Trondheim	196	85	Husby (1986)
USA, Montana	190	*c* 100+	Todd (1968)
Canada, Alberta	166	89	Dhindsa & Boag (1990)[2]

Notes: Adult weight is mean of male and female weight (Appendix 2). For UK studies mean adult weight = 240 g (see Appendix 2).

(1) The data in this study may be biased upwards since 1 or 2 eggs were removed (for chemical analysis) from most clutches.

(2) The data from this study were for 20-day-old chicks, and may underestimate the true fledging weight.

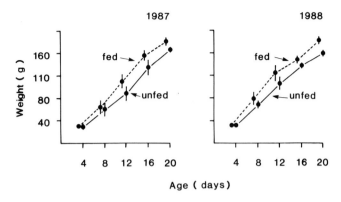

Fig. 72. *Growth of nestling North American Black-billed Magpies in two years, showing the difference between parents provided with extra food (fed) and unfed control birds. In both years the difference between these two categories was significant ($p < 0.05$) from the twelfth day onwards. (Drawn from data in Dhindsa & Boag, 1990.)*

idea that food availability is reflected by the chick's weight at or near fledging is nicely illustrated by Dhindsa and Boag's (1990) study, in which parent magpies provided with additional food reared significantly heavier offspring (by 10–13%) than control pairs without extra food (Fig. 72).

NESTLING MORTALITY

In Tatner's (1984) study the average size of brood within a few days of hatching was 3.42 chicks ± 1.57 SD, but this fell to 2.79 ± 1.47 just before fledging at day 27: a mean daily percentage loss of 7.5%. A similar reduction in brood size occurred between hatching (3.5) and day 14 (3.1 chicks, or 7.3% per day) in our study (Appendix 6). Some of these losses occurred as a result of predation and desertion, but most others were due to starvation. Tatner (1982a) found, not unexpectedly, that chicks which were underweight for their age (see Fig. 71) were significantly more likely to disappear before fledging than chicks of above-average weight. These losses were almost certainly due to starvation, and occurred mainly among the youngest chicks (Fig. 73).

The fact that starvation is a major factor causing chick mortality among magpies has also been demonstrated experimentally. Högstedt (1981b) provided some magpies with extra food throughout the breeding season. These birds suffered significantly fewer clutch or brood losses (5 (25%) out of 20 nests), compared with unfed pairs (18 (56%) out of 32 nests). However, the number of young fledged per successful nest (i.e. rearing at least one chick), did not differ significantly between the two categories—fed: 3.1 and unfed: 3.0. Chicks from pairs provided with extra food also tended to be heavier (197 g ± 74.4) than those from unfed broods (189 g ± 89.8), although the difference was not statistically significant. Högstedt (1981b) suggested that

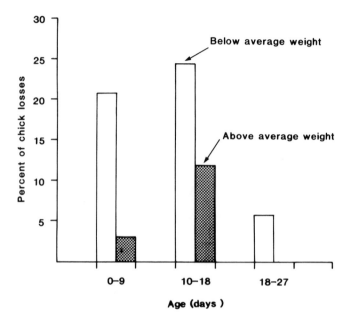

Fig. 73.   *Mortality of nestling European magpies in relation to weight, for three different age-classes. In each case, chicks below average weight within a brood were more likely to disappear. (Redrawn from Tatner 1982a.)*

the difference in breeding failure between the fed and unfed birds was due to a combination of interrelated factors, including predation and food shortage. Magpies given extra food, he argued, were able to spend more time at the nest and were therefore better able to deter predators than unfed birds, which had to forage further afield. He also noted that chick mortality, particularly among the unfed birds was especially high during periods of bad weather. Several factors could account for this. First, food is less abundant at such times: pitfall sampling showed that invertebrates were less abundant when the weather was cool and wet (Högstedt 1981b). Second, during bad weather both adults and young use more energy simply to maintain condition, and so a shortage of food would have increased the likelihood of mortality (Mugaas & King 1981). Clearly, birds provided with additional food were buffered from the vagaries of bad weather.

In another study Hochachka and Boag (1987) provided magpies with extra food, this time in North America. Their results also showed that breeding performance improved when additional food was provided, but in a different way from Högstedt's (1981b). Hochachka and Boag (1987) found that supplemental feeding had no effect on the proportion of pairs which fledged young, but significantly increased the average number of young fledged per nest (Fig. 74). In Dhindsa and Boag's (1990) study additional food significantly increased the rate at which chicks gained weight (Fig. 72), as well as

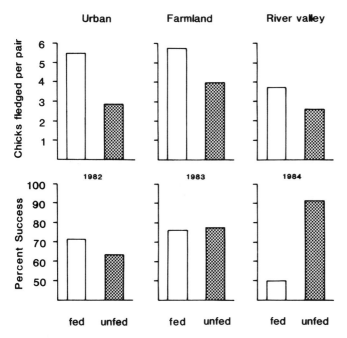

Fig. 74.   *Breeding success of experimentally fed and unfed control pairs of North American Black-billed Magpies. The top line shows the mean number of chicks fledged per pair in urban, farmland and river valley areas in 1983 (the differences between fed and unfed are significant* p < 0.01*). The bottom line presents data for three different years for all habitats combined, and shows that the proportion of pairs rearing young was no greater among fed pairs than it was for control pairs. From Hochachka & Boag (1987).*

increasing the average number of young fledged per (successful) nest, from 2.8 to 4.8 ($p < 0.05$).

BROOD REDUCTION

It may appear odd, at first sight, for magpies to lay six or more eggs, but to rear only three or four chicks. However, the reduction in brood size that occurs during the nestling period may be part of the magpie's overall breeding strategy. It has been suggested, initially by David Lack (1954), that if the food supply during the chick-rearing period is variable it may be impossible for birds to predict at the time of egg laying how many chicks they will be able to rear. They get round this problem by laying a relatively large clutch and starting to incubate before the last egg is laid. The result is that the chicks hatch asynchronously and are therefore of different sizes. If feeding conditions during chick rearing turn out to be good, then all or most of the young may be reared. If, on the other hand, food is scarce some of the young, usually the smallest, will die of starvation. This is advantageous for the parents because it results in a few large, but well-fed chicks being reared.

The idea that brood reduction in Black-billed Magpies might be adaptive has been tested by Husby (1986), working with urban magpies in the vicinity of Trondheim, central Norway. To do this Husby created three categories of nest; (a) those with chicks added to replace any dying naturally, (b) unmanipulated control nests, and (c) nests where the brood size was experimentally reduced by removing chicks. He then compared the survival of the young magpies from these three groups. An important aspect of this study, which had not previously been included in brood reduction studies of other species, was that chick survival was measured well beyond fledging. Indeed, if the study had terminated when the chicks left the nest, there would have been no detectable effect of the experimental treatment, since the mortality rate of the nestlings was similar in all three categories up to that stage (Table 18). However, after fledging the mortality rate of the young birds was significantly higher for those broods where chick numbers had been maintained at a high level (i.e. group (a), above). By the time these chicks were independent of their parents at 80 days old, the mean brood size had declined from 4.0 to 1.1 (72.5% mortality). Moreover, there was a significant negative correlation between the size of these broods and the survival of their chicks ($r = -0.60$, 7 d.f., $p < 0.05$); in other words, the larger the brood the greater the mortality. In contrast, broods in the control group (b) declined from 3.2 to 1.6 young (50% loss), and in group (c) broods decreased from 2.2 to 1.4 young (36% loss), and in neither case was there any correlation between brood size and survival (Table 18). These results support the idea that brood reduction is an adaptive strategy by magpies, and Husby suggests that it works in the following way. Magpies whose broods were maintained at the original size must have had to work harder to feed their brood while they were in the nest. As a result these parents would have been less able to meet the demands of feeding their young after fledging.

TABLE 18: *Results from Husby's (1986) brood reduction experiment with Black-billed Magpies. This shows that nests in which natural losses were experimentally replaced, were much less successful than control nests and those in which chick numbers were experimentally reduced.*

	Nestlings replaced	Control	Nestlings removed
Number of nests	10	26	5
Mean clutch size	6.6	6.8	6.8
Brood size at hatch	5.2	6.0	6.0
Brood size after			
manipulation	5.2	4.0	2.6
after 24 days	4.0	3.2	2.2
after 80 days	1.1	1.6	1.4
Mean weight at 24 days	190.2	195.7	183.2
Percentage nests with losses	100	81	60
Percentage young dying (N)	79 (52)	60 (104)	46 (13)

POST-FLEDGING CARE

Those chicks that survive to three weeks of age stand a good chance of fledging successfully, at about 27 days (Buitron 1988). Although it has been known for a long time that Black-billed Magpies look after their chicks for several weeks (Linsdale 1937), few studies have examined this part of the breeding cycle. In our study area dense leaf-cover and tall grass in midsummer made observation of fledglings almost impossible. However, Buitron (1988) working in South Dakota was able to study this stage in some detail. For the first two weeks after fledging the young stayed close to their nest, but after that the family started ranging over a wider area. Both parents looked after all the chicks and fed them for the first four weeks after fledging (Fig. 69). The chicks became independent about six weeks after leaving the nest, at about 70 days old. Verbeek (1973) states that young Yellow-billed Magpies become independent of their parents at 49 days old, just three weeks after leaving the nest, but subsequent observations indicate that this is probably a mistake.

Magpies do more than simply feed their fledged offspring, they also protect them from predators. Buitron (1983b) found in her study area a wide range of birds and mammals that would readily make a meal out of young, or indeed adult magpies. These included Prairie Falcons, Red-tailed Hawks, Northern Harriers, Cooper's Hawks, Golden Eagles, Bald Eagles, Great Horned Owls, coyotes and bob cats. Magpies often responded to the presence of these species by mobbing them, although the response varied according to the type of predator and the stage of the breeding cycle.

There is good evidence that the animals which magpies mob are potentially lethal. Adult magpies are regularly killed by Goshawks in Sweden (Chapter 6), and female European Sparrowhawks will occasionally kill magpies (M. McGrady, pers. comm.); in southern England a Common Buzzard was seen to swoop down and catch a magpie that had been tree topping (G. Jackson, pers. comm.), and there are reports of Golden Eagles taking magpies in North America (McGahan 1968). Fledgeling magpies are probably especially vulnerable to predators, because their ability to fly is rather poor for some time after leaving the nest. A study of Buzzards in Wales found that fledgeling magpies were the single most important part of the diet (Dare 1989). Buitron (1983b) recorded a Red-tailed Hawk taking a young bird on the day it fledged. In our study, K. Clarkson (pers. comm.) saw a stoat kill recently fledged chicks. Presumably predators like coyotes, red foxes, or bob cats would opportunistically take young magpies too. Eggs and nestlings are also vulnerable, and nest predators include owls, squirrels and crows. A summary of the main predators and the stages of the breeding cycle when magpies are most vulnerable from Buitron's (1983b) study is given in Table 19.

Magpies mob potential predators by calling, swooping close and even attacking them. Buitron (1983b) found that the calls uttered in response to predators consisted of either the familiar harsh rattle or a more staccato chatter (Fig. 75). Further studies by Stone and Trost (in press) have shown that there is in fact a gradation between these two types of call and that the

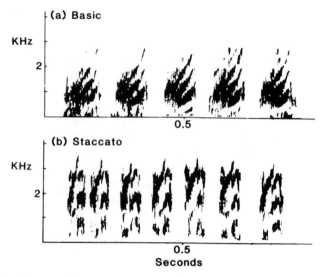

Fig. 75.　*Sonagrams of North American Black-billed Magpie alarm calls used in mobbing predators: (a) basic, (b) staccato. From Buitron (1983b).*

rattle (the 'basic call') was given when mobbing a predator, and the staccato call as a more general alarm. When magpies were mobbing they sometimes approached potential predators very closely and pulled at their fur or feathers. Buitron (1983b) records how magpies mobbing a coyote pulled at its tail, and there are a number of observations of magpies tweaking and tugging at the feathers of perched raptors and corvids. Mobbing predators in this way is potentially quite dangerous since perched or even flying raptors sometimes lunge at mobbing magpies. Although Buitron (1983b) never saw magpies captured during these activities, there are records of other species being

TABLE 19: *Summary of the responses of Black-billed Magpies in Dakota to different predators according to the stage of the reproductive cycle*

Type of predator	Stage in greatest danger						Stage of maximum response by parents	Effectiveness of response
	Eggs	Nestlings		Fledgelings				
		Young	Old	Young	Old	Adult		
Squirrels	+	+	?				Eggs	Always
Crows	+	+	?				Eggs	Usually
Coyotes				+			All stages, but especially young fledglings	Usually
Flying raptors			?	++	+	+	Nestlings Young fledglings	Often
Perched raptors	?	+	+	++	+	+	All stages?	Usually

From Buitron (1983b). + indicates that mobbing occurred. ++ indicates a stronger response.

caught and killed whilst mobbing raptors. It follows therefore that this behaviour must be advantageous, and the most likely benefit derived from mobbing is that it drives the predator away, and reduces the likelihood of predation. It may also deter predators from hunting in that area again.

Buitron (1983b) showed that different species or types of predator pose different threats at different stages of the breeding cycle, and magpies responded to them accordingly. The intensity of the magpie's response closely matched the risk that each predator posed. For example, crows and squirrels were egg predators and magpies responded towards them most intensely during the egg stage, and virtually ignored them at other times. The greatest threat to fledgelings was flying raptors, and adults were most responsive to these during the late nestling period and after fledging (Fig. 76). Verbeek (1973) made similar observations for Yellow-billed Magpies. Perched raptors posed a threat to nestling, fledgling and adult magpies, and Buitron (1983b) found that these were mobbed at all times. The response of magpies also differed to the various raptors. For example, eagles were never chased or dived at, and falcons and buzzards were treated differently, with falcons being more likely to elicit staccato calls (79% of occasions), than buzzards (41%). Buitron (1983b) discovered that the anti-predator behaviour of magpies was almost always successful in driving squirrels away from the nest, and was usually effective against crows, coyotes and perched raptors. In Europe, magpies were much less successful at deterring Carrion Crows from their nests (see Chapters 5 and 7).

RESPONSE TO HUMANS

Anyone who has climbed to a few Yellow-billed or Black-billed Magpie nests to ring chicks will know that parent birds can sometimes respond very vigorously to a human 'predator'. However, the way magpies treat people at the nest varies markedly. On our ringing visits some birds would simply slink away, others would sit in a tree 10–20 m away continuously uttering their alarm chatter, while yet others would confidently approach to within a metre or so, calling loudly. Linsdale (1937) states that of about fifty Black-billed Magpie nests that he checked the adults mobbed him closely at only three.

When magpies approached closely to mob a human they either hammered at branches with their bill, or ripped off small pieces of bark or nearby twigs. I got the impression that their vicious pecking at branches was a displacement activity and was what magpies would have liked to have done to me. Another impression that I got was that magpies could actually recognize me, and when I was simply making observations away from nests were much more tolerant of my presence than of other people walking about the study area. Buitron (1983b) also noticed this and found that for about two days following one of her nest checks the magpies were rather wary of her. She then tried visiting the nest in disguise (wearing a particular jacket and a scarf over her head and nose). On the following day, out of disguise, the magpies responded to her as

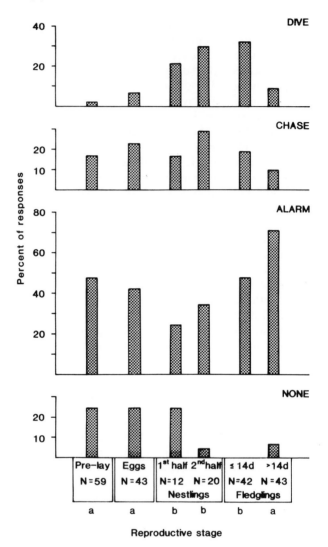

Fig. 76.   *Responses of North American Black-billed Magpies to potential predators (flying raptors) in relation to the stage in the breeding cycle. Responses were: none, alarm, chase and dive in increasing order of intensity. The most intense responses occurred when parents had chicks. From Buitron (1983b).*

normal as she continued to make observations! Buitron also noticed, as we had done, marked differences between pairs in the way they responded during nest visits. She found that birds breeding in areas remote from human activity rarely approached within 4 m, whereas those which were used to humans, were much less wary and often came much closer than this. Two birds even touched her during their mobbing!

SUMMARY

Magpie chicks hatch blind, naked and helpless and are brooded by the female. Brooding decreases with age until by 15 days old they are brooded for only 10% of the time. Chicks are usually fed two to five times per hour, with the male making more feeds than the female. Over the entire breeding season his energy expenditure is 30% greater than the female's. Chicks weigh about 7 g at hatching and reach about 180 g at 18–20 days old. Fledging probably occurs at this weight at around 27 days. Hatching is asynchronous and results in a weight hierarchy within the brood, with the smallest, lightest chicks most likely to die. Asynchronous hatching, achieved by delaying the start of incubation, is an adaptation to unpredictable food supplies during chick rearing. Provision of additonal food reduces chick mortality. Post-fledging care lasts about six weeks. The anti-predator behaviour of parents with fledged chicks is described.

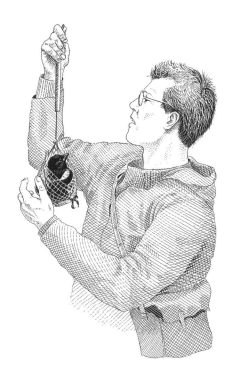

CHAPTER 9

The breeding cycle: breeding success

One crow perched quietly near the nest while the other drew off both the magpies to a distance in pursuit of it. Then the crow which had perched hurried to the magpie nest, left unattended, and obtained an egg which it carried off. This drew the attention of the two magpies to the retreating bird and permitted the first crow to return and make off with another egg.

Raspail (1888)

Given that a pair of magpies have built a nest and laid a clutch of eggs, what are their chances of successfully rearing young and what factors affect their chances of success? Breeding success in magpies, and most other birds, has been measured in three main ways: (a) the average number of chicks raised to fledging age per pair, (b) the average number of chicks raised per successful pair (i.e. excluding pairs which failed entirely), and (c) the proportion of pairs rearing at least one chick to fledging. A further measure of reproductive success is (d) the number of offspring which survive to breed that a particular

bird produces during its lifetime. The latter is referred to as lifetime reproductive success, and is the one which has most biological significance since it is
the best measure of a bird's genetic contribution to future generations.

BREEDING SUCCESS

Information on breeding success of magpies, from a number of studies in
both Europe and North America, shows that magpies usually raise between
one and two chicks to fledging (Table 20). However, approximately half the
pairs fail to rear any young at all, while the rest raise between two and four
chicks. There does not appear to be any consistent difference between the
success of magpies in Europe and North America. However, before we
examine the factors that influence breeding success, it is important to consider
whether the data in the table are comparable. There are several potential
sources of bias. First, success is expressed as the number of chicks that survive
to fledge, but different observers have defined 'fledging' in different ways. In
most studies the final nest check has been made some time before fledging

TABLE 20: *Breeding success of Black-billed Magpies in various studies*

Location	Chicks/ pair	Chicks/ successful pair	% pairs successful (N)	Reference
Europe				
UK, Sheffield	1.81	3.18	57.4 (409)	This study
UK, Sheffield, urban	1.97	3.00	65.7 (35)	Eden (1985b)
UK, Anglesey	—	—	63.7 (405)	Seel (1983)
UK, Bristol	0.81	1.91	42.4 (33)	Vines (1981)
UK, Manchester	1.55	2.79	40.4 (94)	Tatner (1982a)
UK, Skomer Island	2.45	2.96	82.3 (29)	S. Sutcliffe, pers. comm.
UK, Scotland	2.1	4.2	68.2 (22)	Love & Summers (1973)
Ireland, Dublin	1.48	2.71	55.0 (93)	Kavanagh (1986)
France, Paris Basin	1.1	2.9	35.3 (40)	Balanca (1984b)
Denmark	1.44	4.55	31.7 (104)	A. P. Møller, pers. comm.
Sweden, Revinge	1.3	3.0	43.7 (32)	Högstedt (1981b)
Netherlands	1.0–1.9	2.0–3.3	54.8 (73)	Baeyens (1981c)
Norway, Trondheim	—	3.2	63.8 (127)	T. Slagsvold, pers. comm.
Spain, Carceres	1.58	3.90	40.4 (52)	T. Redondo, pers. comm.
Spain, Cordoba I	1.45	3.75	38.7 (137)	Arias de Reyna *et al.* (1984); T. Redondo, pers. comm.
Spain, Cordoba II	2.84	3.98	71.0 (87)	T. Redondo, pers. comm.
North America				
USA, South Dakota	2.5	4.4	60.7 (56)	Buitron (1988)
USA, Utah	2.2	4.0	56.5 (184)	Reese & Kadlec (1985)
USA, Montana	—	3.5	73.5 (699)	Brown (1957)
Canada, Alberta	—	2.9–3.8	64.3 (70)	Hochachka & Boag (1987)

Note: Cordoba I = Espiel; Cordoba II = Cardena.

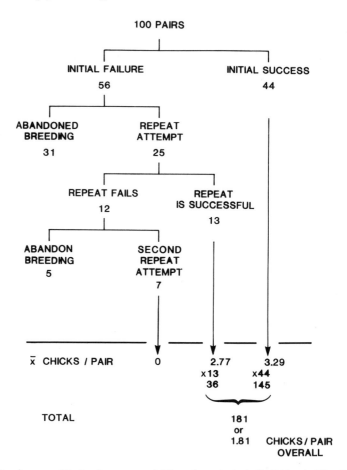

Fig. 77.   *Summary of the breeding success and failure of magpies in the Sheffield study. The scheme shows the average situation for a population of 100 pairs.*

because of the nasty habit some young magpies have of 'exploding' from the nest if they are disturbed. Love and Summers (1973) last checked nests when the young were 10 days old, and in our study we last visited chicks to ring them when they were 14 days old. In contrast, Högstedt (1981b) was able to record the number of 25-day-old chicks present in his nests. Obviously if the last check is made a long time before fledging this will overestimate breeding success. Another potential source of bias concerns repeat nests. If these are overlooked, as they probably often are, breeding success will tend to be underestimated. Seel's (1983) data for example are primarily from first nests, so his figure of 64% successful nests must be regarded as a minimum. Since repeat nests are infrequent among North American magpies this bias may only affect European studies.

In our study, pooling data for all years, breeding success averaged 1.81

chicks per pair, or 3.18 chicks per successful pair, or expressed as the proportion of pairs producing some chicks: 57% (235 out of 409) (Fig. 77). Success measured as the average number of chicks (per successful nest) at 14 days after hatching, varied between years, from 2.6 in 1986 to 3.9 in 1983 (Appendix 7). The only environmental factor which correlated with this measure of breeding success was the amount of rain during the 14 days prior to fledging (total rainfall, $r = 0.82$, 5 d.f., $p < 0.05$; days of rain, $r = 0.75$, 5 d.f., $p < 0.1$). Presumably this effect occurs because rainfall increases food abundance for magpies, probably by driving invertebrates to the soil surface, as noted by Verbeek (1973) for Yellow-billed Magpies. In addition, increased breeding success in wet summers is consistent with the idea that summer drought can stop breeding altogether in some areas (see Chapter 12).

SEASONAL CHANGES IN BREEDING SUCCESS

In each of the nine years for which we had data, the number of chicks reared per pair was negatively correlated with laying date, but in only two years was the effect significant. However, pooling data for all years, but using the same pairs only once (taken at random from the data available), and expressing laying date as a deviation from the annual median, showed a significant negative correlation ($r = -0.321$, 208 d.f., $p < 0.001$) (Fig. 78). However, although this relationship is significant, it is clear that laying date explains relatively little (10.3% in fact) of the variation in breeding success.

A number of other studies have found that magpie breeding success declines through the season (Fig. 78). The extent of these declines vary considerably in some areas, such as North America (e.g. Reese & Kadlec 1985), the decline was quite pronounced, while in others the decline was slight. A seasonal decline in breeding success is a fairly common pattern among birds and there are several explanations for its occurrence. First, young birds bred relatively late in the season, laid relatively small clutches, and had low success (see below). Second, it could be caused by a seasonal decline in clutch size. As shown earlier (Chapter 7), in several studies, including ours, there was a tendency for clutch size to decrease through the season. Obviously, the fewer eggs that are laid the fewer chicks can be fledged. The importance of this effect can be estimated by looking at the proportion of nests rearing at least one chick through the season. In our study clutch size showed a weak seasonal decline (Chapter 7), but there was also a significant seasonal decline in the proportion of pairs producing young (Fig. 78). Seel's (1983) study also showed a significant decline in clutch size through the season as well as a decline in the proportion of successful nests (Fig. 78). In contrast, although Tatner (1982a) found breeding success to decline through the season, when he allowed for the seasonal decline in clutch size the seasonal change in breeding success was no longer significant.

The third factor that can contribute towards a seasonal decline in breeding success is the effect of repeat breeding attempts, since these are slightly less

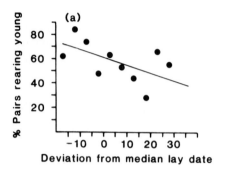

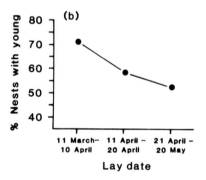

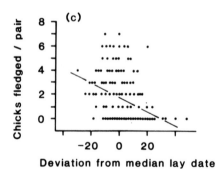

Fig. 78.   *Seasonal declines in magpie breeding success. (a) Shows that the proportion of pairs rearing young in the Sheffield study declined significantly with later laying (data for 389 breeding attempts using pairs only once: linear trend in proportion* p < 0.002*). (b) Shows a similar pattern for Seel's (1983) data* ($\chi^2 = 8.2$, 2 d.f., p < 0.05*). (c) Data from the Sheffield study for the mean number of chicks fledged per pair (using each pair only once)* (r = −0.32, 208 d.f., p < 0.001*). There are two separate effects: the chances of rearing any young declines through the season (a and b), as does the mean number of young reared per brood (c).*

successful than first attempts (see below). The fourth factor is bird or territory quality. A poor-quality bird or a bird in a poor territory may both breed late and rear few young. A discussion of the effect of territory quality on breeding success is deferred until later (see Chapter 10).

The final factor concerns environmental conditions, but may be linked with bird age or quality. If there is an optimum time period in which to rear young (see Chapter 5), for example when ground invertebrates are most abundant, then any bird laying relatively late, so that its chicks hatch after this time, may experience a declining food supply and be less able to rear its young. A poor-quality bird may be unable to accumulate nutrients fast enough early in the season to be able to breed at the optimum time, with the result that its chicks hatch later and survive less well. However, the data on food abundance for magpies in Britain (see Fig. 62) shows no marked decrease until very late in the season, so this explanation appears unlikely at first sight. However, food abundance is not necessarily the same as food availability, and while invertebrates may continue to be abundant through the summer (as measured by pitfall trapping), they may become less accessible to foraging magpies. This may occur because the vegetation increases in length through the summer, and as we have seen, magpies avoid foraging in this habitat. Whatever the cause, chicks which hatch early in the season have the greatest chance of becoming dominant members of the non-breeding flock (see Chapter 4), and surviving to breed (Chapter 6). Among Black-billed Magpies in North America, the evidence suggests that food availability peaks and then decreases more sharply than it does in mid- and northern latitudes in Europe, and late breeders are relatively unsuccessful as a result.

SUCCESS OF REPEAT BREEDING ATTEMPTS

Differences in success between first and repeat breeding attempts in our study are summarized in Table 21. Considering both the number of chicks fledged per pair, and per successful pair, repeat nests were less successful than first atempts in six out of the eight years. The effect was not particularly pronounced, however. In terms of the proportion of pairs rearing some young,

TABLE 21: *Summary of breeding success of Black-billed Magpies for first and repeat nests in the Sheffield study*

Measure of success	First nests	Repeat nests
Chicks per pair	1.84	1.39
Chicks per successful pair	3.29	2.77
Percentage pairs rearing at least one chick	57.7	48.0

Note: Data pooled over all years.

repeat nests were less successful than first nests in five out of the eight years, but again this was not statistically significant. Other studies have found repeat nesting attempts to be less successful than initial ones (e.g. Tatner 1982a).

CAUSES OF BREEDING FAILURE

In our study we defined a breeding attempt as an event in which a female laid at least one egg in a nest. We recorded 236 (54.6%) failures out of 432 breeding attempts, and for each of these had a reasonably good idea about what caused the failure (Table 22). Combining data for all years we found that 88% (207 out of 236) failures occurred at the egg stage, during laying or incubation, and just 12% during the chick stage. While these figures indicate a higher rate of loss during the early stages of breeding, it is important to take into account the number of days over which failure *could* have occurred. The

TABLE 22: *Causes of magpie breeding failure in the Shef-field study*

Stage of cycle	Cause	No of failed nests (%)	% of all nests
Laying and incubation			
	Desertion	69 (29.2)	(16.0)
	Predation	52 (22.0)	(5.1)
	Egg disappeared	26 (11.0)	(6.0)
	Robbed by man	25 (10.6)	(5.8)
	Eggs 'infertile'	17 (7.2)	(3.9)
	Nest collapse	13 (5.5)	(3.0)
	Nest destroyed	2 (0.8)	(0.5)
	Female died	1 (0.4)	(0.2)
	Tree felled	1 (0.4)	(0.2)
	Eggs broken	1 (0.4)	(0.2)
Hatching and chick rearing			
	Predation	15 (6.3)	(3.5)
	Starvation	10 (4.2)	(2.3)
	Female shot	1 (0.4)	(0.2)
	Chicks shot	1 (0.4)	(0.2)
	Female died	1 (0.4)	(0.2)
	Chicks stolen	1 (0.4)	(0.2)

Notes: Data are combined over all years of the study. The total number of nests which failed was 236 and the total nests followed was 432. Over all, 207 nests failed during laying and incubation, and 29 failed during hatching and chick rearing. Note that this information provides only an indication of the factors causing mortality. Some of those listed here are not independent – see text.

laying and incubation period span 24 (i.e. 6 + 18) days and the chick-rearing period (in our study) just 14 days. The daily percentage loss (L) can be calculated from the formula: $L = 1 - (N_1/N_2)^{(1/d)} \times 100$, where N_1 is the initial number, N_2 the final number, and d the duration of the interval. For the egg stage the average daily loss was 2.75%, and for the nestling period just 1%.

Part of this difference is due to the fact that vulnerable nests have failed by the time the chick-rearing period is reached. In addition, the factors associated with nest failure may also account for the difference. In all years desertion was an important cause of nest failure, but it occurred only during the egg stage. Overall, 16% of all nests were deserted. Of all the failures at the egg stage (207), 69, or 33% were due to desertion. The other important factor causing failure was predation (mainly by Carrion Crows – see Chapter 5), and this could occur at any stage of the breeding cycle. Overall, 22% of breeding attempts failed at the egg stage because of predation, and a quarter of all failures at this stage (i.e. 52 out of 207) were due to predation. Eggs also simply disappeared from nests and this could have been due either to predation or to robbery by humans. Our estimates for the incidence of predation are therefore minimum ones. Failure during the chick stage was infrequent. Predation occurred in just 3.5% of all breeding attempts, but accounted for 48% (i.e. 15 out of 29) of all failures at this stage. The other major cause of nest failure was chick starvation. In 2.3% of all breeding attempts the entire brood starved to death, accounting for one-third (10 out of 29) of all failures during the chick stage.

Other studies have identified the causes of nesting failure and some of these are summarized in Table 23. Not unexpectedly, the relative importance of the different mortality factors varied between studies. For example, Tatner (1982a) found that the main cause of egg loss was through clutches being deserted, whereas Reese and Kadlec (1985) had relatively few deserted clutches. In almost all studies some chicks starved and, as described in Chapter 8, the delay in the start of incubation, to produce asynchronous hatching, is part of the magpie's breeding strategy to cope with starvation. The extent of and type of predation varied between studies, but in almost all studies

TABLE 23: *Main causes of breeding failure among Black-billed Magpies*

Location	Eggs	Chicks	Reference
UK, Sheffield	Desertion Predation	Predation Starvation	This study
UK, Manchester	Desertion	Starvation	Tatner (1982a)
UK, Sheffield, urban	Hatching failure	Starvation	Eden (1985b)
Ireland, Dublin	Disappeared Predation	Predation	Kavanagh (1986)
Netherlands	Hatching failure Desertion	Robbed Starvation	Baeyens (1981c)
USA, Utah	Disappeared	Starvation	Reese & Kadlec (1985)

of European magpies, Carrion Crows are considered to be the most important predator. In the early years of our study 'predation' by boys was a significant cause of failure. However, a re-education programme by one of my students changed all that! Although it is relatively easy to categorize the factors responsible for nest failures, in reality it is difficult to identify them accurately since many are interrelated. For example, predation may be a consequence of reduced food availability, which in turn may be dependent upon weather conditions. If cold and wet conditions decrease the abundance of ground invertebrates, adult magpies may have to spend more time foraging for both themselves and their chicks. During such periods offspring may receive less food, but will also be much more vulnerable to predation, for example by crows, simply because their parents spend more time foraging and less time near the nest. In cases like this it is impossible to identify any single factor responsible for chick deaths.

THE EFFECT OF AGE ON BREEDING

Magpies first breed in their first or second spring (Chapter 4), and may breed for five or more breeding seasons. As in many other birds, age has a marked effect on several aspects of magpie breeding biology. In our study first-year birds laid later than older birds, and indeed the timing of breeding advanced consistently with increasing age. First-year birds laid on average about ten days after the median laying date for any particular year, whereas the oldest birds in our population laid about five days before the median (Fig. 79). Clutch size also increased with age, with first-year birds laying an average clutch of about four eggs, and 4-year-olds laying about six eggs. Birds of 5 or

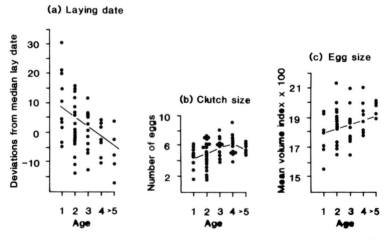

Fig. 79.   *Age and breeding performance in magpies (data from the Sheffield study). (a) Breeding occurs earlier with age, (b) clutch size increases with age, up to age 4, and (c) egg size increases with age. From Birkhead & Goodburn (1989).*

more years laid slightly smaller clutches than 4-year-old magpies. The average size of eggs laid by magpies also increased with age (Fig. 79). All these effects could have arisen as a result of increasing experience among the birds. Because age and experience usually increase hand in hand, it is often difficult to separate their effects. A further contributory factor could be territory quality since some birds at least changed territories during their lives. However, the effect of territory quality on egg size is probably not a straightforward one. As Clarkson (1984) showed, in the year following a change of territory egg size decreased, before continuing to increase as the bird got older (Fig. 80).

Breeding success also increased with age. First-year magpies were relatively unsuccessful at fledging young, and overall less than 20% of those that laid managed to rear young. However, with increasing age the proportion of pairs hatching and fledging young, and the mean number of chicks fledged per pair increased, at least until the age of 4. Birds older than this showed either similar

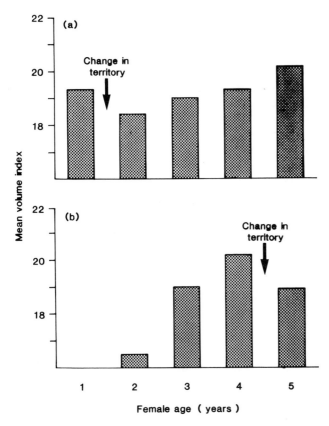

Fig. 80.   *Changes in egg size (volume index) following a change in territory. (a) and (b) are two different females and in both examples, from the Sheffield study, a change in territory resulted in a decrease in egg size. From Clarkson (1984).*

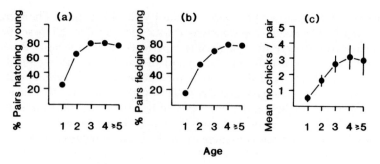

Fig. 81.   *Changes in breeding success with age for magpies in the Sheffield study. (a) The proportion of pairs hatching young, (b) the proportion of pairs fledging young, and (c) the mean number (± SE) of chicks fledged per pair. From Birkhead & Goodburn (1989).*

or slightly reduced breeding success (Fig. 81). Once again, experience could account for these patterns. In addition, though, the changes in timing of breeding, clutch and egg size with age may also have played a part. One might imagine that magpies that wait until their second year before breeding do so to gain experience, despite losing one breeding season. However, although birds breeding for the first time at age 2 breed earlier, with larger clutches of larger eggs than birds breeding in their first year, they do no better than 2-year-olds that have bred previously (Table 24). This suggests that the reason birds delay breeding is because they are unable to obtain a territory.

Studies of magpies elsewhere confirm several of the age-related patterns we detected. Buitron (1988) found that first-year females in North America laid smaller clutches (5.3 eggs) and fledged fewer young (1.0) than older females (6.6 eggs and 2.5 chicks, respectively). Reese and Kadlec (1985), also in North America, compared the breeding biology of different combinations of different

TABLE 24: *Differences in clutch size and laying date for male and female magpies in the Sheffield study, breeding for the first time in their first or second year, and for two-year-old birds (which first bred in their first year)*

Sex	Variable	Bred in first year				Bred in second year			Two years old		
		Mean	SD	(N)		Mean	SD	(N)	Mean	SD	(N)
Male	Clutch	4.33 ±	1.22	(9)	**	5.65 ±	1.03	(23)	5.40 ±	1.14	(5)
	Lay date[1]	8.8 ±	11.70	(9)		2.3 ±	9.39	(23)	2.80 ±	4.15	(5)
Female	Clutch	4.70 ±	0.89	(12)	**	5.83 ±	1.19	(12)	5.57 ±	1.27	(7)
	Lay date	7.5 ±	13.10	(12)		5.2 ±	12.5	(12)	6.1 ±	13.90	(7)

Notes: ** indicates a significant difference. Tests for clutch size were *t* tests, for laying date, Mann-Whitney U tests. (1) The difference in laying date for males first breeding at 1 and 2 was almost significant ($p = 0.062$).
(1) Laying dates are expressed as deviations from the annual median.
None of the differences between sexes within years were significant.

TABLE 25: *Effect of age of male and female partner on breeding performance of Black-billed Magpies in Utah*

Pair composition		Sample sizes	Laying date	Clutch size	No. young fledged	No. young per successful nest	Percentage nests successful
Male	Female						
First-year	First-year	10–20	April 15	6.2	1.9	3.9	50
First-year	Adult	5–9	April 13	6.4	2.2	4.0	56
Adult	First-year	6–7	April 17	6.6	3.6	4.2	86
Adult	Adult	26–33	April 10	6.9	3.3	4.1	82

Notes: Significant differences: 2 adults laid earlier than all other pair combinations. Adult male and young female and two adults had a significantly higher proportion of successful nests compared with the rest.
From Reese & Kadlec (1985).

age-classes of magpies. Two first-year birds breeding together laid later, had smaller clutch sizes and had a lower chance of rearing any offspring than other categories. At the other extreme, two older birds breeding together bred earliest, laid the largest clutches and had a relatively high chance of rearing young. Interestingly, of the two categories, consisting of one old and one young bird, the combination of older male and first-year female was the more successful, and despite later breeding, was just as successful as two older birds (Table 25). Högstedt (1981a) also looked at the effect of age and experience on breeding biology. As in our study he was able to follow known-age birds, and found, like us that clutch size increased with age up to about the fourth or fifth breeding attempt and then levelled off or even decreased very slightly. Breeding success followed a similar pattern, increasing up to about the fifth breeding attempt and then levelled off.

LIFETIME SUCCESS

Once they survive their first year, magpies can expect to live for a further two or three seasons on average, and a very small proportion of birds may breed for ten seasons (see Chapter 6). The number of offspring which they produce during their lifetime is one of the best measures of their evolutionary success (Clutton-Brock 1988; Newton 1989; Birkhead & Goodburn 1989). One of the surprising results to emerge from studies of lifetime reproductive success is the relatively low success of some individuals, and the small proportion of birds which actually make a contribution to subsequent generations. In our study only half of all magpies which survived to breed produced any offspring (Fig. 82).

The single most important factor affecting the number of offspring magpies rear during their lifetime is longevity. No bird which bred for only a single

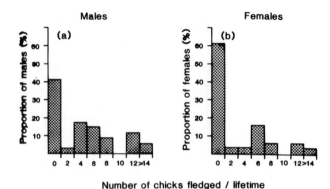

Fig. 82.   *Lifetime reproductive success for (a) male (N = 36) and (b) female magpies (N = 28) in the Sheffield study. In both cases about half of all birds failed to leave any descendants, and a few were relatively successful. From Goodburn (1987).*

season produced any offspring which survived to breed. But the longer a magpie survived the greater were its chances of leaving descendants. A similar pattern existed for both males and females (Fig. 83), but this assumes that males were always the fathers of the offspring they reared. As Chapter 3 shows, this might not have always been the case. Similarly, since eggs are sometimes moved between nests, females may not have always been the mothers of the young they reared (Chapter 7).

Since lifespan has such an important effect on lifetime success, Goodburn and I tried to predict, retrospectively, which birds would be long-lived. To do this we divided magpies into two groups, those which survived for a maximum of three years, referred to as short-lived birds, and those which survived more than three years, which we called long-lived individuals. Comparing the first breeding attempt of these two categories of birds we found that short-lived birds had significantly poorer territories than long-lived birds (see Chapter 10 for measures of territory quality). Perhaps as a consequence of this, the short-lived birds also produced significantly smaller clutches than long-lived birds, and were less likely to fledge any young (Table 26). These effects could be due to differences either in the quality of the territories the birds bred in, or to differences in the quality of the birds themselves, or both. The information does not allow us to separate these two possibilities. This is because inherently good-quality birds might obtain good territories. On the other hand, a bird of indifferent quality might reproduce well if it succeeds in obtaining a good territory (Birkhead & Goodburn 1989).

YELLOW-BILLED MAGPIES

Information about the breeding success of Yellow-billed Magpies comes from Hastings Reservation and adjacent areas and is summarized in Table 27.

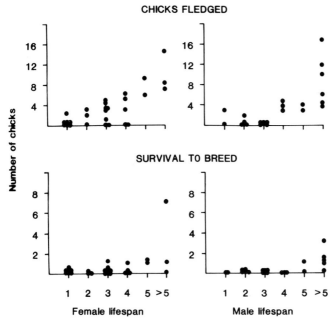

Fig. 83.   *Relationship between lifespan and breeding success for female (left) and male (right) magpies in the Sheffield study. Upper graphs show success in terms of number of chicks fledged, and lower graphs show success in terms of the number of recruits (i.e. the number of chicks surviving to breed). In all four cases success increases significantly with lifespan. From Birkhead & Goodburn (1989).*

TABLE 26: *Comparison of characteristics of short- and long-lived magpies*

Variable	Short-lived $\bar{x} \pm SD$ (N)	Long-lived $\bar{x} \pm SD$ (N)
Hatch date[1]	5.91 ± 7.57 (32)	3.84 ± 5.93 (25)
Territory quality[2]	41.28 ± 31.24 (24)	59.82 ± 25.39 (29)
Lay date[3]	7.35 ± 9.79 (31)	5.00 ± 10.9 (32)
Clutch size[4]	4.90 ± 1.49 (31)	5.74 ± 1.21 (31)
Fledging success[5]	26% (7/27)	74% (14/19)

Notes: Data are for dead and alive birds combined (see text).
From Birkhead & Goodburn (1989).
(1) Hatch date of short- and long-lived birds, expressed as deviations from the annual median, the difference is not significant (Mann-Whitney U test, $p = 0.34$).
(2) Territory quality: this is the percentage of grazing land in the birds' first breeding territory; the difference is significant ($t = 2.31$, 51 d.f. $p < 0.05$; analysis on arcsin transformed data).
(3) Lay date of first breeding attempt, expressed as deviation from the annual median laying date: the difference is not significant (Mann-Whitney U test, $p = 0.44$).
(4) Clutch size in first breeding attempt; $t = 2.43$, 60 d.f. ($p < 0.02$).
(5) Percentage of pairs, fledging at least one chick ($\chi^2 = 3.71$, 1 d.f., $p < 0.1$).

TABLE 27: *Breeding success of Yellow-billed Magpies at Hastings Reservation, California*

Year	Chicks/ pair	Chicks/ successful pair	% pairs successful
1968	2.0	3.5	57 (4 of 7)
1969	3.2	3.2	100 (5 of 5)
1970	2.1	3.0	71 (5 of 7)
1971	0.5	2.0	25 (3 of 12)
1981–1985	2.60 ± 2.87	3.83 ± 2.73	67.8 (N = 140)

Data for 1968 to 1971 inclusive from Verbeek (1973); data from 1981 to 1985 inclusive from Reynolds (1990): values are means ± SD.

Verbeek's (1973) results were based on rather few nests, but are similar to those obtained by Reynolds (1990). The number of chicks fledged per successful pair is similar to that for Black-billed Magpies (see Table 20). The very low success in 1971 occurred as a result of nine of twelve pairs abandoning their small young. This was a cool, dry spring and food may have been particularly scarce.

Climbing to a Yellow-billed Magpie nest located in the uppermost clump of mistletoe. (Photo: K. Clarkson).

SUMMARY

Several studies show that on average each pair of magpies produces 1–2 chicks per season. About half of all pairs fail to rear any young at all, and the rest produce 2–4 chicks. Within a season birds breeding relatively late are less successful then early breeders, for a variety of reasons. Factors responsible for breeding failure include desertion, predation and starvation of chicks – the relative importance of these is difficult to determine. Several breeding parameters, including success, increase or improve with age. The number of fledged young produced in a lifetime varies markedly between individuals. About half of all magpies leave no descendants. The longer a magpie lives the greater is its chance of contributing to future generations.

CHAPTER 10

Factors affecting success: bird and territory quality

Now there's no bird in all the deserts of the West who can look down his beak at other animals as well as brother Magpie. With his great long black-and-white tail, his cocky eye, and lofty opinion of himself, he's hard to beat.

From *Meditations with the Navajo*, Hausman (1987)

For birds which occupy an all-purpose territory the quality of that territory could play an important role in their daily lives and have important consequences for their breeding success and survival. Three studies of magpies in northern Europe have recognized that breeding territories differ in quality. There have been no attempts to examine territory quality among birds in North America presumably because the type of territory used by these birds is so different (see Chapter 2). The criteria used to assess territory quality vary between the three studies. Baeyens (1981b) divided territories into two classes: class I were those occupied throughout the year, whereas class II were abandoned outside the breeding season. Møller (1982a) classified territories according to the number of years they were occupied during a ten-year period. Group I were occupied for only a single breeding season, group II for 2 to 7 years and group III for 8 to 10 years. In our study Goodburn (1987) also used the number of years a territory was occupied over a nine-year period as a measure of its quality. Short-term territories were those used for up to four out of the nine study years, long-term territories were used for five to nine years. These ways of classifying territories seem intuitively sensible since good-quality areas are likely to be defended throughout the year (Baeyens's study), or more consistently between years (Møller's and our studies), than poor areas. The fact that in all three studies territory quality, as defined above, was positively correlated with breeding success confirms the usefulness of this system.

Here I will describe the situation in our study area and then draw some comparisons with Baeyens's and Møller's studies. There were three questions relating to territory quality which we tried to answer: (a) Are some territories occupied more often than expected by chance? (b) Is breeding success related to territory occupancy, and if so, how? (c) Do territories which are occupied for different numbers of years differ in their physical characteristics?

To answer the first question we looked at the frequency with which 140 territories were occupied over the nine-year period and compared it with the pattern expected if territories were occupied at random. This clearly showed that some territories were occupied more than expected while others were used less often than expected (Fig. 84). This strongly indicates that some territories

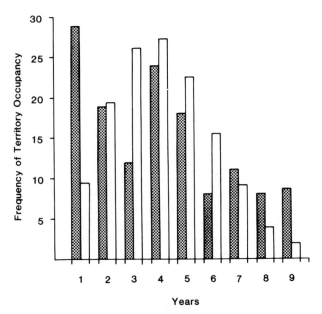

Fig. 84. *Frequency distribution of the number of years 140 magpie territories in the Sheffield study were occupied (shaded), compared with a random (Poisson) model (open). The difference between the observed and expected is significant ($\chi^2 = 93.4$, 8 d.f., p < 0.001). From Goodburn (1987).*

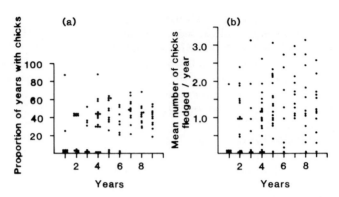

Fig. 85.   *Relationships between the number of years territories were occupied in the Sheffield study and (a) the proportion of years in which at least one chick fledged from that territory (r = 0.343, 119 d.f., p < 0.001), and (b) the mean number of chicks fledged per pair (r = 0.443, 127 d.f., p < 0.001). From Goodburn (1987).*

were more attractive than others – a result also found by Newton (1986) in his study of Sparrowhawks.

As indicated above, the number of years a particular territory was occupied was positively correlated with breeding success, both in terms of the proportion of years in which some young were raised (Fig. 85a) and the mean number of young fledged each year (Fig. 85b). It is possible that these effects could have arisen because the same individuals occupied the same territory year after year and simply reflect the birds' increasing age or experience (see Chapter 9). To avoid this problem we excluded individuals which had bred in the same territory for three or more years and re-ran the analysis. The effect of territory occupation and success was still apparent ($r_s = 0.515$, $N = 79$, $p < 0.001$), confirming that this was a real effect.

We tested the idea that territories occupied for different numbers of seasons differed in their physical attributes by looking at the habitat composition of territories. This was done by using a large-scale aerial photograph of the study area and measuring the proportion of each territory made up of different habitats, such as woodland, grazing land, buildings and so on. A comparison of short- and long-term territories showed only a single significant difference: the proportion of grazing land in long-term territories was greater than in short-term territories (Table 28). The amount of grazing land was also correlated with the length of territory occupancy (Fig. 86). Grazing land is grassland occupied by livestock, usually horses or cattle. The animals keep the grass short and their droppings help to attract many of the invertebrates, like dung flies and beetles, that magpies eat. Since magpies spend much of their time foraging in such areas (Chapter 5), the importance of grazing land is not unexpected. However, it does provide an objective means of assessing territory quality. As expected, breeding success was positively correlated with the relative amount of grazing land in the territory (Fig. 87). It is interesting to note that the amount of grazing land explains only 6% of the variation in

TABLE 28: *Habitat composition of 140 magpie territories in the Rivelin Valley (1978–1986). (Areas expressed as a mean percentage of the total territory area)*

| Habitat variable | Length of territory occupancy | | | | |
| | Short-term | | Long-term | | |
	Mean	SD	Mean	SD	Means
Dense wood	15.21	19.50	12.41	19.80	13.8
Thin wood	15.29	15.08	10.17	10.49	12.7
Grazing land*	38.92	31.50	51.16	27.80	45.0
Scrub	7.16	14.51	5.96	8.81	6.6
Road	5.99	5.85	6.57	5.14	6.3
Buildings	11.19	21.23	10.56	18.36	10.9
Allotments	4.26	11.54	3.31	10.20	3.8
Grass	4.12	13.16	0.51	1.82	2.3
Altitude (m)	189.0	48.54	182.0	44.79	185.5

Note: This is the only difference between short- and long-term territories ($p < 0.05$).
From Goodburn (1987).

breeding success (Fig. 87), suggesting that other factors, as yet undetermined, are also important.

In Baeyens's (1981b) study, habitat differences between good- and poor-quality territories were not examined in detail. The only differences were that permanently occupied, class I territories were closer to areas of human activity

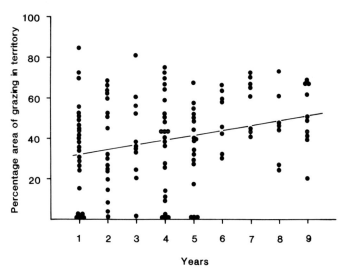

Fig. 86. *Relationship between the number of years a territory was occupied in the Sheffield study and the percentage of that territory composed of grazing land ($r = 0.253$, 138 d.f., $p < 0.01$). From Goodburn (1987).*

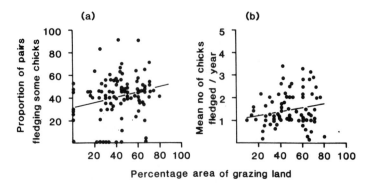

Fig. 87.   *Relationship between the percentage of grazing land in territories and breeding success: (a) proportion of pairs rearing at least one chick (r = 0.239, 101 d.f., p < 0.02), and (b) mean number of chicks fledged per pair (r = 0.247, 83 d.f., p < 0.025). From Goodburn (1987).*

and had less open space than class II territories. Breeding success was significantly greater in class I territories than class II (Table 29) and there are several, interrelated reasons for this. Class I territories were more likely to be occupied by birds older than two years, and perhaps as a result were more likely to build domed nests. In addition, being closer to buildings they suffered less disturbance from Carrion Crows (Table 29).

Møller (1982a) recorded the habitat characteristics in territories occupied for different numbers of years. He found positive relationships between the duration of occupancy and the amount of grassland, the occurrence of farmyards, dunghills and roads, and negative relationships between occupancy and the occurrence of cereals, stubble and ploughed or harrowed fields (Fig. 88). The association between human activity and occupancy is similar to the result obtained by Baeyens, and the effect of grassland is similar to our study. Also in agreement with Baeyens's study is the seasonal pattern of occupancy. Møller found that class III territories were occupied more

TABLE 29: *Differences in good (class I) and poor (class II) Black-billed Magpie territories in Baeyens's study in the Netherlands*

	Class I	Class II
Percentage occupied by adults	54 (21/39)	24 (9/38)
Percentage pairs rearing some young	54 (30/55)	18 (6/34)
Percentage nests domed	87 (41/47)	53 (15/28)
Percentage nests near human habitation	83 (39/49)	61 (17/28)
Percentage nests disturbed by Carrion Crows	11 (5/47)	39 (11/28)

Notes: From Baeyens (1981c).
All differences statistically significant.

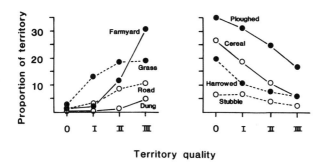

Fig. 88. *Relationships between territory quality (I = 'poor' to III = 'good', and 0 = houses and farms not used for breeding by magpies) and habitat variables, in Denmark. Territory quality improved with increasing area of farmyard, grass, roads, or dung heaps, and decreased with increasing amounts of land which was ploughed, growing cereals, harrowed, or stubble. (Drawn from data in Møller 1982a.)*

frequently than class II territories throughout much of the year. A comparison with class I territories is inappropriate, since by definition they were less likely to be occupied throughout the year than the other two categories. Breeding started earlier in class III and II territories than in class I, and was directly related to the duration of occupancy. As in the other studies, breeding success was correlated with occupancy: 59% of pairs in class III territories raised some offspring, compared to 27% in class II and just 8% in class I. The reasons for this effect may have been similar to those recorded in Baeyens's study, since nests in class III territories were placed closer to houses, than those in either class I or II territories. This in turn may have provided some protection from crows.

In conclusion it is clear that magpie territories differ in their quality and that this affects the breeding success of their owners. Similar effects have been recorded in other species, such as the Wheatear (Brooke 1979) and the Sparrowhawk (Newton 1976). The results from three studies of magpies suggest that the quality of their territory is determined by two factors: the food supply and safety from nest predators. Territory quality may also influence the survival of adult birds (Högstedt 1981a).

TERRITORY QUALITY, BIRD QUALITY AND BREEDING SUCCESS

Territory quality is clearly an important determinant of breeding success. Further evidence for this comes from Högstedt's (1980c) study of magpies in southern Sweden, in which he examined the variation in the size of magpie clutches in relation to territory quality. Many years previously, David Lack (1948, 1954) suggested that the size of clutch a bird species produces is that which on average results in the largest number of surviving young. Högstedt (1980c) extended Lack's idea, suggesting that instead of there being a single optimal clutch size for a particular species, there were several optimal clutch sizes, and that the number of eggs laid by a female should match either her

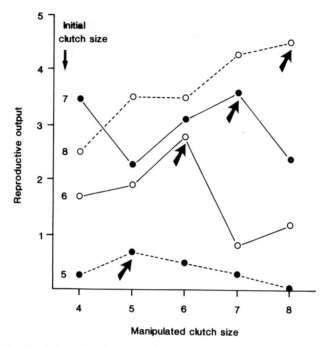

Fig. 89.   *Clutch size and breeding success of magpies. Each line shows the reproductive success for a particular initial clutch size after it was experimentally reduced, increased, or left as a control. The arrows indicate the highest breeding success for each line. In each case the control (i.e. the original) clutch size was the most productive, neither removal nor adding of extra eggs improving reproductive output. Redrawn from data in Högstedt (1980c).*

ability as a parent or the amount of food available. In other words, in good-quality territories, with a rich food supply, magpies should lay larger clutches because they will be able to rear more young than they would in poorer territories.

To test the idea that magpies adjust their clutch size according to territory quality, Högstedt manipulated magpie broods by adding or removing chicks. Regardless of their initial clutch size, pairs which were given additional chicks were less successful at rearing young. Indeed, the clutch sizes originally laid by the females were the most productive ones (Fig. 89). Högstedt then went on to examine clutch size in relation to particular females and the territory they bred in. His results showed that most (86%) of the variation in clutch size occurred as a result of differences in territory quality, and only 14% was attributable to differences between females. These results support the idea that there is no single optimal clutch size, but a range of clutch sizes each adapted to the quality of a particular territory. A similar result had previously been obtained for Great Tits (Perrins & Moss 1975).

After seeing Högstedt's interesting results we decided to examine our own data to determine whether a similar situation existed. We used a slightly

TABLE 30: *Variables used in repeatability analysis of Sheffield magpies*

Variable	Definition
Laying date	Date of the first egg of the first clutch in a particular season
Clutch size	Total number of eggs in the first clutch of a particular breeding season
Mean egg-volume index	The mean egg-size ($l \times b^2$; where l is egg length and b is egg breadth) of each clutch
Hatching success	Total number of chicks hatched, expressed as a proportion of the total clutch size, in a particular breeding season
Fledging success	Total number of chicks which survive to day 14, expressed as a proportion of the total clutch size in a particular breeding season
Mean chick weight	Mean weight of chicks at 14 days post-hatching
Hatching survival	Total number of chicks surviving to one year, expressed as a proportion of the total number of chicks hatched in a particular breeding season
Fledgling survival	Total number of chicks surviving to one year, expressed as a proportion of the total number of chicks fledged in a particular breeding season

different approach from Högstedt's: ours involved looking at how consistent certain breeding variables were for particular females and particular territories. Eight variables were examined, all of which are measures of breeding performance. These were: clutch size, laying date, egg size, hatching success, fledging success, chick weight at day 14, survival of chicks hatched, and survival of chicks fledged (Table 30). We then examined these in relation to three types of situation: (i) where the same birds bred in the same territory over several years, (ii) where the same birds bred in different territories, and (iii) where the same territories was occupied by different birds. In this way we were able to disentangle the effects of bird and territory quality. For example, if clutch size was determined largely by territory quality, as Högstedt found, then clutches laid in the same territories should be very similar regardless of which birds were involved. On the other hand if clutch size was primarily determined by the female rather than the territory then we would expect little consistency in clutch size when different females laid in the same territory. The measure of consistency which we used is referred to as 'repeatability' (Lessells & Boag 1987), and can be expressed as a percentage: 100% indicating perfect consistency or repeatability, and 0% indicating a total lack of repeatability.

The first step was to consider the same birds breeding in the same territory in order to identify the breeding variables worth examining further. With the same female in the same territory in different years, five of the eight breeding variables showed significant repeatability (clutch size, laying date, egg size, hatching success and fledging success). For males, only egg size and laying date showed significant repeatability (Table 31). This indicates that female effects, that is female quality, exerted a stronger effect than the male on the various breeding characteristics. One might assume that the timing of

TABLE 31: *Summary of results from the repeatability analysis*

Parameter	Bird effects[1]		Territory effects[2]	
	Male	*Female*	*Male*	*Female*
Lay date	NS	NS	NS	19.0*
Clutch size	NS	65.0**	some	17.0*
Egg size	NS	65.0***	NS	NS
Proportion of chicks hatched	69.0**	NS	NS	NS
Proportion of chicks fledged	NS	NS	NS	NS
Proportion of fledglings surviving to 1 year	75.0*	NS	NS	NS

Notes: Values are repeatabilities and only significant effects are shown.
(1) Same birds in different territories.
(2) Same territories occupied by different birds.
*** $p < 0.001$, ** $p < 0.01$, * $p < 0.05$.
NS = no significant effect.

breeding or egg size could be determined only by the female, but this overlooks the fact that the male can exert an indirect effect by providing the female with food or allowing her to forage in the best locations.

When the same female bred in different territories during the course of her life, repeatability was maintained for both clutch size and egg size. In both cases about 65% of the variability in these characteristics was attributable to a female effect. In order to assess the effect of territory we then looked at those cases where the same territory was occupied by different birds. This showed that there was significant repeatability for clutch size and laying date, but not egg size. Interestingly however, these territory effects were relatively small, accounting for just 19% of the variation in timing of breeding and 17% in clutch size. Overall, it is apparent that female quality accounted for most of the variation in clutch size and egg size, while territory quality had only small effects on clutch size and laying date, and no effect on egg size.

Let us turn now to the effects of male quality. For the same males in different territories, there was significant repeatability for hatching success and fledgeling survival. For the same territories occupied by different males, there was a suggestion that territory quality had a small effect on the size of clutches laid in them.

We can summarize these results by considering each of the breeding variables in order to examine the relative contribution of bird and territory effects. Laying date was controlled mainly through territory quality: when the same territory was occupied by different females the repeatability of laying date was 19%. In contrast, the laying dates of the same females breeding in different territories showed no repeatability. There was therefore a relatively small effect of territory quality, but no effect of female quality on the timing of breeding. This suggests that food levels in the territory during the pre-laying period play a part in determining when females lay. This idea is supported by two facts: first, that females advance their timing of breeding when provided with additional food (Chapter 7), and second, the observation that the pre-laying period is precisely the time when magpies most actively defend their territory (see Chapter 3).

The main factor affecting clutch size was female quality, (65%), with a small (17%) effect of territory quality. Egg size was also primarily determined by female quality (65%). This could arise, in part at least, through the effect of female body size. Clarkson (1984) found a significant correlation between female wing length and mean egg volume index in the same population. Male quality appeared to have a marked effect upon breeding success and the survival of fledglings, with respective repeatabilities of 69% and 75%. When the same territories were occupied by different males repeatability values were non-significant, indicating a minimal effect of territory quality on these variables. Since the male makes the major contribution to the care and rearing of young (Chapter 8), these effects are not unexpected.

Our results, summarized in Table 31, clearly differ from those of Högstedt (1980c). In his study, territory quality was the most important factor affecting clutch size, whereas in ours bird quality was much more important than the effects of territory. Why should this be so? Although the two studies differ in the type of analysis used to examine repeatability (see Goodburn 1987, 1991) this should not have affected the results. The studies did differ in several other respects. First, the population density in our study area (19–32 pairs/km^2) was at least three times as high as that in Högstedt's study (4.0–7.1 pairs/km^2; G. Högstedt, pers. comm.). Second, predation of adult magpies was virtually non-existent in our study, but in Sweden frequent predation by Goshawks may have created more territorial vacancies than in Sheffield.

The higher population density in our study could have affected our results in several ways. First, intense competition for space and frequent territorial intrusions may have reduced any advantages of being in a good-quality territory because the birds spent so much time defending it. The effects of territory quality may therefore have been minimized relative to Högstedt's study. There is some evidence for this idea, derived from a comparison of the high- and low-altitude parts of our study area. In the low-altitude area breeding density was high (Chapter 2), and territorial incidents averaged 1.2 per pair per hour. In contrast, in the high-altitude area, where breeding density was low (Chapter 2), territorial interactions were almost non-existent (F. M. Hunter, in Birkhead *et al.* 1986). Since the breeding density of birds on the valley tops was so much lower than in the centre of our study area we assumed that that area was less suitable for magpies. Accordingly we also expected breeding success to be lower. In fact it was not: in the high-density area 40% of pairs reared chicks to fledging, and 33% of pairs did so in the low-density area (not significantly different). Breeding success at high altitudes may be limited by lack of resources, food, or nest sites, whereas in the valley bottom pressure from territorial intruders may limit breeding success.

A further possibility which could account for the difference between Högstedt's results and ours concerns the opportunities for birds to move between territories. In our study the high population density may have resulted in fewer chances for birds to change territories. In Högstedt's study the lower population density, together with relatively frequent predation, would create more territory vacancies, more opportunities for birds to move, and therefore the increased likelihood of breeding in a wide range of territories. Data which G. Högstedt kindly provided confirmed that his females moved more frequently than ours. In Sweden, 22% of 65 females bred in different territories compared with 13% of 83 females in our study. However, while this result is suggestive, the difference is not statistically significant ($\chi^2 = 1.78$, 1 d.f., NS).

SUMMARY

Some magpie territories are occupied significantly more than expected by chance, whereas others are occupied less than expected. The number of years for which a territory is occupied is positively correlated with the breeding success of the magpies living in it. This probably occurs because the amount of suitable foraging area within the territory is also correlated with the number of years it is used for breeding. The contribution of territory quality to breeding success was small (6%). The relative importance of territory and bird quality

to reproductive performance was investigated. The breeding parameters of male and female magpies breeding in different territories, and different magpies breeding in the same territories were compared. This confirmed that in the Sheffield study, territory quality had a negligible effect on breeding performance compared with individual bird quality.

CHAPTER 11

Magpies and man

*Over much of its range, where it appears in moderate numbers, the bird
is not an outstanding agricultural pest or a serious menace to other wild
birds, and the present study has revealed that there are times when its
influence may even be decidedly beneficial.*

Kalmbach (1927)

Magpies have long been familiar to man: the Romans kept them as pets to
warn of the approach of strangers. Illustrations of them feature in the 14th
century Holkham Bible and Arundel Psalter, and in the 15th century
paintings by Hieronymus Bosch. Chaucer wrote about the 'joly pie' in his
Parlement of Foules (*c*. 1381), and Rowley writing in 1605 referred to someone
being 'As merry as a magge pie'. The very name 'Mag'-pie is a reflection of its
familiarity (Chapter 1); the habit of giving popular animals human names in
the late Middle Ages was common, hence, 'Jack'-daw, 'Tom'-tit and 'Jenny'-
wren. Moreover, the magpie's multitude of alternative names throughout its
range attests to its abundance and popularity. Newton and Gadow (1896)

describe it as being, prior to the 18th century, the 'cherished neighbour of every farmer'. This reputation was well justified since the magpie is an attractive, confident bird which helps to clear up man's waste and will eat large numbers of potentially harmful insects and rodents. However, with the increase in game preservation in the 18th and 19th centuries the magpie ceased to be popular in Europe because of its habit of taking gamebird eggs and chicks.

The North American Indians of the Plains area regularly used the feathers and carcasses of magpies as ornaments, particularly those worn in war. One artefact which I examined consisted of a scalp and several narrow buckskin straps beautifully decorated with forty magpie tail feathers. For the Plains Indians, magpies seem to have been associated with war because as carrion eaters they were frequently seen at battlefields.

Magpies have never been eaten with any regularity. Some boys I met in Portugal told me how they killed magpies with catapults in order to eat them. On the Aran Islands, Republic of Ireland, magpies are reputed to make 'a lovely pie', whenever they are unfortunate enough to turn up there (M. E. Birkhead, pers. comm.).

MAGPIES AND FARMING

I doubt whether magpies are anything but a local and infrequent nuisance to farmers these days, but their past reputation still lingers. The fact that magpies sometimes steal fruit and the eggs of poultry, and can attack livestock, has given them a bad reputation. Interestingly however, the conflict with man's agricultural practices is most prevalent in North America. This in turn may be due to differences in agricultural practices or to the behaviour of the magpies in the two areas.

The magpie's liking for wild fruits has already been mentioned (Chapter 5), but they can also cause damage to cultivated fruits, especially cherries. That this is not a recent problem is nicely illustrated by William Lawson's *A New Orchard and Garden*, written in 1618: 'Your cherries when they bee ripe, wil draw all the blacke-birds, Thrushes and May-pyes [magpies] to your Orchard' (Roach 1963). In North America too, Black-billed Magpies can constitute a local nuisance in cherry orchards (Kalmbach 1927).

In some areas where poultry are kept in open-topped pens magpies learn to steal their eggs, food and sometimes young chicks. In our study area a small poultry farm was established during the latter half of the study. The pens were all open and magpies quickly started to utilize the food provided for the chickens. Indeed the presence of this superabundant food source acted as a focus for one of the non-breeding flocks (see Chapter 4). The farmer was concerned about the amount of food taken by the thirty or so magpies which visited the farm to feed. The problem could have been avoided by covering the tops of the pens, though this remedy would certainly have reduced the farmer's profits. Kalmbach (1927) describes how in the early part of this century

European magpie scavenging on a dead sheep. (Photo: M. Wilkes).

magpies in North America were considered to be serious predators of poultry and young chicks. He reports that on some ranches several hundred young chickens could be killed in a season, and describes one instance where magpies destroyed 100 chicks in a single day. Again, covered pens would have eliminated the problem, but instead most people resorted to 'an inexpensive poisoning campaign'.

The effect of magpies on larger livestock was sometimes thought to be more serious. In Britain the magpie is not considered to be a serious nuisance to livestock – that role is reserved for the larger and more powerful Carrion Crow, which sometimes attacks newly born lambs (Murton 1971). In North America it is, or was, a rather different story. Linsdale (1937) describes a number of cases from the late 19th century in which magpies attacked horses, mules, cattle and sheep. In most cases the magpies pecked at existing injuries such as sores, galls, or warbles on the backs of the livestock. Most attacks also seemed to have occurred during the winter months when food was difficult for magpies to find. For the farmers and mule-packers magpies were a serious problem, enlarging wounds and in some cases apparently even killing the animals as a result. The following account is from British Columbia in the days of the Wild West:

> To the packer the [black-billed] magpies are dire enemies. If a pack-mule or horse has a gall, and happens to be turned out to graze with the wound uncovered, down come the magpies on its back; clinging with their sharp claws, reckless of every effort to displace them, they peck away at the wound; the tortured beast rolls madly, and for a short time the scoundrels are obliged to let

go, but only to swoop down again the instant a chance offers. This repeated agony soon kills an animal, unless the packers rescue it. . . . We had frightful trouble with magpies at our winter mule camp near Colville. They gradually accumulated, to eat the offal and what there was besides, until they were in hundreds, and became perfectly unbearable. Shooting them was only wasting ammunition. The packers were driven almost to a state of revolt. We had an old maimed suffering mule which was to be killed, so the packers gave it a ball containing a large dose of strychnine; death was immediate, and the carcass, ere ten minutes had lapsed, was covered with magpies working at the eyes, lips, sores and soft skin inside the thighs. It was the most singular spectacle I ever witnessed. One after the other birds rolled from off the dead mule, and as they fell and died, others greedily took their vacant places; and so this terrible slaughter went on until heaps of dead magpies nearly buried the body of the mule. . . . It was a terrible revenge – how far justifiable is a matter of opinion.

(Lord 1866)

There are also cases of magpies injuring sheep in a similar way: in Montana magpies pecked holes in the backs of newly shorn sheep. In some instances this behaviour extended further:

For some reason the kidneys are particularly favored tid-bits, and the birds were quick to learn the location of these organs in the animal's body and the ease with which they could penetrate to them by drilling a shallow hole just at the side of the spine in the lumbar region, through this they would peck away piecemeal, first the overlying tissues, then the toothsome fatty layer, and then work into the kidney itself. The wretched sheep would become weaker and weaker, soon sink by the wayside, and in the absence of prompt human intervention the end was not long delayed.

(Berry 1922)

Despite the unpleasant nature of these attacks, it is important to note that they all occurred well over one hundred years ago and some of them are probably exaggerated. Modern husbandry has all but eliminated such attacks. The magpies that are seen perched on the backs of farm animals these days are either using the animal as a convenient perch whilst foraging, or they may be removing ticks or other parasites. Hewett (1843) recorded that magpies sit on the backs of sheep to 'observe the grasshoppers which the flock disturb as they feed, and on which these birds feast luxuriously'. They were also thought to be 'of service in ridding cattle of maggots embedded in their hide, and sheep it will free from lice' (Yarrell 1843). Magpies also occasionally take wool or hair from livestock for nesting material. At the present time the effect of magpies on agriculture appears to be minimal in both Europe and North America. Given the large quantities of insects they consume (see Chapter 5), and their liking for small mammals, they are probably more useful than harmful.

MAGPIES AND GAME PRESERVATION

In Europe and North America magpies have long been considered serious predators of eggs and young gamebirds, particularly pheasants and partridges. However, it is clear from the numerous analyses of the magpie's diet that although these items are eaten, they form only a small proportion of the magpie's diet. None the less, from the gamekeeper's point of view the loss of any gamebird eggs or young can appear to be a serious problem. An account, written over 150 years ago states:

> To all kinds of eggs they [magpies] are destructive. Even the nest of the smallest bird does not escape their minute observation. To their rapacious appetite a great many partridges and pheasants, and several other birds, fall an easy prey. Day after day, I have observed them in pursuit of the same covey; and they never appeared to be satisfied until the poor birds were extirpated.
>
> (Weir, in MacGillivray 1837)

Similarly, Johns (1862) wrote: 'Partridges and pheasants are watched to their retreat and plundered mercilessly of their eggs and young'. Not surprisingly, magpies featured on every gamekeeper's gibbet, and in some areas still do. Emotions still run high when magpies are mentioned: 'Ask any gamekeeper, sportsman, farmer or many a garden-birdwatcher which single bird species upsets him or her most these days, and surely the magpie will feature among the top three' (Shedden & Fenwick 1988). Less restrained is Llewellyn (1989) writing in *Country Living*: 'Right thinking Victorians didn't have any hesitation in preserving ... gamebirds by letting daylight into every magpie unwise enough to show itself above the parapet'.

It is actually difficult to assess just how much of a threat magpies are to gamebirds. In heavily keepered areas *all* potential predators are removed, so it is impossible to determine which one is the main culprit. Vesey-Fitzgerald (1946) in his book *British Game*, concludes that while magpies undoubtedly take the odd gamebird chick, overall they do not do much harm. In contrast, predators which kill adult partridges or pheasants, such as the fox, stoat and cat are a much more serious threat simply because of their effect on gamebird populations. Both the Carrion Crow and magpie are considered to be vermin, and although the magpie is considered to be less of a threat both are still persecuted. In North America magpies are thought to be more important predators of game than either Common Crows or raccoons (Jones & Hungerford 1972).

The gamekeeper's objective is to eliminate all potential predators during the partridge and pheasant breeding season. As far as European magpies are concerned, to hope for anything else would be unrealistic, given the current increase in numbers. One keeper informed me that of the sixty-odd magpies he killed each season (on a 25 km^2 estate), all were replaced by immigrants by the following breeding season. In other words despite systematic destruction, magpie numbers are maintained by birds from nearby unkeepered areas. Exactly the same type of effect occurs among some birds of prey (e.g. sparrowhawk: Newton 1986).

Keepers have employed a variety of techniques to control magpie numbers. The most effective, but illegal, method involves poison baits, usually a chicken or pheasant egg laced with highly toxic phosdrin or alpha-chloralose. Although the latter substance does not kill birds outright it renders them unconscious and they eventually die of hypothermia. Phosdrin on the other hand kills very rapidly. Some birds are shot opportunistically, incubating or brooding females are shot on the nest, and occupied nests are destroyed. In the past magpies were sometimes lured within shooting range by 'calling them up', or by presenting a decoy owl. A tame owl was used if available, but failing that a stuffed one would work just as well. Nowadays, plastic decoy owls of various 'species' are available. In the past, gin-traps were used to catch magpies and although these are now banned in Britain, they are apparently still used in North America for the same purpose (Jones & Hungerford 1972).

The magpie is considered to be a relatively easy species to control by gamekeepers, and the presence or absence of magpies on an estate is a good indication of how well the keeper is doing his job. The ease with which magpies can be killed explains why they were so successfully eradicated from much of Britain during the last century. It is interesting that with the advent of increased 'vermin control' during the last century the magpie's behaviour altered. Newton and Gadow (1896) write:

> Since the persecution to which the Pie has been subjected in Great Britain, its habits have undoubtedly altered greatly in character. It is no longer the merry, saucy hanger-on of the homestead as it was to writers of former days, who were constantly alluding to its disposition, but is becoming the suspicious thief, shunning the gaze of man, and knowing that danger may lurk in every bush.

Charles Darwin (1872) commented on how wary the magpie was in England and how tame it was in Norway, where it was not persecuted. That intense shooting can have this effect on magpies was demonstrated during a visit to Portugal: I heard magpies on several occasions but hardly ever saw them (or any other birds). Only after discovering that bird shooting was a national pastime, did I realize the reason for the magpies' furtiveness.

The legal situation regarding the shooting of magpies in Europe has changed. Until recently in Britain, any landowner could kill magpies on his land. However, since the formation of the European Community, all European birds, including magpies and crows, are now legally protected. There has been considerable concern among British politicians, many of whom enjoy hunting, shooting and fishing, that magpies in Britain might be afforded legal protection. In the House of Lords on 4 May 1989 Lord Stanley asked the British Government whether it would 'resist any attempts to make it more difficult to control pests . . . listed on the Wildlife and Countryside Act 1981, in particular magpies and carrion crows'. The minister of state for the Department of the Environment, the Earl of Caithness, replied that the government had no intention at present of altering the 'pest schedule'. The strength of feeling against the magpie was illustrated by comments made by various others present: Lord John-Mackie described it as the 'biggest possible killer of bird life', and Lord Winstanley proposed 'capital punishment for the thieving and murderous magpie'. The Earl of Swinton asked if members of the European Commission interested in protecting magpies might be allowed to view for themselves 'the preponderance of these horrible magpies which live all over the land'.

The magpie is, surprisingly, a new pest for the present-day keepers: magpies had been eliminated from large parts of Britain by previous generations of gamekeepers. It is only with the increase in magpie numbers since the 1960s that they have started to become a problem again and new techniques have been devised to cope with them. For example, as an alternative to the illegal poison bait method, the Game Conservancy in Britain has been testing the Larsson trap, for controlling magpie numbers. This technique, which is similar to the approach we used in our study (see Chapter 1), does catch magpies, but involves maintaining decoy birds and is time-consuming. I doubt whether it will ever be as attractive to gamekeepers as using poison baits. Another alternative which has been tested in continental Europe and in North America is the use of 'avicides', drugs for specifically killing or repelling birds: several of these substances are very effective (e.g. Guarino 1967; Kalotas & Nikodemusz 1982).

MAGPIES IN TOWNS

As part of their increase across much of Europe (see Chapter 6) magpies now breed regularly in suburban and urban areas. Although they breed in towns in areas other than Europe (e.g. Canada: Hochachka & Boag 1987; South Korea: Doo-Pyo & Koo 1986), it is only in western Europe that they are considered by some people to be a pest. The tendency for magpies to breed in

Suburban habitat of North American Black-billed Magpies: part of David Boag's study area Edmonton, Canada. (Photo: D. Boag).

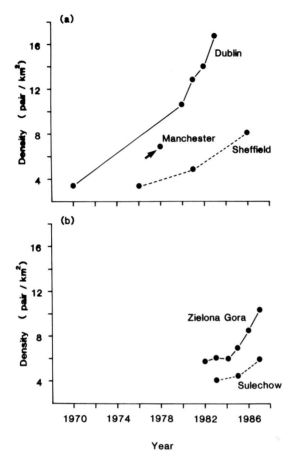

Fig. 90. *Changes in urban magpie population density in (a) British Isles, and (b) in western Poland. For Sheffield the census prior to 1976 showed an average density of 1.4 pairs/km² in 1946 (Clarkson & Birkhead 1987). Data for Dublin is from Kavanagh (1987) and for Manchester from Tatner (1982c). Data for Poland from L. Jerzak (pers. comm.).*

urban areas was first noted in the British Isles in the 1950s and 1960s (Parslow 1973), and has continued to the present. The pattern of suburban population growth in Sheffield and Dublin is shown in Fig. 90. Qualitative observations suggest similar population expansions in other towns in the British Isles, including London, Birmingham and Aberdeen. The increase in the numbers of urban magpies elsewhere in Europe has been monitored, for example in Berlin (Witt 1985, 1989) and several towns in Poland (L. Jerzak pers. comm.).

The rate of increase in magpies in suburban England is twice that in rural habitats (Fig. 48), and has raised a number of questions, particularly about the possible effect of magpies on songbirds. The expansion of urban magpie numbers has not occurred, as some people think, because magpies have moved from rural to urban areas: the increase is simply part of the overall population

Magpie nest in a man-made site: a railway watch-tower in Sheffield. (Photo: D. Hollingworth).

expansion. That said, conditions for magpies in urban areas must be better than they are in more rural habitats. The magpie's ability to utilize the urban environment has hinged on there being suitable nesting sites and food supplies. In many towns, nest sites are now plentiful since as part of the redevelopment following the Second World War there were extensive tree-planting programmes. The species of tree varied from city to city: in Manchester, poplars were the most commonly planted species, whereas in Sheffield sycamore and lime were used (Tatner 1982b; Clarkson 1984). From the magpie's point of view this has made little difference since they can build in most tree species. About twenty years after they were planted, in the early 1960s, these trees began to reach a size suitable for magpies to nest in, and have ever since provided an abundance of nest sites. Indeed, in Tatner's (1982b) study in Manchester, the abundance of trees was the main factor determining the density of breeding magpies. Even in the absence of trees magpies can sometimes find suitable alternative nesting sites, and there are increasing numbers of records of nests made on man-made structures. These include telegraph poles, electricity pylons, British Rail watch-towers, cranes, and even

Magpie nest on a man-made structure: an electricity pylon, in Sheffield. (Photo: T. R. Birkhead).

A magpie nest in the heart of urban Sheffield. Magpies are remarkably adaptable and can exist in even the most unpromising habitats. (Photo: T. R. Birkhead).

inside large factories (Kulczycki 1973). In addition, magpies sometimes use man-made materials for constructing their nests. Keith Clarkson found three such nests in adjacent trees and presumably built by the same pair over several years, in a heavily industrial part of Sheffield. The framework of the nests was made from wire of various sorts, and the 'mud' bowl, from papier mâché. In each case the finished product was an incredibly solid structure.

In addition to requiring somewhere to nest, magpies also need feeding areas close-by. In suburbia neatly mown lawns and grass verges provide the perfect feeding habitat. In more urban areas parks often fulfil this need. However, urban magpies sometimes seem to be able to exist with the smallest patch of grassland in their territories, presumably because other food sources are available. In Sheffield magpies breed successfully in some of the most industrial and least attractive parts of the city, which at first glance seem to offer very little in the way of feeding habitat. However, being opportunists, magpies can often do very well where other species might fail.

The magpie's food-hoarding habit has undoubtedly played an important role here, enabling the birds to exploit any temporary abundance of food, such as human refuse. Despite their abundance in towns magpies are still wary of people, and in most areas they have not attained the tameness of species like the Blackbird. Instead the magpie's suburban feeding strategy seems to be based on stealth, often visiting gardens early in the morning while there are few people around. They either collect invertebrates from lawns and flower-beds or take the food from bird tables provided for other species. In the latter case they can rapidly remove and hoard all the food they need for the day. In some industrial parts of Sheffield the local magpies have become popular with workmen who share their sandwiches with them. In rural areas magpies have only ever been seen hoarding food in the ground (Chapter 5), but in urban or suburban areas they hoard food on the roofs of buildings, under the eaves and in gutters. Presumably magpies in built-up areas treat roof-tops as part of the 'ground'. By hoarding in such places they need to spend only a short time hiding food each day, but can recover and eat it at their leisure with little risk of disturbance. The abundance of food, both natural and unnatural, in suburban gardens must also play a role in the magpie's survival and breeding success. Indeed, Balança (1984a) found that in his suburban study area in France 40% (by weight) of the diet of magpie chicks was from food provided by man. In addition, the fact that cities are a few degrees warmer than surrounding rural areas, due to the 'heat island effect' (see Chapter 7), must also contribute to the magpie's success there. However, life for city magpies is not completely idyllic. The urban environment exposes them to one predator from which they would normally be quite safe. In much of Britain magpies have few natural predators, but in towns their habit of feeding in gardens and on bird tables makes them vulnerable to cats. There are increasing numbers of records of cats killing magpies.

It is not clear at present how the rapid rate of population growth has arisen. Eden (1985b) compared the breeding biology of magpies in Sheffield with those in our nearby rural study population and found that although the urban magpies bred slightly earlier in the year, the breeding success of urban birds (1.97 chicks per pair) did not differ significantly from that of rural birds (1.72 chicks per pair). As Chapter 6 shows, breeding success is just one component of population dynamics, and urban magpies might survive better than those in rural areas. This is likely to be true if shooting is an important mortality factor in rural areas. The high rate of population increase in towns compared with rural Britain supports this idea. A detailed population study of colour-marked birds in an urban area is needed to check this.

The main problem associated with magpies in cities is their supposed effect on suburban songbirds. Magpies certainly take the eggs and young of songbirds (e.g. Mizera 1988), but in most areas they probably pose no serious threat to songbird populations. The 'problem' of magpies and songbirds has two components: an emotional one arising from seeing nestlings being killed, and a concern for long-term trends in songbird numbers. When magpies rob a nest of eggs or young it is often a noisy and conspicuous affair. The parent birds mob the magpies noisily, quickly drawing the observer's attention to the scene. The sight of one or a pair of magpies killing young birds while the parents fly around helplessly can be rather unpleasant and can arouse strong feelings. One writer, referring to magpies as 'black and white brutes', described the situation thus: 'All along the hedges, the ground has been littered with the grisly remains of what would have been next year's song birds'. Unfortunately, it is the manner in which magpies act as predators which creates part of the problem. If a Sparrowhawk swoops down across the garden and plucks a fledgling Starling off the bird table, most birdwatchers are delighted. Unlike a magpie, the raptor has performed some marvellous aerobatics, made a 'clean' kill and removed the luckless victim out of sight. None the less, the end-result is the same. Because such an obvious double standard exists, one cannot really discuss magpies and songbirds from such an emotional perspective.

The second aspect of the problem is whether magpies have, or could, reduce the numbers of songbirds. Each spring in recent years the national press in Britain has contained numerous letters, stating that a local songbird population has been reduced in numbers, and that it is all due to magpies. There is relatively little quantitative information on magpie predation on songbirds. Møller (1988) looked at nest predation on Blackbirds breeding in clumps of elm trees on Danish farmland. The potential nest predators which occurred in the area included Hooded Crows, Jays, Jackdaws and magpies. Of these, magpies were the most abundant and accounted for the majority of nest failures: 87% of all corvids in the area were magpies, and these were responsible for 96% of all nest losses – only slightly higher than one would expect from their abundance. Nest predation was most frequent in small patches of woodland, and the presence of breeding magpies in the woodland resulted in an increased failure rate (Fig. 91). In small clumps of trees Blackbirds were more likely to build their nests in concealed sites, such as inside buildings or in coniferous trees, than in larger woods. Surprisingly, the

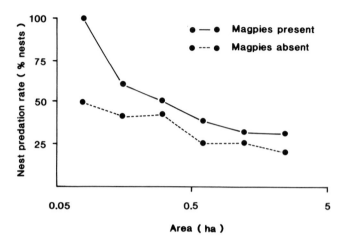

Fig. 91. *Magpie predation on Blackbird nests with eggs in Denmark in relation to size of wood (area) and the presence or absence of magpies breeding in the same wood. In both cases predation decreased with size of wood, but predation was consistently higher where magpies were present. (Redrawn from Møller 1988.)*

TABLE 32: *Breeding success and causes of breeding failure among the four commonest songbird species breeding in British gardens.*

Measure	Blackbird	Song Thrush	Robin	Dunnock
No. of nests checked	375	89	50	47
No. successful	183	43	33	30
(%)	(49)	(48)	(66)	(64)
No. fail	192	46	17	17
No. of failed nests predated (%)	125	30	10	9
No. times predator seen	(65)	(65)	(59)	(53)
	39	9	0	0
Predator:				
Magpie	26	5		
(%)	(67)	(55)		
Cat	6	0		
(%)	(15)			
Carrion Crow	3	3		
(%)	(8)	(33)		
Jay	2	0		
(%)	(5)			
Stoat or weasel	1	1		
(%)	(2)	(11)		
Man	1	0		
(%)	(2)			

Note: From Gooch, Birkhead & Baillie (unpublished).

presence of magpies in a wood had no effect on where Blackbirds placed their nests, so it seems as though Blackbirds responded more to habitat character-istics than predators when selecting a nest site.

A survey of the breeding success of British suburban songbirds by Stephen Gooch, Stephen Baillie and myself (unpublished) found that although mag-pies were among the most frequently observed nest predators, breeding success was still relatively high (Table 32). In a study of the breeding success of urban birds in Solacz, Poland, Mizera (1988; pers. comm.) suggested that magpies were responsible for the breeding failure of most open-nesting songbirds. He also found that as magpie numbers increased the breeding success and numbers of Blackbirds decreased (Fig. 92). However, in another study, in Berlin, Witt (1989) found no evidence that increasing magpie numbers had any deleterious effect on songbird numbers.

In order to assess whether magpies might be responsible for any widespread declines in songbird populations in England, Stephen Gooch, Stephen Baillie and I used the British Trust for Ornithology's data on breeding success and

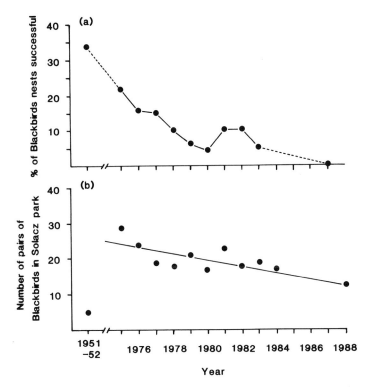

Fig. 92. *(a) Changes in the breeding success of Blackbirds in Solacz area of Poland (r = −0.914, 9 d.f., p < 0.01), and (b) changes in the number of Blackbirds breeding in Solacz park, Poznan, Poland (r = −0.783, 9 d.f., p < 0.01: No. of Blackbirds = −0.9 × year + 92.41). The decreases in breeding success and numbers are thought to be due to an increase in magpie numbers in the same area: from 2 pairs in 1963, 4 pairs in 1969 to 13 pairs in 1982 (Mizera 1988; pers. comm.).*

population levels to test four ideas. We predicted that if magpies were having a negative effect on songbirds the following should be true: (a) Songbird nest mortality should increase as magpie population density increases. (b) Songbird nest mortality should be higher when magpies are more abundant. (c) Changes in songbird breeding density should be inversely related to changes in magpie density. (d) Changes in songbird density should be inversely related to the rate of increase in magpie numbers. There was no evidence that any of these predictions was true. We looked at breeding success and population status of eleven common songbird species, which we thought might be vulnerable to magpies. These were: Blackbird, Song Thrush, Mistle Thrush, Dunnock, Robin, Chaffinch, Greenfinch, Goldfinch, Skylark, Wren and Yellowhammer. The results are for birds in rural England, mainly on farmland and woodland, and were as follows for each prediction. (a) Nine of the eleven songbird species showed no change in nest mortality with increasing magpie density, and two showed significantly reduced nest mortality as magpies became more abundant! (b) The nest mortality of all songbird species was not related to magpie density. (c) Songbird populations actually did better (not worse), i.e. they increased more, or decreased less, in areas where magpie density was higher; Witt (1989) also found this effect in Berlin. (d) There was no evidence that the rate of change in songbird numbers was in any way related to the rate of change in magpie numbers (Gooch *et al.* 1991). Overall, this analysis provides good evidence that, despite people's fears, magpies have had no detectable effect on songbird breeding success or population levels in rural habitats. We are currently investigating the situation in British suburban habitats.

It seems likely that the most serious threat to songbirds in the suburban environment is the domestic cat. A study of cat diets in a village in southern England by Churcher and Lawton (1987) showed that 35% of all prey items were birds, and most of these were House Sparrows. Most predation on birds occurred during the winter months, presumably when small mammals, the cats' other main prey, were scarce. On average each cat was known to have killed about six birds each year, and it was clear that cats were a major mortality factor for House Sparrows. No less than one-third of all sparrow deaths were caused by cats. The fact that cats kill birds mainly during the winter means that they take mainly adults, and therefore are more likely to reduce the population than a predator like a magpie which takes mainly eggs or young.

The figures from this study probably underestimate the impact that cats have on suburban songbird populations. First, the number of prey items brought home by cats may be only half what are actually caught (George 1974). Second, several studies have shown that in more urbanized areas the proportion of birds taken by cats is even greater. C. Howes (pers. comm.) found that in northern England the proportion of birds in the cat's diet increased with increasing urbanization, and that in suburban areas they made up 35% of all prey items.

Colin Howes kindly allowed Ian Massie and I to analyse his data on cats and we found that in urban areas there was an average of 74 cats per magpie territory (5 ha), and in suburban areas 25 cats per territory. The urban cats killed an average of 8.4 birds each per year, so in total cats killed 622 birds per magpie territory over the year. In suburban areas each cat killed an average of 16.4 birds per year; a total of 415 birds were killed by cats per territory. The House Sparrow was the main prey in both urban (77%) and suburban areas (53%). Blackbirds formed 7% of cats' diets in urban areas and 10% in suburban areas. The Starling formed 4% of the diet in urban areas and 11% in suburban areas. We do not know how many eggs or young birds magpies kill, but it is probably insignificant compared with what is taken by pet cats.

SUMMARY

Prior to the widespread rearing of game, magpies were popular birds, but they are now regarded by many as 'vermin'. Their habit of eating carrion and taking the eggs or young of songbirds has not improved their image. There is little evidence that magpies currently pose anything other than a local threat to poultry farmers or fruit growers, and the number of invertebrates that magpies eat probably compensates for any damage they do. The increase in magpie numbers in towns in the British Isles has caused concern for their effect on songbirds. Although magpies take songbird eggs and young, these items form only a very small proportion of their diet. An analysis of the trends in magpie numbers and in the numbers and breeding success for eleven species of English songbird, provided no evidence that magpies had any effect on songbirds.

CHAPTER 12

Comparisons and conclusions

The magpies constitute a group of birds peculiarly suitable for a comparative study.

Linsdale (1937)

The aim of this final chapter is to draw together some of the material presented earlier and make some comparisons between what probably might as well be three species: the European Magpie, the North American Black-billed Magpie and the Yellow-billed Magpie. In the following discussion I refer to these as three 'types' of magpie, but I use the term only as a matter of convenience. Any comparisons between the different types of magpie are bound to be somewhat speculative, for several reasons. First, despite the various detailed studies which have been undertaken, we still have a great deal to learn about magpies. Second, as yet, no one person has made detailed, comparative field studies of

European magpie portrait. (Photo: M. Wilkes).

Yellow-billed Magpie portrait. (Photo: T. R. Birkhead).

both the North American species and any of the Eurasian races of magpie. Third, it is difficult to distinguish between genuine genetic differences and those which occur in response to the very different climatic and environmental regimes experienced by each type. With these provisos, I attempt to identify the main differences between the three types of magpies for which we have most information and offer explanations wherever possible, or at least suggest ideas that might be worth exploring.

I have divided the magpies' biology into three broad areas: (a) population and breeding biology, (b) territoriality, and (c) other aspects of social behaviour. In order to facilitate comparisons I have summarized the main similarities of and differences between the three types of magpies in Tables 33–35.

TABLE 33: *Comparison of the population biology and breeding biology of Black-billed and Yellow-billed Magpies*

Feature	Black-billed Magpie in Europe	Black-billed Magpie in North America	Yellow-billed Magpie
Body weight (g)	200+	180	160
Habitat	Grassland	Grassland	Grassland savannah
Climate	Warm–cool summer Mild–cold winter	Warm–hot summer Cold winter	Hot summer Warm winter
Nest site	Bush or tall tree	Bush or tall tree	Tall tree
Nest type	Domed, sometimes open	Domed	Domed
Breeding season	April	April	April
Clutch size	6	6.5	6.5
Egg weight (g)	10	9.5	8.3
Fresh egg weight as % female weight	4.4–5.1	5.0–5.8	5.7
Incubation (days)	*c.* 22	*c.* 22	*c.* 22
Hatching	Asynchronous	Asynchronous	Asynchronous
Brood reduction?	Yes	Yes	Yes
Fledging period	25	25	25
Post-fledging care (days)	42	35–42	?
Age at independence (d)	80	60–70	?
No. of broods	1	1	1
Repeat nesting	Yes	Some	Some
Seasonal decline in breeding success	Slight	Yes	Some
Population breeding season	Very long	Long	Short
Breeding success (chicks per successful pair)	3.3	4.0	2.6
Natal dispersal	Slight	Yes	Slight
Breeding dispersal	Slight	Some	Slight
Adult moult	Late June–late Sept.	Late June–late Sept.?	Mid-May–end October
Post-juvenal moult	May–August	May–August	Mid-July–mid-November

POPULATION AND BREEDING BIOLOGY

The three magpie types differ in body size, with those in Europe being the largest and the Yellow-billed being the smallest. For the European magpie, body size varies between populations, being somewhat larger in cooler climates. The difference between the three types could also be a response to climatic conditions. The body size differences which exist are consistent with the idea that they are correlated with summer (but not winter) temperatures, which are hottest in California (Yellow-billed), followed by the rest of North America, and then Europe. In Chapter 1 I used wing length as an index of body size (because data are available for both species and all races of *Pica pica*), and looked at the correlation between this and summer temperature. The result was somewhat equivocal: the correlation was in the predicted direction (i.e. with smaller-winged birds in warmer climates), but it was not statistically significant.

There are two reasons for this result. (i) Wing length may be a poor index of body size because the relative size of wings may differ between populations or species. The few cases where we have data on both wing length and body weight support this idea. For example, Yellow-billed Magpies and magpies in England have almost identical wing lengths, but the Yellow-billed Magpie is substantially lighter in body weight, indicating that it has relatively long wings (Appendix 3). Measuring body size in birds is not straightforward, but I suspect that a clearer relationship between temperature or latitude would emerge if we used body weight instead of wing length. These data exist for the two North American magpie species, but for very few races of *P. pica*. The

TABLE 34: *Comparison of territory types used by Black-billed and Yellow-billed Magpies*

Feature	Black-billed Magpie in Europe	Black-billed Magpie in North America	Yellow-billed Magpie
Breeding unit	Single pair	Single pair	Colonies of 5–30 pairs
Nest spacing	Even	Aggregated in habitat	Aggregated
Mean nearest distance between nests (m)	100	80	50
Territory size (ha)	5	0.3	1.2
Home range size (ha)	5	40	40
Seasonal pattern of territory occupancy	Throughout year	Breeding season only	Throughout year
Seasonal pattern of territory defence	Pre-laying	None?	Pre-laying
Territorial interactions	Frequent	Infrequent	Frequent
Territory function	Pre-laying food supply and/or mate guarding	Nest defence	Pre-laying food supply and/or mate guarding
Feeding areas	Within territory	Up to 400 m from nest	Within territory and communal flock areas

available information indicates a negative correlation between weight and summer temperature. (ii) It is difficult to obtain good information on the sorts of temperatures that magpies in different parts of the range experience: I suspect the information available is not particularly precise. For example, the

TABLE 35: *Summary of the visual displays and other behaviours performed by Black-billed Magpies in Europe and North America and Yellow-billed Magpies*

Type of behaviour	Display	Black-billed Magpie in Europe	Black-billed Magpie in N. America	Yellow-billed Magpie
Aggression and submission	Upright	+	+	+
	and feathers fluffed	+	+	+
	Wing-flirting	+	+	+
	Tail-flirting	+	+	+
	Tail-up	−	−	+
	Displacement bill-wiping	+	+	+
	pecking	+	+	+
	Nictitating membrane blink	+	+	+
	Wing-flash	+		+
	Head-up	+	+	+
	Stretch	+	+	+
	Parallel walk	+	+	+
	Tree-topping	+	+	+
	Ceremonial gatherings	+	−	−
Sexual behaviour	Allopreening	+	+	+
	Billing	+		+
	Tugging	+		+
	Wing-flirting	+	+	+
	Tail-flirting	+	+	−
	Tail-spreading	+	+	−
	Courtship feeding	+	+	+
	Female begging	+	+	+
	Nictitating membrane blink	+	+	
	Pre-copulatory behaviour:			
	Male wing-quiver	+	+	+
	Tilting	+	+	+
	Circling	+	+	+
	Babble singing	+	+	+
	Extra-pair courtship and copulation	+	+	+
	Mate guarding by following	+	+	+

Notes: Terminology is primarily from Verbeek (1972b) and Baeyens (1979).
+ the display occurs; − the display does not occur; a blank: no information.
Note that some displays (e.g. wing-flirting) can be used in either aggressive/submissive or sexual contexts.

race *asirensis* has a small, rather poorly known range in the Asir Mountains of south-west Arabia, and no meteorological information appears to be available for that area.

The age at which magpies first start to breed varies between different areas. Our birds started breeding at either 1 or 2, and G. Högstedt (pers. comm.) found most of his birds in Sweden breeding at 2 or more years old. Most Yellow-bills probably start breeding at 2 (Verbeek 1973). Reese and Kadlec (1985) found a very high proportion (40%) of first-year North American Black-billed Magpies breeding. However, in Buitron's (1988) study only 9% of breeding birds were first-years. The age of first breeding may differ according to local conditions. It seems unlikely that any consistent difference in the age of first breeding exists between European and North American Black-billed Magpies.

One consistent difference between North American magpies and those in Europe to emerge from this study is the difference in nest construction. North American Black-bills and Yellow-bills almost always build domed nests, whereas in some European populations 20% or more of nests may be undomed. This difference could be due to genetic differences between the three types of magpie, but given that nest predation by Carrion Crows is a serious mortality factor in almost all European populations examined, it is surprising that any magpies there build open nests.

The clutch of North American Black-billed Magpies averages about 6.5 eggs, about half an egg larger than the clutch of European magpies. Although there is a slight latitudinal trend in clutch size within Europe, with somewhat larger clutches in the north, it is very unlikely that the higher clutch size among North American magpies is part of this overall trend. Most North American populations which have been studied are at the same or lower latitudes, and experience warmer summer temperatures, than the European ones. However, latitudinal trends in clutch size are thought to be related to seasonal patterns of productivity: at higher latitudes there is a large, seasonal peak of food abundance and birds in those regions are therefore capable of rearing more offspring, hence their bigger clutches (Ashmole 1963). The observed pattern of clutch size variation in magpies may be consistent with Ashmole's hypothesis. Within Europe clutch size increases from south to north, as predicted, but with one exception. In southern Spain clutch size is larger than expected from this relationship (Chapter 7). This area has warmer, drier summers than most of the rest of Europe. Similarly, the two magpie species in North America also experience relatively warm, dry summers and produce relatively large clutches. It might be that in climates with a summer drought, the seasonal pattern of productivity, particularly of soil-surface invertebrates, also shows a large spring peak. Additional evidence for this idea comes from the duration of magpie breeding seasons, which are protracted in mid- and northern European latitudes compared with those in southern Europe and North America. Consistent with these observations is that in North America the seasonal decline in breeding success appears to be more pronounced than among European magpies. The implication here is that birds which breed late miss the peak of food abundance and suffer reduced success as a consequence. All these factors taken together indicate that the seasonal pattern of food abundance in areas with warm or hot summer climates (i.e. southern Europe and North America) is shorter and possibly more pronounced than it is in areas with cooler summers. Detailed information on the seasonal patterns of food availability for different magpie populations is needed to test this idea.

The sparse information available suggests that young Black-billed Magpies in North America move much further and show greater natal dispersal than magpies in western Europe. The difference in climatic regimes between the two areas, with the colder winters in much of the North American magpie's range, undoubtedly accounts for part of this difference. However, whereas young magpies either disperse or have relatively large home ranges, adult birds are thought to be sedentary. Presumably, young birds move further afield because they are less capable of competing for food with older birds when food is scarce. Winter conditions are much less harsh in the Yellow-billed Magpie's range, and this may account for the lack of dispersal among young birds. In addition, however, the more restricted geographic range of this species may also limit the movements of young individuals.

TERRITORY

Nest spacing and the types of territories utilized by the three types of magpies differ fairly consistently (Fig. 93). Yellow-billed Magpies breed in small, loose colonies, in which each pair defends a territory of about 1.2 ha during the breeding season. Birds visit their territories throughout the year, and most boundaries are established in the autumn.

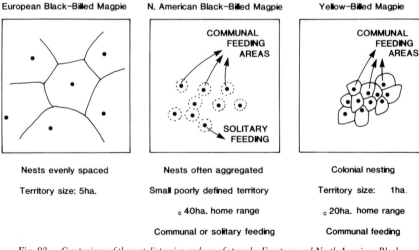

Fig. 93.   *Comparison of the nest dispersion and use of space by European and North American Black-billed Magpies and the Yellow-billed Magpie.*

North American Black-billed Magpie nests are aggregated, but generally less so than Yellow-billed Magpies, although the distances to their nearest neighbours can be similar (Chapter 2). In some cases at least, the clumping of nests occurs because nesting habitat is also clumped, and within suitable nesting habitat nests are regularly spaced. North American Black-billed Magpies show either no territorial defence or defend a relatively small area (about 0.3 ha) around their nest only during the breeding season. Despite the proximity of neighbouring pairs, territorial interactions are relatively infrequent. Breeding birds forage mainly outside their territories, and usually as pairs. The foraging areas of adjacent pairs overlap and in some areas at least they forage in flocks at communal feeding areas in the same way as Yellow-billed Magpies (E. Stone, pers. comm.). Because Black-billed Magpies in North America and Europe have been considered to be the same species it has usually been assumed that they behave in an identical manner. This has resulted in a certain amount of confusion in the literature, but it is now clear that the two are very different and in terms of their social system North American Black-billed Magpies are more similar to Yellow-bills than they are to European magpies.

In southern Europe magpie nests are aggregated, as in North America. Although the territorial behaviour of southern European magpie populations has not been studied in detail, the spatial distribution of nests implies a different system from magpies elsewhere in Europe. In mid- and northern European latitudes magpies defend classical all-purpose territories; Hinde's (1956) 'type A territory'. As a result nests are regularly spaced. Some territories are occupied throughout the year and most actively defended during the pre-laying period. All breeding and feeding activities take place within the territory and during the breeding season breeding birds forage alone or in pairs within the territory. In high-density populations at least, territorial interactions are both vigorous and frequent. Competition for space is often intense, and young birds attempt to obtain territories by force, through 'ceremonial gatherings'. It is interesting that ceremonial gatherings have not been reported for North American Black-billed or Yellow-billed Magpies. In these two types the territory comprises only a small area around the nest: it would hardly be worth competing viciously for such a small territory which contains few or no resources.

Why should such differences in territoriality exist? Are the differences genetic, or are they imposed on the birds by different environmental pressures? Short of transplanting magpies between continents, it will be difficult to determine the extent to which these differences are inherited. However, the role of environmental factors, such as nest sites, food and predation, can be explored rather more easily. An obvious starting-point would be to compare these aspects of magpie ecology in southern Spain and North Africa with that of magpies further north in Europe.

Using existing information we can consider why Yellow-billed Magpies breed colonially. Many bird species nest in colonies and there have been a number of explanations for why they should do so. These include: (a) a shortage of nest sites, (b) protection from predators, and (c) aggregated and unpredictable food supplies. Verbeek's (1973) study indicates that the trees suitable for nesting were not limiting, so we can exclude that possibility. Yellow-billed Magpies may be more vulnerable than Black-billed Magpies to predators such as snakes (see Chapter 7), so they may breed in colonies in order to reduce the risk of predation. However, the food supply is the factor most commonly regarded as being responsible for spacing patterns among birds and other animals (e.g. Lack 1968). Verbeek's results show that food supplies for Yellow-billed Magpies are patchily distributed in both space and time.

There are at least two ways in which patchy, unpredictable food and colonial breeding are linked. First, by breeding together Yellow-bills can exploit the food-finding potential of other colony members. Peter Ward and Amotz Zahavi (1973) proposed that a major advantage of breeding in colonies was that the breeding site could serve as a centre for information exchange, with unsuccessful individuals following successful ones to food sources. As Verbeek (1973) has described, Yellow-billed Magpies certainly do follow each other between the colony and feeding areas, so this idea seems plausible. If birds rely to some extent on others to help them find food, then it is important for all individuals to be at a similar stage in the breeding cycle. In the Yellow-billed Magpie's case, this is likely to be especially important since in addition to food being patchily distributed, its seasonal pattern of abundance is concentrated. It is not surprising to find therefore that Yellow-bills breed relatively synchronously.

An alternative explanation for breeding synchrony is that it occurs only because the seasonal pattern of food availability is highly synchronous. It should be possible to distinguish between these two explanations: if the seasonal pattern of food availability was the main factor causing synchrony, then Yellow-billed Magpie colonies over a wide area should have very similar median laying dates. If the information-centre idea is important, it would not matter if different colonies bred at different times and we might expect the median laying dates between colonies to differ. The data to make this comparison are not currently available.

The second association between patchy food and coloniality is an idea proposed by Henry Horn (1968). He suggested that to minimize the average distance birds have to fly between their nest and feeding areas, they should breed together (i.e. in a colony) in the centre of a group of food patches. As we have seen (Chapter 2), Reynolds (1990) has tested the idea for Yellow-billed Magpies, and confirmed that this is what occurs.

The nest-spacing patterns in North American Black-billed Magpies indicates that in some areas the distribution of their food supplies in both space and time are similar to that of the Yellow-billed Magpie. Unfortunately, there is virtually no detailed, quantitative evidence for this. Measuring the availability and abundance of any species' food supply is one of the major problems that has faced field ornithologists (e.g. see Orians 1980).

Heads of juvenile North American Black-billed Magpies (females on left, males on right) to show the individual variation in feather loss during moult (see text). (Photos: C. Trost).

In northern and mid-European latitudes the magpie's territory contains a suitable breeding site and often a year-round food supply. Overall, food must be fairly evenly distributed so that areas of about five hectares in extent provide sufficient for two adults and some offspring. Under these circumstances, if the habitat was fairly uniform we would expect nests to be regularly spaced. In most cases they are, but breeding habitat is rarely uniform and in a few cases this sometimes results in nests being either randomly spaced or (more rarely), aggregated.

Two features emerge from this comparison of magpie social systems. First, both species are extremely flexible in their patterns of nest spacing. Second, birds at the southern limit of their distribution tend to nest in a more aggregated manner than those further north. In North America Yellow-bills occur further south than most Black-bills and breed colonially. Within Europe and North Africa, magpies in southern Spain (see Chapter 2), tend to breed closer together than the same species further north. Another feature which may be associated with this pattern is the fact that both the Yellow-billed Magpie in North America and the North African race of the Black-billed Magpie have colourful patches of bare skin on their faces, yellow in one case, blue in the other. Lisa Reed and Chuck Trost (pers. comm.) have suggested that this may increase the variability in the appearance of birds and aid individual recognition. They suggest that this may be an adaptation to the greater sociality shown by these birds. They also point out that a similar effect occurs in their Black-billed Magpies during a period of greater sociality during the autumn. At that time magpies moult and often lose many of the feathers from their face giving them a rather odd, if somewhat individualistic appearance. It would be interesting to determine the function of the bare facial skin patches in magpies and in particular to determine what role they play in individual recognition.

SOCIAL BEHAVIOUR

There are two aspects of behaviour to discuss: the nature of the visual and vocal signals used in communication, and the frequency with which social interactions occur. The main factor determining the latter, during the breeding season at least, is the distribution of nests. As I have shown, the three types of magpie differ in this respect.

In terms of their communication system it is probably premature to make such comparisons. In the absence of a detailed comparative study, by the same person, it is extremely difficult to assess how similar or dissimilar the three types of magpie are. Moreover, published descriptions and my own experience of visual signals are restricted to the European magpie and the Yellow-billed Magpie. Nevertheless, in Table 35 I have, as far as is possible, indicated the major behavioural similarities and differences of the three types. It is clear that all types of magpie have much in common in terms of their visual communication system. In addition, it is interesting that despite the differences in their spacing patterns, extra-pair courtship and copulation attempts are frequent in all three types.

One of the more ornithologically orientated pioneers in North America, Prince Maximilian, commented on the difference between the voices of the European and North American Black-billed Magpies: 'provisions sometimes procured us a visit from the forward magpies, which, without the least shyness, perched on the stem of the boat, and uttered their note, which is quite different from that of the European bird' (Maximilian 1833, in Thomas & Ronnefeldt 1976). The few people that have had an opportunity to listen to the three types of magpie have commented on the similarity between the two North American species (Brooks 1931) and how these differ from the European magpie

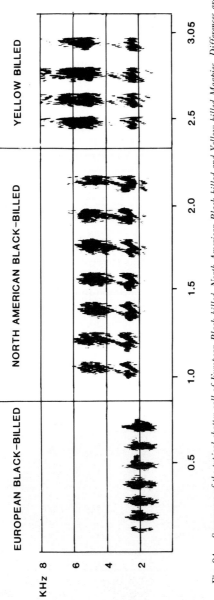

Fig. 94. Sonagrams of the typical chatter call of European Black-billed, North American Black-billed and Yellow-billed Magpies. Differences are apparent between all three types, but the two American types have slower, higher pitched calls (from Birkhead & Enggist-Dublin, unpublished).

(Goodwin 1986). Although a detailed comparative study is still needed, the available information suggests that all three types of magpie make calls of similar structure in similar circumstances, but that some differences between the types exist. Peter Enggist-Dublin and I made and compared sonagrams of the typical chattering call of all three magpie types. As Fig. 94 shows, the two North American species are much more similar to each other than either is to the European magpie. The chattering of the European magpie is generally faster (with about twice as many 'elements' per unit time), and lower pitched than the two North American species. Differences in vocalizations also exist between other races of magpies.

The differences in voice are just one further feature that distinguishes the two North American magpies from the European magpie. As the previous chapters have shown, the Yellow-bill and North American Black-bill are remarkably similar in most behavioural and ecological features so far examined. These observations raise the question of whether it is still valid to regard the North American Black-billed Magpie as the same species as the European magpie (or to put it another way, whether the Yellow-bill deserves specific status). There are several ways to test these ideas. If Voous (1960) is right and the last glaciation eliminated magpies from North America (except for what are now Yellow-bills), only for Black-bills to recolonize from Asia after the ice had retreated, then we might expect Asian magpies to be more similar in their behaviour and ecology to North American Black-bills than they are to European magpies. This would make an interesting project for someone in Kamchatka. Another approach would be to make a biochemical (i.e. DNA) comparison of the different races and species of magpie to determine their evolutionary relationships.

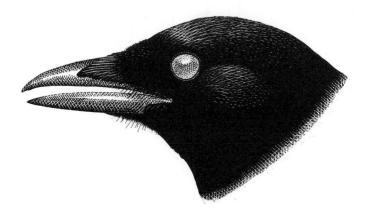

CONCLUSION

It is clear from the number of references used in writing this book that a considerable body of information exists on the behaviour and ecology of magpies. It is also clear that if we are going to be able to interpret the behavioural features we see, then there is still a lot more to learn. One advantage of trying to make a comparative study, as in this final chapter, is that it highlights those areas where information is lacking. If nothing else, I hope that this book stimulates both professional and amateur ornithologists to get out into the field and try to fill some of these gaps.

Geographical variation in magpies

A number of races of magpie *Pica pica* have been recognized, and the number varies between different authors (Diederich 1889; Stegmann 1927, 1931; Kleiner 1935; Linsdale 1937; Bahrmann 1968; Dementiev & Gladkov 1970). The simplest and most coherent account is that of Vaurie (1959) who recognizes 13 races; in his *Crows of the World* Goodwin (1986) follows Vaurie. Geographical races of *Pica pica* have been identified on the basis of morphological characteristics, such as body size (usually measured as wing length) and plumage characteristics, such as the colour of the gloss on the 'black' wing and tail feathers, or the relative amount of white on the wing and rump. There has been much discussion about whether dividing species (of any animal) into geographical races is of any value. The aim of this appendix is simply to examine the extent of geographical variation in magpies. As will become apparent, the available information is far from complete and there is a good study waiting for someone who cares to take on a thorough examination of this topic.

To get a feel for the geographical variation and the different races I examined and measured most of the skins of adult (i.e. more than 1 year old) magpies in the British Museum (BM). These had been divided into Vaurie's races by Derek Goodwin (who worked at the BM) and for convenience I used his categories. In doing this I was able to check (and in most cases confirm) the trends identified by Vaurie (1959). I also made a few additional observations which might be useful to anyone who decides to look at geographical variation in more detail.

I have used the same three measures that Vaurie (1959) used: wing length (mm), relative tail length (i.e. tail length expressed as a percentage of wing length), and the relative amount of white in the wings. For the latter, Vaurie apparently assessed it qualitatively, whereas I calculated a simple index. I measured the length of the black tip on the longest primary, subtracted this from the wing length (which also measured the longest primary), and expressed this value as a percentage of the overall wing length. An index of 100% would mean there was no black tip to the longest primary (or indeed any of the primaries). Smaller values indicate a smaller proportion of white in the wing.

The results provide some indication of the variation in these three characters. However, it is important to note that while the British Museum holds specimens of all the races recognized by Vaurie (1959), some are represented by only two or three adult specimens. Moreover, some races cover vast geographical areas (see Fig. 1), and there may well be variation within these areas. As Vaurie points out, some races, such as *galliae*, are not particularly distinct.

Figure 95 shows the differences in wing length, relative tail length and white index, for all races of *Pica pica* and for the Yellow-billed Magpie. In terms of wing length the two extremes are *mauritanica* from North Africa, which has the shortest wings of any race, and *bottanensis* from Tibet, which has the longest wings. Vaurie (1959) suggested that within Europe and North Africa there was a cline of increasing wing length from south to north. Figure 95 indicates that if we exclude *mauritanica*, there is not much evidence for a cline in the other races. Vaurie also suggested that wing length increased from west to east across Europe and Asia, but there is even less indication of this in my

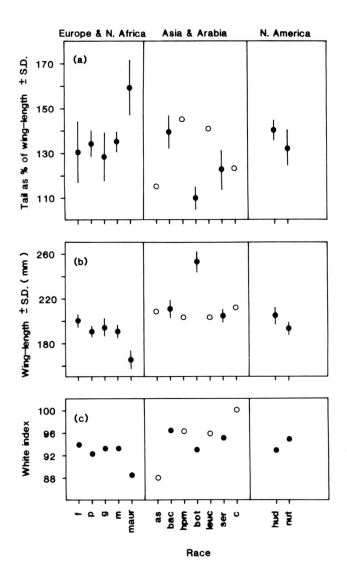

Fig. 95. *Variation in (a) relative tail length, (b) average wing length, and (c) amount of white on the wing of different races of* Pica pica *and the Yellow-billed Magpie. All values are means. Small samples (less than 5 individuals) are represented by open circles. Measurements are from adult birds from the British Museum (Natural History). Races of* P. pica *are as follows: f =* fennorum, *p =* pica, *g =* galliae, *m =* melanotos, *maur =* mauritanica, *as =* asirensis, *bac =* bactriana, *hpm =* hemileucoptera, *bot =* bottanensis, *leuc =* leucoptera, *ser =* sericea, *c =* camtschatica, *hud =* hudsonia. *nut =* Pica nuttalli.

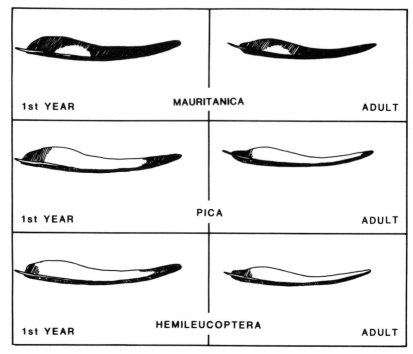

Fig. 96.   *Variation in the shape and the relative amounts of black and white on the first (outermost) primary of three races of adult and first-year Black-billed Magpies (see text).*

data. However, since races do not occur in sequence from west to east it might have been better to ignore races and simply look at the relationship between wing length and longitude. In terms of relative tail length, *mauritanica* has the longest tail, and as Vaurie noticed, *bottanensis*, the shortest.

Vaurie states that the relative amount of white on the wing increases from west to east through Europe and Asia. My results confirm this general pattern: most of the Asian races have a higher white index than the European races. Using my index the three specimens of the most easterly race, *camtschatica*, all had a white index of 100. The two most southerly races, *mauritanica* (N. Africa) and *asirensis* (Arabia), have the lowest values. These are both very dark races, and *mauritanica* also has a completely black rump, and a greater area of black on the lower breast than most other races. The relative amount of black or white on the wing may create a problem in terms of using the outermost primary for ageing birds (see Chapter 1). I noticed that *mauritanica* (N. Africa) has so much black on its outermost primary that it was impossible to separate first-year from older birds (see Fig. 96).

The other feature I noticed was that the adults of some races had black only on the outermost vane of their first primary, the inner edge being completely white. For example, 21 out of 24 (87%) *bactriana* were like this. All first-year *bactriana*, however, had black on both sides of the rachis. None of the 12 adult nominate *pica* in the BM were of this type, and nor were any of the *pica* I have examined in the field. Similarly all 10 adult *bottanensis* had black on both sides of the rachis. In adult *sericea* 8 out of 24 (33%) had black only on the outermost vane.

DESCRIPTIONS OF RACES

Pica pica pica: (Linnaeus 1758; type locality: Sweden) Striking black and white plumage (see photographs in Chapter 1). Head and body black. Underparts (excluding under tail coverts) white, scapulars white, inner vanes of primaries also white. Coverts and tail black but with green, blue, or purple gloss. Six pairs of tail feathers, middle pair are the longest. Sickle-shaped outermost primary. Throat feathers have a hairy texture with a grey rachis. Upper part of rump dirty white or grey. Iris dark brown. Bill, legs and feet black. Nictitating membrane white with a bright orange oval spot (measuring approximately 3.5 × 6 mm).

P. p. fennorum: (Lonnberg 1927; type locality: Viborg district, SE Finland) Differs from nominate race by having a greater 'white index' for the wing (above), and paler rump.

P. p. galliae: (Kleinschmidt 1917; type locality: NE France) Differs rather little from the nominate race. Vaurie (1959) states that it has less white on the wing, but my white index does not show this (See Fig. 95). Apparently slightly smaller than the nominate race.

P. p. melanotos: (Brehm 1857; type locality: Madrid-Toledo, Spain) Almost always black rump, but otherwise differs relatively little from *galliae* (Vaurie 1959). However, the few body weights available (Appendix 3) indicate that it is considerably smaller than the nominate race. Interestingly, Vaurie states that some individuals possess a small bare patch of skin behind the eye (see *mauritanica*, below).

P. p. mauritanica: (Malherbe 1843; type locality: Oran and Bone, Algeria) A very small race with small wings, and a relatively long tail (Fig. 95). The small body size is apparent from an examination of museum skins, but as far as I am aware, no measurements of body weight are available. Rump always black. Cobalt blue patch of bare skin behind the eye. Gloss on the tail sometimes bronze.

P. p. bactriana: (Bonaparte 1850; type locality: Kandahar, Afghanistan) Differs from races described above by having a higher white index. Inner secondaries show a green rather than blue gloss (Vaurie 1959).

P. p. hemileucoptera: (Stegmann 1928; type locality: Nishneudinsk, Siberia) Vaurie states: 'larger than *bactriana* and white area in the primaries larger'. The number of examples of this race in the BM is small, and my white index was almost identical to that for *bactriana*.

P. p. leucoptera: (Gould 1862; type locality: eastern Siberia) This race is larger than *hemileucoptera* and has even more white on the wing (Vaurie 1959). My results are based on just two individuals, so I cannot add anything useful to this.

P. p. bottanensis: (Delessert 1840; type locality: Bhutan) At last, a really distinctive race: the largest race (although no body weights available), with a very long wing and a relatively short tail (Fig. 95).

P. p. sericea: (Gould 1845; type locality: Amoy, China) Described by Vaurie as similar to the nominate race but with a relatively shorter tail (Fig. 95). No weight data. Two previously recognized races, *P. p. janowski* and *P. p. anderssoni* are now regarded as *P. p. sericea*.

P. p. camtschatica: (Stejneger 1884; type locality: Kamchatka) The race with the greenest gloss on the tail and wing, and with the greatest white index (Fig. 95). No weight data.

P. p. asirensis: (Bates 1936; type locality: Sahra, Asir Mountains, Saudi Arabia) Another very distinctive race. Discovered and described only in 1936 (Bates 1936; Meinertzhagen 1954). Confined to the Asir Mountains in south-west Saudi Arabia (Hollom *et al.* 1988), where it occurs in juniper scrub between 7000 and 9200 feet (2400–3000 m). This relict population is the most isolated of all magpie races, and Voous (1960) has suggested that it became isolated at the height of the last glacial period, along with a few other vertebrates (including a lizard and a toad). Bruno Pambour has sent me a tape-recording of this magpie's chatter call and it is markedly different from that of magpies in Britain and elsewhere in western Europe. This magpie's range is thought to cover an area about 200 km by 40 km, running north-west to south-east along the escarpment of the Asir Mountains, from 19°23'N, 42°03'E to 18°00'N, 42°45'E (J. Gasperetti, pers. comm.). There are only two specimens in the BM, but these indicate a relatively short tail and very low white index (similar to *mauritanica*). Overall, a very dark magpie, with smaller areas of white than other races (Goodwin 1986).

P. p. hudsonia: (Sabine 1823; type locality: Saskatchewan) Similar to the nominate race, but smaller (see Appendices 2, 3 and 4), with a proportionately longer tail and slightly longer wings. Distinct pale rump. Several features (colour of the iris, mouth and bill tip) show seasonal variation in adults (C. Trost and C. Webb, pers. comm.); this may well be true in other races.

Pica nuttalli: (Audubon 1836; type locality: Santa Barbara, California) Although not regarded as a race of *Pica pica*, a brief description is included here for completeness. Smaller than almost all races of *P. pica* in terms of body weight (see Appendix 3). Given its small body size it probably has relatively long wings (Fig. 95). The average wing length is almost the same as for *P. p. pica* in our study area, yet the Yellow-billed Magpie, at 160 g, weighs only 67% of our magpies (240 g): (weights here are means of male and female weights). The relatively longer wing of Yellow-billed Magpies is probably related to their colonial breeding and the increased time they have to spend flying between the colony and feeding area as a consequence (see Chapters 5 and 8). Relative tail length in the Yellow-billed Magpie is similar to *P. pica* (Fig. 95). Bill yellow, patch of bare yellow skin behind the eye. The yellow patch is relatively small, and sometimes difficult to see during the breeding season, but is more conspicuous during the moult. Linsdale (1946) states that the soles of the feet are yellow, but this was not the case in the birds I examined in the field during the breeding season. Iris dark brown, and nictitating membrane, as in *P. pica*, with a bright orange spot. Compared with the European Magpie, Yellow-bills have a noticeable green gloss to the feathers on the top of the head, and a much brighter blue gloss on the secondaries.

APPENDIX 2: *Morphological characteristics of male and female Black-billed Magpies*

	Ireland[1] *Pica pica pica*						Canada[2] *P. p. hudsonia*						USA[3] *P. p. hudsonia*					
	Male			*Female*			*Male*			*Female*			*Male*			*Female*		
	$\bar{x}$	SD	(N)	$\bar{x}$	SD	(N)	$\bar{x}$	SD	(N)	$\bar{x}$	SD	(N)	$\bar{x}$	SD	(N)	$\bar{x}$	SD	(N)
Weight (g)	241.5	17.02	(95)	203.5	14.32	(107)	192.6	17.2	(48)	181.4	28.2	(22)	187.8	10.5	(41)	166.7	12.4	(30)
Wing (mm)	192.1	4.76	(96)	181.7	4.18	(107)	207.1	4.3	(48)	192.4	3.2	(22)	206.5	4.8	(41)	196.7	5.9	(30)
Tail	243.4	12.52	(86)	231.3	8.82	(99)	293.4	14.1	(48)	260.4	21.8	(22)	285.3	17.3	(41)	264.1	18.6	(30)
Bill length	27.0	1.46	(95)	24.6	1.19	(100)	44.4	1.6	(48)	40.5	2.0	(22)	33.8	2.0	(41)	30.6	2.1	(30)
Bill depth	13.6	0.47	(94)	12.5	0.50	(101)	13.4	0.7	(48)	12.5	0.4	(22)	—	—		—		
Head length	74.7	2.14	(94)	69.9	1.65	(99)	—			—			—			—		
Tarsus	—			—			50.7	2.2	(48)	45.9	2.5	(22)	50.4	1.51	(41)	48.0	1.56	(30)

Notes: (1) from Kavanagh (1986); (2) from Scharf (1987); (3) from Reese & Kadlec (1982).
All measurements except weight (g) in mm.

APPENDIX 3: *Body weight of male and female magpies in various locations*

	Male						Female						Reference
	Adult			First-year			Adult			First-year			
	x̄	SD	N	x̄	SD	N	x̄	SD	N	x̄	SD	N	
Europe													
Black-billed Magpie													
UK, Sheffield	248	13	12	240	18	4	233	11	11	205	22	7	Birkhead *et al.* (1986)
Ireland, Dublin	241	17	95	224	17	27	203	14	107	194	17	48	Kavanagh (1986)
Netherlands (a)	238	19	7	233	41	16	208	18	11	206	14	11	Baeyens (1979)
(b)	230	19	16	—	15	—	209	11	9	—	—	—	J. Walters, pers. comm.
UK, all	239	15	23	229	15	6	221	24	43	213	32	7	Seel (1976)
Norway: Trondheim	248	—	14				213	—	14	—	—	—	T. Slagsvold, pers. comm.
Sweden: Revinge	236	16	56				204	14	37	—	—	—	G. Högstedt, pers. comm.
Spain: all	217	31	4				174	19	13	—	—	—	F. Alvarez, pers. comm.
North America													
Black-billed Magpie													
Canada, Edmonton	193	17	48				181	28	22				Scharf (1987)
USA, South Dakota	204	10	10				164	10	13				Buitron (1988)
USA, Utah	188	10	41				167	12	30				Reese & Kadlec (1982)
USA, Washington	183	9	6				162	8	4				Mugaas & King (1981)
USA, Montana	188	18	29				171	15	26				Todd (1968)
Yellow-billed Magpie													
USA, Hastings, California	165	—	—				145	—	15				Verbeek (1973)
USA, Hastings, California	175	9	17				146	12	15				Linsdale (1937; p. 129)
USA, Hastings, California	166	9	27				142	6	21				M. D. Reynolds, pers. comm.

APPENDIX 4: *Differences in body weight and size between adult and first-year Black-billed Magpies in two studies*

Location	Measure	Adult Mean ± SD		Male first-year Mean ± SD	First-year as % of adult	Adult Mean ± SD		Female first-year Mean ± SD	First-year as % of adult
Ireland									
	Weight	241.4 ± 17.0	**	224.2 ± 17.2	92.8	203.4 ± 14.3	**	193.8 ± 16.8	95.3
	Wing length	192.1 ± 4.8	**	185.9 ± 4.2	96.8	181.7 ± 4.2	**	177.2 ± 5.9	97.5
	Tail length	243.4 ± 12.5	**	224.1 ± 13.6	92.1	231.3 ± 8.8	**	211.1 ± 12.4	91.3
	Bill length	27.0 ± 1.5	**	26.2 ± 1.3	97.0	24.6 ± 1.2		24.5 ± 1.1	99.6
	Bill depth	13.6 ± 0.5		13.1 ± 0.6	96.1	12.5 ± 0.5	*	12.2 ± 0.5	98.0
	Head length	74.7 ± 2.1	**	72.8 ± 2.3	97.5	69.6 ± 1.6		69.6 ± 1.9	99.6
	Tarsus	—		—	—	—		—	—
Edmonton, Canada									
	Weight	192.6 ± 17.2		197.5 ± 25.6	102.5	181.4 ± 28.2		170.9 ± 16.1	94.2
	Wing length	207.1 ± 4.3	*	204.0 ± 6.5	98.5	192.4 ± 3.2		195.7 ± 4.7	101.7
	Tail length	293.4 ± 14.1	***	260.2 ± 24.2	88.7	260.4 ± 21.8		253.9 ± 12.6	97.5
	Bill length	26.3 ± 1.6	*	26.5 ± 1.1	100.8	23.6 ± 1.6		25.4 ± 3.9	107.6
	Bill depth	14.4 ± 0.7		14.3 ± 0.7	99.3	13.3 ± 0.4		13.4 ± 0.6	100.7
	Head length	—		—	—	—		—	—
	Tarsus	50.7 ± 2.2		50.3 ± 1.9	99.2	45.9 ± 2.5		48.3 ± 2.8	105.0

Notes: Data for Ireland from Kavanagh (1986). Asterisks show statistically significant differences between age classes within sexes (* <0.05, ** <0.01, *** <0.001). Sample sizes: adult male: 95, first-year males: 107, first-year females: 48.
Data for Edmonton from Scharf (1987); conventions as above. Sample sizes: adult males: 48, first-year males: 24, adult females: 22, first-year females: 39.
Note that the greatest percentage difference between age-classes is for tail length. Note also that the difference between age-classes is greatest for the Irish sample.

APPENDIX 5: *Mean weight of 14-day-old magpie chicks in the Sheffield area*

Year	Mean weight (g)	SD	N (broods)
1979	155.5	24.4	11
1980	141.7	27.5	26
1981	147.2	26.6	48
1983	166.3	24.7	42
1984	156.3	23.5	48
1985	161.3	25.5	33
1986	146.9	29.6	15

Difference between years $F_{6,216} = 3.56$, $P < 0.005$.
No data for 1982.

APPENDIX 6: *Differences in number of Black-billed Magpie chicks hatched and fledged in the Sheffield study*

Year	N	Chicks hatched[1] Mean ± SD	N	Chicks fledged[2] Mean ± SD	Percentage difference
1979	11	4.27 ± 1.35	10	3.90 ± 1.52	8.7
1980	28	3.28 ± 1.51	28	3.00 ± 1.33	8.5
1981	50	2.94 ± 1.49	50	2.74 ± 1.37	6.8
1982	32	3.19 ± 1.31	22	2.95 ± 1.46	7.5
1983	50	3.76 ± 1.71	42	3.48 ± 1.66	7.4
1984	55	3.85 ± 1.57	48	3.32 ± 1.40	13.8
1985	35	3.57 ± 1.52	32	3.22 ± 1.24	9.8
1986	33	3.12 ± 1.62	25	2.64 ± 1.68	15.4
Mean		3.50		3.16	9.73

Data exclude total failures (i.e. zero values excluded).
[1] Analysis of variance (excluding zeros): $F_{7,286} = 2.48$, $p < 0.025$.
[2] Analysis of variance (excluding zeros): $F_{7,249} = 1.56$, NS.

APPENDIX 7: *Breeding success of Black-billed Magpies in the Sheffield study*

Year	Number of pairs	Chicks fledging/ all pairs Mean ± SD	Chicks fledging/ successful pair Mean ± SD	Pairs rearing some chicks N (%)
1979	18	1.26 ± 2.30	3.90 ± 1.52	10 (55.6)
1980	47	1.78 ± 1.80	3.00 ± 1.33	28 (59.6)
1981	83	1.65 ± 1.71	2.74 ± 1.37	50 (60.2)
1983	72	2.03 ± 2.14	3.48 ± 1.66	42 (58.3)
1984	81	1.93 ± 1.96	3.32 ± 1.40	48 (59.0)
1985	56	1.86 ± 1.84	3.22 ± 1.24	32 (57.0)
1986	52	1.27 ± 1.76	2.64 ± 1.68	25 (48.0)

Note: No data for 1982. Data include repeat nests.

APPENDIX 8: *Breeding success for first and repeat breeding attempts within a season, for magpies in the Sheffield study*

Year	N	a	b	c	N	a	b	c
		First attempts				Repeat attempts		
1979	16	2.25 ± 2.35	4.00 ± 1.58	56 (9)	2	1.50 ± 2.21	3.0	50 (1)
1980	39	2.03 ± 1.86	3.16 ± 1.31	64 (25)	8	0.63 ± 0.92	2.0	38 (3)
1981	39	1.46 ± 1.68	2.59 ± 1.44	56 (22)	44	1.82 ± 1.74	2.85 ± 1.33	64 (28)
1983	60	2.03 ± 2.10	3.33 ± 1.69	62 (37)	12	1.75 ± 2.30	4.20 ± 1.30	42 (5)
1984	75	2.03 ± 1.99	3.78 ± 1.43	61 (46)	6	0.67 ± 1.03	2.00	33 (2)
1985	41	1.73 ± 1.90	3.23 ± 1.34	54 (22)	15	2.20 ± 1.70	3.00 ± 1.18	66 (10)
1986	38	1.32 ± 1.89	2.78 ± 1.86	50 (19)	14	1.14 ± 1.41	2.17 ± 1.17	43 (6)

(a) Chicks fledged per all pairs.
(b) Chicks fledged per successful pair.
(c) Percentage (*N*) of pairs rearing some chicks. No data for 1982.
Note: values in columns a and b are means ± SD.

List of Latin Names

BIRDS

Blackbird, European *Turdus merula*
Buzzard, Common *Buteo buteo*
Chaffinch *Fringilla coelebs*
Chicken *Gallus domesticus*
Chough, Red-billed *Pyrrhocorax pyrrhocorax*
Crow, Carrion *Corvus corone corone*
Crow, Common *Corvus brachyrhynchos*
Crow, Hooded *Corvus corone cornix*
Cuckoo, European *Cuculus canorus*
Cuckoo, Great Spotted *Clamator glandarius*
Dunnock *Prunella modularis*
Eagle, Bald *Haliaeetus leucocephalus*
Eagle, Golden *Aquila chrysaetos*
Falcon, Prairie *Falco mexicanus*
Flycatcher, Pied *Ficedula hypoleuca*
Goldfinch *Carduelis carduelis*
Goshawk *Accipiter gentilis*
Greenfinch *Carduelis chloris*
Guillemot, Common *Uria aalge*
Gull, Herring *Larus argentatus*
Harrier, Hen (=Northern Harrier)
 Circus cyaneus
Hawk, Cooper's *Accipiter cooperi*
Hawk, Red-tailed *Buteo jamaicensis*
Jackdaw *Corvus monedula*
Jay, European *Garrulus glandarius*
Jay, Florida Scrub *Aphelocoma coerulescens*
Kestrel, European *Falco tinnunculus*
Kiwi, Brown *Apteryx australis*
Koel *Eudynamis honorata*
Magpie, Black-billed *Pica pica*
Magpie, Yellow-billed *Pica nuttalli*
Mallard *Anas platyrhynchos*
Moorhen *Gallinula chloropus*
Murre, Common *Uria aalge*
Nutcracker, Clark's *Nucifraga columbiana*
Nutcracker, European *Nucifraga caryocatactes*
Owl, Great Horned *Bubo virginianus*
Pheasant *Phasianus colchicus*
Pigeon, Wood *Columba palumbus*
Raven *Corvus corax*

Red-winged blackbird *Agelaius phoeniceus*
Robin *Erithacus rubecula*
Rook *Corvus frugilegus*
Sandpiper, Spotted *Tringa macularia*
Skylark *Alauda arvensis*
Sparrow, House *Passer domesticus*
Sparrow, Tree *Passer montanus*
Sparrowhawk, European *Accipiter nisus*
Starling, European *Sturnus vulgaris*
Swallow, Cliff *Hirundo pyrrhonota*
Thrush, Mistle *Turdus viscivorus*
Thrush, Song *Turdus philomelos*
Tit, Great *Parus major*
Vulture, Turkey *Cathartes aura*
Wheatear *Oenanthe oenanthe*
Woodpecker, Acorn *Melanerpes formicivorus*
Wren *Troglodytes troglodytes*
Yellowhammer *Emberiza citrinella*

OTHER ANIMALS

Bobcat *Lynx rufus*
Coyote *Canis latrans*
Fox, Red *Vulpes vulpes*
Mole *Talpa europaea*
Mouse, Wood *Apodemus sylvaticus*
Prairie-dog *Cynomys ludovicianus*
Rabbit *Oryctolagus cuniculus*
Raccoon *Procyon lotor*
Shrew, Common *Sorex araneus*
Slug *Arion* Spp.
Snake, Gopher *Pituophis melanoleucus*
Snake, King *Lampropeltis getlus*
Squirrel, Ground *Spermophilus beecheyi*
Stoat *Mustela erminea*
Weevil *Philopedon plagiatus*

PLANTS

Alder *Alnus glutinosa*
Birch, Silver *Betula pendula*
Blackthorn *Prunus spinosa*
Dogwood *Cornus sanguinea*
Elder *Sambucus nigra*

Elm, Jersey *Ulmus wheatleyi*
Hawthorn *Crataegus monogyna*
Holly *Ilex aquifolium*
Lichen, Lace *Ramalina menziesii*
Lime *Tilia vulgaris*
Mistletoe *Phorandendron villosum*
Mistletoe *Viscum album*
Oak, Holm *Quercus rotundifolia*

Oak, Live *Quercus agrifolia*
Oak, Valley *Quercus lobata*
Poplar, Lombardy *Populus nigra 'italica'*
Poplar, Manchester *Populus nigra*
Seabuckthorn *Hippophae rhamnoides*
Spindle *Euonymus europaeus*
Sycamore *Acer pseudoplantanus*
Whitebeam *Sorbus aria*

References

ALVAREZ, F. & ARIAS DE REYNA, L. (1974). Reproducción de la urraca (*P. pica*) en Doñana. *Doñana Acta Vertebrata*, 1: 77–95.

ALVAREZ, F., ARIAS DE REYNA, L. M. & SEGURA, M. (1976). Experimental brood parasitism of the Magpie (*Pica pica*). *Animal Behaviour*, 24: 907–916.

ARIAS DE REYNA, L. M., RECUERDA, P., CORVILLO, M. & AGUILAR, I. (1982). Reproducción del críalo (*Clamator glandarius*) en Sierra Morena Central. *Doñana Acta Vertebrata*, 9: 177–193.

ARIAS DE REYNA, L. M., RECUERDA, P., CORVILLO, M. & CRUZ, A. (1984). Reproducción de la urraca (*Pica pica*) en Sierra Morena (Andalucia). *Doñana Acta Vertebrata*, 11: 79–92.

ARMSTRONG, E. A. (1940). *Birds of the Grey Wind*. Oxford University Press, London.

ASHMOLE, N. P. (1963). The regulation of numbers of tropical oceanic birds. *Ibis*, 103: 458–473.

BAEYENS, G. (1979). Description of the social behavior of the Magpie (*Pica pica*). *Ardea*, 67: 28–41.

BAEYENS, G. (1981a). The role of the sexes in territory defence in the Magpie (*Pica pica*). *Ardea*, 69: 69–82.

BAEYENS, G. (1981b). Functional aspects of serial monogamy: the magpie pair-bond in relation to its territorial system. *Ardea*, 69: 145–166.

BAEYENS, G. (1981c). Magpie breeding success and carrion crow interference. *Ardea*, 69: 125–139.

BAEYENS, G. & KONING, F. (1982). Broedsucces bij Eksters. *Argus*, 7: 5–7.

BAHRMANN, U. (1956). Welchen Einfluss hatte der Winter 1955/1956 auf den Brutzyklus der Elster? *Falke*, 3: 195–198.

BAHRMANN, U. (1968). *Die Elster Pica pica*. Die Neue Brehm Bücherei, Wittenberg, Lutherstadt.

BALANÇA, G. (1984a). Le régime alimentaire d'une population des pies bavardes (*Pica pica*). *Gibier Faune Sauvage*, 3: 37–61.

BALANÇA, G. (1984b). Le déterminisme du succès de la réproduction chez une population de pies bavardes (*Pica pica*). *Gibier Faune Sauvage*, 4: 5–27.

BALANÇA, G. (1984c). La sélection des sites d'alimentation par une population des pies bavardes (*Pica pica*). *Gibier Faune Sauvage*, 2: 45–77.

BALDA, R. P. (1980). Recovery of cached seeds by a captive *Nucifraga caryocatactes*. *Zeitschrift Tierpsychology*, 52: 331–346.

BATES, G. L. (1936). On interesting birds recently sent to the British Museum by Mr H. St J. B. Philby. *Bulletin of the British Ornithologists' Club*, 52: 17–21.

BERRY, S. S. (1922). Magpies versus livestock: an unfortunate new chapter in avian depredations. *Condor*, 24: 13–17.

BIRKHEAD, T. R. (1979). Mate-guarding in the magpie *Pica pica*. *Animal Behaviour*, 27: 866–874.

BIRKHEAD, T. R. (1982). Timing and duration of mate-guarding in Magpies (*Pica pica*). *Animal Behaviour*, 30: 277–283.

BIRKHEAD, T. R. (1988). Behavioral aspects of sperm competition in birds. *Advances in the Study of Behaviour*, 18: 35–72.

BIRKHEAD, T. R. & CLARKSON, K. (1985a). Ceremonial gatherings of the Magpie (*Pica pica*): territory probing and acquisition. *Behaviour*, 94: 324–332.

BIRKHEAD, T. R. & CLARKSON, K. (1985b). The Magpie as an aid to teaching behaviour and ecology. *Journal of Biological Education*, 19: 163–168.

BIRKHEAD, T. R. & GOODBURN, S. F. (1989). Magpie. In: *Lifetime Reproduction in Birds* (Ed. I. Newton). Academic Press, London.

BIRKHEAD, T. R., EDEN, S. F., CLARKSON, K., GOODBURN, S. F. & PELLATT, J. (1986). Social organization of a population of magpies *Pica pica*. *Ardea*, 74: 59–68.

BIRKHEAD, T. R., ATKIN, L. & MØLLER, A. P. (1987). Copulation behaviour of birds. *Behaviour*, 101: 101–138.

BOCK, C. E. & LEPTHIEN, L. V. (1975). Distribution and abundance of the Black-billed Magpie (*Pica pica*) in North America. *Great Basin Naturalist*, 35: 269–272.

BOSSEMA, I. (1979). Jays and oaks: an eco-ethological study of a symbiosis. *Behaviour*, 70: 1–117.

BOSSEMA, I., ROELL, A. & BAEYENS, G. (1986). Adaptations to interspecific competition in five corvid species in the Netherlands. *Ardea*, 74: 199–210.

BRIGGS, J. J. (1849). The birds of Melbourne. *Zoologist*, 7: 2475–2493, 2559–2565, 2603–2611.

BROOKE, M. DE L. (1979). Differences in the quality of territories held by wheatears (*Oenanthe oenanthe*). *Journal of Animal Ecology*, 48: 21–32.

BROOKS, A. (1931). The relationships of the American magpies. *Auk*, 48: 271–272.

BROWN, C. R. & BROWN, M. B. (1988). A new form of reproductive parasitism in cliff swallows. *Nature* (London), 331: 66–68.

BROWN, J. L. (1969). Territorial behavior and population regulation in birds. *Wilson Bulletin*, 81: 293–329.

BROWN, J. L. (1987). *Helping and communal breeding in birds*. Princeton University Press, Princeton, NJ.

BROWN, R. H. (1924). Field-notes from Cumberland. *British Birds*, 17: 222–228.

BROWN, R. L. (1957). The population ecology of the magpie in western Montana. p. 32. Unpubl. MS Thesis, Montana State University.

BUITRON, D. (1983a). Extra-pair courtship in Black-billed Magpies. *Animal Behaviour*, 31: 211–220.

BUITRON, D. (1983b). Variability in the responses of Black-billed Magpies to natural predators. *Behaviour*, 87: 209–236.

BUITRON, D. (1988). Female and male specialization in parental care and its consequences in Black-billed Magpies. *Condor*, 90: 29–39.

BUITRON, D. & NUECHTERLEIN, G. L. (1985). Experiments on olfactory detection of food caches by Black-billed Magpies. *Condor*, 87: 92–95.

BURKE, T. (1989). DNA fingerprinting and other methods for the study of mating success. *Trends in Ecology and Evolution*, 4: 139–144.

BUTLIN, S. M. (1971). Food hiding by the Magpie. *British Birds*, 64: 422.

CHARLES, J. K. (1972). Territorial behaviour and the limitation of population size in the crow *Corvus corone* and *Corvus cornix*. Unpubl. Ph.D. Thesis, Aberdeen University.

CHURCHER, P. B. & LAWTON, J. H. (1987). Predation by domestic cats in an English village. *Journal of Zoology* (London), 212: 439–455.

CLARK, P. J. & EVANS, F. C. (1954). Distance to nearest neighbour as a measure of spatial relationships in populations. *Ecology*, 35: 445–453.

CLARKSON, K. (1984). The breeding and feeding ecology of the Magpie *Pica pica*. Unpubl. Ph.D. Thesis, University of Sheffield.

CLARKSON, K. & BIRKHEAD, T. R. (1987). Magpies in Sheffield: a recipe for success. *BTO News*, 151: 8–9.

CLARKSON, K., EDEN, S. F., SUTHERLAND, W. J. & HOUSTON, A. I. (1986). Density dependence and magpie food hoarding. *Journal of Animal Ecology*, 55: 111–121.

CLEGG, T. M. (1962). Pre-coital display of magpies. *British Birds*, 55: 88–89.

CLUTTON-BROCK, T. H. (ed.) (1988). *Reproductive success*. University of Chicago Press, Chicago & London.

COLLINGE, W. E. (1930). The food and feeding habits of some Corvidae. The carrion crow, hooded crow, magpie and jay. *Journal of Ministry of Agriculture*, 1930: 151–158.

CONNOR, R. J. (1965). Notes on the nidification and oology of the Magpie (*Pica pica*) in a locality on the Middlesex/Buckingham border during 1965. *Oologist's Record*, 39: 4–9.

COOKE, A. S. (1979). Population declines of the Magpie *Pica pica* in Huntingdonshire and other parts of eastern England. *Biological Conservation*, 15: 317–324.

COOMBS, C. J. F. (1978). *The Crows: a study of the corvids of Europe*. Batsford, London.

CSIKI, E. (1919). Positive Daten über die Nahrung unserer Vögel – *Pica pica*. *Aquila*, 26: 76–104.

DARE, P. J. (1989). Aspects of the breeding biology of the buzzard *Buteo buteo* in North Wales. *Naturalist*, 114: 23–31.

DARWIN, C. (1871). *The Descent of Man and Selection in Relation to Sex*. John Murray, London.

DARWIN, C. (1872). *The Expressions of the Emotions in Man and Animals*. John Murray, London.

DAVIES, N. B. (1985). Cooperation and conflict among dunnocks, *Prunella modularis*, in a variable mating system. *Animal Behaviour*, 33: 628–648.

DAVIS, D. E. (1955). Determinate laying in barn swallows and black-billed magpies. *Condor*, 57: 81–87.

DAWKINS, R. (1976). *The Selfish Gene*. Oxford University Press, Oxford.

DECKERT, G. (1968). Zur Reviergrösse und Nestbautechnik der Elster (*Pica p. pica* L.). *Beiträge zur Vogelkunde*, 14: 97–102.

DEMENTIEV, G. P. & GLADKOV, N. A. *et al.* (1970). *Birds of the Soviet Union* Vol. 5. Israel Program for Scientific Translation, Keter Press, Jerusalem.

DHINDSA, M. S. & BOAG, D. A. (1989). Influence of age on the flushing distance of marked and unmarked Black-billed Magpies. *Ornis Scandinavica*, 20: 76–79.

DHINDSA, M. & BOAG, D. A. (1990). The effect of food supplementation on the reproductive success of Black-billed Magpies *Pica pica*. *Ibis*, 132: 595–602.

DHINDSA, M. S., BOAG, D. A. & KOMERS, P. E. (1989a). Mate choice in Black-billed Magpies: the role of male quality versus quality of defended resources. *Ornis Scandinavica*, 20: 193–203.

DHINDSA, M. S., KOMERS, P. E. & BOAG, D. A. (1989b). The effect of familiarity with an environment on the dominance relationships between juvenile and adult Black-billed Magpies. *Ornis Scandinavica*, 20: 187–192.

DHINDSA, M. S., KOMERS, P. E. & BOAG, D. A. (1989c). Nest height of Black-billed Magpies: is it determined by human disturbance or habitat type? *Canadian Journal of Zoology*, 67: 228–232.

DIEDERICH, F. (1889). Die geographische Verbreitung der Elster Genus *Pica*. *Ornis*, 5: 280–332.

DIXON, C. (1900). *Among the Birds in Northern Shires*. Blackie, London.

DOO-PYO, L. & KOO, T-H. (1986). A comparative study of the breeding density of magpies *Pica pica sericea* Gould, between urban and rural areas. *Bulletin of the Institute of Ornithology, Kyung Hee University*, 1: 39–51.

DUNN, P. O. & HANNON, S. J. (1989). Evidence for obligate parental care in Black-billed Magpies. *Auk*, 106: 635–644.

EDEN, S. F. (1985a). Social organization and the dispersal of non-breeding magpies *Pica pica*. Unpubl. Ph.D. Thesis, University of Sheffield.

EDEN, S. F. (1985b). The comparative breeding biology of Magpies *Pica pica* in an urban and a rural habitat (Aves: Corvidae). *Journal of Zoology* (London), 205: 325–334.

EDEN, S. F. (1987a). Natal philopatry of the magpie *Pica pica*. *Ibis*, 129: 477–490.

EDEN, S. F. (1987b). Dispersal and competitive ability in the magpie: an experimental study. *Animal Behaviour*, 35: 764–772.

EDEN, S. F. (1987c). The influence of Carrion Crows on the foraging behaviour of magpies. *Animal Behaviour*, 35: 608–610.

EDEN, S. F. (1989). The social organisation of non-breeding magpies *Pica pica*. *Ibis*, 131: 141–153.

EIGELIS, Y. K. (1964). Feeding habits and economic importance of the magpie (*Pica pica* L.) in deciduous and pine stands of the steppe and forest-steppe of the European part of USSR. *Zoological Zhurnal*, 43: 1517–1529.

EIGELIS, Y. K. & NEKRASOV, B. V. (1967). The morphological peculiarities of the buccal cavity in Corvidae as related to food transportation. *Zoological Zhurnal*, 46: 258–263.

ELLENBERG, H., GAST, F. & DIETRICH, J. (1984). Elster, Krähe und Habicht ein beziehungsgefüge aus territorialität, konkurrenz und prädation. *Verhandtlungen der Gesellschaft für Ökologie*, 12: 319–330.

ENGGIST-DUBLIN, P. (1988). Die Lautäusserungen der Elster (*Pica pica*). Beiheft Veröffentlichungen der Landesstelle für Naturschutz und Landschaftspledge. *Baden-Württemberg*, 53: 175–182.

ERPINO, M. J. (1968a). Age determination in the Black-billed Magpie. *Condor*, 70: 91–92.

ERPINO, M. J. (1968b). Nest-related activities of Black-billed Magpies. *Condor*, 70: 154–165.

ERPINO, M. J. (1969). Seasonal cycle of reproductive physiology in the Black-billed Magpie. *Condor*, 71: 267–279.

ETCHÉCOPAR, R. D. & HÜE, F. (1967). *The Birds of North Africa*. Oliver & Boyd, Edinburgh.

FASOLA, M. & BRICHETTI, P. (1983). Mosaic distribution and breeding habitat of the hooded Crow *Corvus corone cornix* and the Magpie *Pica pica* in Padana plain (Northern Italy). *Avocetta*, 7: 67–84.

FLINT, P. R. & STEWART, P. F. (1983). *The Birds of Cyprus, an annotated check list*. British Ornithologists' Union.

GEORGE, W. G. (1974). Domestic cats as predators and factors in winter shortages of raptor prey. *Wilson Bulletin*, 86: 384–396.

GIBSON, B. (1862). Large flocks of Magpies. *Zoologist*, 20: 7881.

GOOCH, S., BAILLIE, S. & BIRKHEAD, T. R. (1991). The impact of magpies *Pica pica* on songbird populations. Retrospective investigation of trends in population density and breeding success. *Journal of Applied Ecology*, in press.

GOODBURN, S. F. (1987). Factors affecting breeding success in the Magpie *Pica pica*. Unpubl. Ph.D. thesis, University of Sheffield.

GOODBURN, S. F. (1991). Territory quality or bird quality? Factors determining breeding success in the magpie (*Pica pica*). *Ibis*, 133: 85–90.

GOODWIN, D. (1952). Notes and display of the magpie. *British Birds*, 45: 113–122.

GOODWIN, D. (1986). *Crows of the World*. British Museum, London (2nd edition).

GUARINO, J. L. (1967). Magpie reduction in an urban roost. *Special Scientific Report, Wildlife*, 104: 5pp.

GWINNER, E. (1966). Über Bau and Funktion einer Nickhautstruktur der Elster (*Pica pica*). *Journal für Ornithologie*, 107: 323–325.

GYLLIN, R. & KALLANDER, H. (1977). Nattlig samvaro, sovstrack ochovernatting has skatan *Pica pica*. *Fauna-Flora*, 72: 18–24.

HANSEN, L. (1950). An investigation of the occurrence, nest-building, etc., of the Magpie *Pica pica* (L). *Dansk Ornitologisk Forenings Tidsskrift*, 44: 150–161.

HAUSMAN, G. (1987). *Meditations with the Navajo*. Bear, Santa Fe, NM.

HAYMAN, R. W. (1958). Magpie burying and recovering food. *British Birds*, 51: 275.

HAYWORTH, A. M. & WEATHERS, V. V. (1984). Temperature regulation and climatic adaptation in Black-billed and Yellow-billed Magpies. *Condor*, 86: 19–26.

HEIM DE BALSAC, H. (1926). Contribution à l'ornithologie de l'Algérie septentrionale. *Revue Française d'Ornithologie*, 10: 383–409.

HENRIKSEN, K. (1989). Yngletaethed og redeforhold hos Husskade *Pica pica* og Gråkrage *Corvus corone cornix* i bymaessig bebyggelse. *Dansk Ornitologisk Forenings Tidsskrift*, 83: 55–59.

HENTY, C. J. (1975). Feeding and food-hiding responses of jackdaws and magpies. *British Birds*, 68: 463–466.

HEWETT, W. (1843). Note on magpies and starlings. *Zoologist*, 1: 351.

HINDE, R. A. (1956). The biological significance of territories of birds. *Ibis*, 98: 340–369.

HOCHACHKA, W. (1988). The effect of food supply on the composition of Black-billed Magpie eggs. *Canadian Journal of Zoology*, 66: 692–695.

HOCHACHKA, W. & BOAG, D. (1987). Food shortage for the Black-billed Magpie (*Pica pica*): an experiment using supplemental food. *Canadian Journal of Zoology*, 65: 1270–1274.

HÖGSTEDT, G. (1980a). Resource partitioning in Magpie *Pica pica* and Jackdaw *Corvus monedula* during the breeding season. *Ornis Scandinavica*, 11: 110–115.

HÖGSTEDT, G. (1980b). Prediction and test of the effects of interspecific competition. *Nature* (London), 283: 64–66.

HÖGSTEDT, G. (1980c). Evolution of clutch size in birds: adaptive variation in relation to territory quality. *Science*, 210: 1148–1150.

HÖGSTEDT, G. (1981a). Should there be a positive or negative correlation between survival of adults in a bird population and their clutch size? *American Naturalist*, 118: 568–571.

HÖGSTEDT, G. (1981b). Effect of additional food on reproductive success in the magpie (*Pica pica*). *Journal of Animal Ecology*, 50: 219–229.

HOLLOM, P. A. D., PORTER, R. F., CHRISTENSEN, S. & WILLIS, I. (1988). *Birds of the Middle East and North Africa*. Poyser, Calton.

HOLYOAK, D. (1967). Breeding biology of the Corvidae. *Bird Study*, 14: 153–168.

HOLYOAK, D. (1968). A comparative study of the food of some British Corvidae. *Bird Study*, 15: 147–153.

HOLYOAK, D. (1971). Movements and mortality of Corvidae. *Bird Study*, 18: 97–106.

HOLYOAK, D. (1974a). Moult seasons of the British Corvidae. *Bird Study*, 21: 15–20.

HOLYOAK, D. (1974b). Territorial and feeding behaviour of the Magpie. *Bird Study*, 21: 117–128.

HORN, H. S. (1968). The adaptive significance of colonial nesting in the Brewer's Blackbird. *Ecology*, 49: 682–694.

HUDSON, W. H. (1934). *British Birds*. Longman, London.

HUNT, J. (1815). *British Ornithology*. Vol. 2. Bacon, Norwich.

HUSBY, M. (1986). On the adaptive value of brood reduction in birds: experiments with the magpie (*Pica pica*). *Journal of Animal Ecology*, 55: 75–83.

HUSTINGS, F. (1988). *European Monitoring Studies on Breeding Birds* (Report). Sovon, Beek-Ubbergen.

JERZAK, L. (1987). Ecology of urban population of Magpie. *Szczecin*, 106: 17–19 (in Polish).

JERZAK, L. (1988). Distribution and nest sites of magpie in non-urban habitats in Poland. *Notatki Ornitologiczne*, 29: 27–41 (in Polish).

JOHNS, C. A. (1862). British birds in their haunts. *London Society for Promoting Christian Knowledge*, 626.

JONES, R. E. & HUNGERFORD, K. E. (1972). Evaluation of nesting cover as protection from magpie predation. *Journal of Wildlife Management*, 36: 727–732.

JOURDAIN, F. C. R. (1915). Notes on the bird life of Eastern Algeria. *Ibis*, 3: 133–169.

KALMBACH, E. R. (1927). The magpie in relation to agriculture. *United States Department of Agriculture Technical Report*, 24: 1–29.

KALOTÁS, Z. & NIKODÉMUSZ, E. (1982). Controlling magpies (*Pica pica* L) and hooded crows (*Corvus corone cornix* L.) with 3-chloro-4-methyl-aniline HCl using egg baits. *Zeitschrift für Angewandte Zoologie*, 69: 275–281.

KAVANAGH, B. P. (1986). Population dynamics of the magpie (*Pica pica*) in an urban environment. Unpubl. Ph.D. Thesis, Dublin University.

KAVANAGH, B. P. (1987). The breeding density of the magpie in Dublin city. *Irish Birds*, 3: 387–394.

KAVANAGH, B. P. (1988). Discriminating the sex of Magpies *Pica pica* from morphological data. *Ringing and Migration*, 9: 83–90.

KEKILOVA, A. F. (1978). An ecology of *Pica pica bactriana* Bonap. in Turkmenistan. *Izvestija Academii Nauk Turkmenskoj SSR ASHABAD*, 15: 61–69.

KLEINER, A. (1935). Systematische Studien über die Corviden des Karpathen-Beckens, nebst einer Revision ihrer Rassenkreise. *Aquila*, XLII–XLV: 114–140.

KLEJNOSTOWSKI, Z. (1971). Biology of Magpie (*Pica pica* L). *Roczniki Wyzszek Szkoly Rolnic. no Poznania*, 56: 69–98.

KNIGHT, R. L. (1988). Effects of supplemental food on the breeding biology of the Black-billed Magpie. *Condor*, 90: 956–958.

KOENIG, W. D. & MUMME, R. L. (1987). *Population Ecology of the Cooperatively Breeding Acorn Woodpecker*. Princeton University Press, Princeton, NJ.

KOENIG, W. D. & REYNOLDS, M. D. (1987). Potential poisoning of yellow-billed magpies by compound 1080. *Wildlife Society Bulletin*, 15: 274–276.

KOMERS, P. E. (1989). Dominance relationships between juvenile and adult black-billed magpies. *Animal Behaviour*, 37: 256–265.

KOMERS, P. E. & BOAG, D. A. (1988). The reproductive performance of black-billed magpies: is it related to mate choice? *Canadian Journal of Zoology*, 66: 1679–1684.

KOMERS, P. E. & DHINDSA, M. S. (1989). Influence of dominance and age on mate choice in black-billed magpies: an experimental study. *Animal Behaviour*, 37: 645–655.

KULCZYCKI, A. (1973). Nesting of the members of the Corvidae in Poland. *Acta Zoologica Cracoviensia*, 17: 583–657.

LACK, D. (1948). Natural selection and family size in the starling. *Evolution*, 2: 95–110.

LACK, D. (1954). *The Natural Regulation of Animal Numbers*. Oxford University Press, Oxford.

LACK, D. (1968). *Ecological Adaptations for Breeding in Birds*. Methuen, London.

LAKHANI, K. H. & NEWTON, I. (1983). Estimating age-specific bird survival rates from ring recoveries – can it be done? *Journal of Animal Ecology*, 52: 83–92.

LESSELLS, C. M. & BOAG, P. T. (1987). Unrepeatable repeatabilities: a common mistake. *Auk*, 104: 116–121.

LINSDALE, J. M. (1937). The natural history of magpies. *Pacific Coast Avifauna*, 25: Berkeley, CA.

LINSDALE, J. M. (1946). In: A. C. Bent, *Life Histories of North American Jays, Crows and Titmice. United States National Museum Bulletin*, 191: 155–183.

LLEWELLYN, S. (1989). Black and white bandits. *Country Living*, 101–102.

LOCKWOOD, W. B. (1984). *The Oxford Book of British Bird Names*. Oxford University Press, Oxford.

LOMAN, J. (1985). Social organisation in a population of the hooded crow. *Ardea*, 73: 61–75.

LORD, J. K. (1866). *The Naturalist in Vancouver Island and British Columbia*. Richard Bently, London.

LOVE, J. A. & SUMMERS, R. W. (1973). Breeding biology of magpies in Aberdeenshire. *Scottish Birds*, 7: 399–403.

MCGAHAN, J. (1968). Biology of the Golden Eagle. *Auk*, 85: 1–12.

MACGILLIVRAY, W. (1837). *A History of British Birds, Indigenous and Migratory; including their organization, habits, and relations; remarks on classification and nomenclature; an account of the principal organs of birds, and observations relative to practical ornithology*. Scott, Webster & Geary, London.

MAY, L. (1989). Population density and nest-site selection of magpies *Pica pica* L. in an urban environment. Unpubl. M.Sc. Thesis, Manchester Polytechnic.

MAYAUD, M. (1933). Notes et remarques sur quelques corvides. IV. La Pie *Pica pica* L. *Alauda*, 5: 362–382.

MEINERTZHAGEN, R. (1954). *Birds of Arabia*. Oliver & Boyd, Edinburgh & London.

MILLAR, J. B. (1964). Autumn movements of young magpies. *Bird Banding*, 35: 265.

MINTON, C. D. T. (1958). Magpie's rapid replacement of dead mate. *British Birds*, 51: 309.

MIZERA, T. (1988). An ecological study of the synanthropic avifauna of the Solacz District of Poznan in 1975–1984. *Acta Zoologica Cracoviensia*, 31: 3–64.

MOHOLT, R. K. & TROST, C. (1989). Self advertisement: relations to dominance in Black-billed Magpies. *Animal Behaviour*, 38: 1079–1088.

MØLLER, A. P. (1978). Husskadens *Pica pica* bestandstaethed redeplacering og bestandsaend-ringer i Danmark. *Dansk Ornitologisk Forenings Tidsskrift*, 72: 197–215.

MØLLER, A. P. (1982a). Characteristics of Magpie *Pica pica* territories of varying duration. *Ornis Scandinavica*, 13: 94–100.

MØLLER, A. P. (1982b). Yngletidspunkt, traekbevaegelser, dodelighed og dodsarsager hos Husskade (*Pica pica*). *Flora og Fauna*, 88: 39–45.

MØLLER, A. P. (1983a). Habitat selection and feeding activity of the magpie, *Pica pica*. *Journal für Ornithologie*, 124: 147–161.

MØLLER, A. P. (1983b). Changes in Danish farmland habitats and their populations of breeding birds. *Holarctic Ecology*, 6: 95–100.

MØLLER, A. P. (1985). Communal roosting in the magpie (*Pica pica*). *Journal für Ornithologie*, 126: 405–419.

MØLLER, A. P. (1987a). Intruders and defenders on avian breeding territories: the effect of sperm competition. *Oikos*, 48: 47–54.

MØLLER, A. P. (1987b). Extent and duration of mate guarding in swallows *Hirundo rustica*. *Ornis Scandinavica*, 18: 95–100.

MØLLER, A. P. (1988). Nest predation and nest site choice in passerine birds in habitat patches of different sizes: a study of magpies and blackbirds. *Oikos*, 53: 215–221.

MOUNTFORD, G. (1958). *Portrait of a Wilderness: the story of the Coto Doñana Expeditions*. Hutchinson, London.

MUGAAS, J. N. & KING, J. R. (1981). Annual variation of daily energy expenditure by the Black-billed Magpie: a study of thermal and behavioral energetics. *Studies in Avian Biology*, 5: 78.

MURTON, R. K. (1971). *Man and Birds*. Collins, London.

NEWTON, A. & GADOW, H. (1896). *A Dictionary of Birds*. Black, London.

NEWTON, I. (1986). *The Sparrowhawk*. Poyser, Calton.

NEWTON, I. (1989). *Lifetime Reproduction in Birds*. Academic Press, London.

NIETHAMMER, G. & MERZINGER, E. (1943). Über Beteiligung am Brutgeschäft der Elster nach Alter und Geschlecht. *Beitrage zur Fortpflanzungs Biologie der Vogel mit Berucksichtigung der Oologia*, 19: 21–22.

ODUM, E. P. & KUENZLER, E. J. (1955). Measurement of territory and home range size in birds. *Auk*, 72: 128–137.

ORIANS, G. H. (1980). *Some Adaptations of Marsh-nesting Blackbirds*. Princeton University Press, Princeton, NJ.

OWEN, D. H. (1956). Food of nestling Jays and Magpies. *Bird Study*, 3: 257–265.

PARKER, H. (1984). Effect of corvid removal on reproduction of willow ptarmigan and black grouse. *Journal of Wildlife Management*, 48: 1197–1205.

PARSLOW, J. L. F. (1967). Changes in status among breeding birds in Britain and Ireland. *British Birds*, 60: 261–285.

PARSLOW, J. L. F. (1973). *Breeding Birds of Britain and Ireland*. Poyser, Berkhamsted.

PERRINS, C. M. (1965). Population fluctuations and clutch-size in the Great Tit, *Parus major*, L. *Journal of Animal Ecology*, 34: 601–647.

PERRINS, C. M. & BIRKHEAD, T. R. (1983). *Avian Ecology*. Blackie, Glasgow. 221pp.

PERRINS, C. M. & MOSS, D. (1975). Survival of young Great Tits in relation to age of female parent. *Ibis*, 116: 220–224.

RASPAIL, X. (1888). Sur le nid de la pie et la déstruction de ses oeufs par la corneille (*Corvus corone*). *Bulletin de Société de Zoologie de France*, 13: 126–129.

RASPAIL, X. (1901). Cérémonie de secondes noces chez les garruliens (*Pica caudata* et *Garrulus glandarius*). *Bulletin de Société de Zoologie de France*, 26: 104–109.

REDONDO, T. & CARRANZA, J. (1989). Offspring reproductive value and nest defense in the magpie *Pica pica*. *Behavioural Ecology and Sociobiology*, 25: 369–378.

REEBS, S. G. (1986). Sleeping behavior of Black-billed Magpies under a wide range of temperatures. *Condor*, 88: 524–526.

REEBS, S. G. (1987). Roost characteristics and roosting behavior of Black-billed Magpies *Pica pica*, in Edmonton, Alberta. *Canadian Field Naturalist*, 101: 519–525.

REEBS, S. G. & BOAG, D. A. (1987). Regurgitated pellets and late winter diet of Black-billed Magpies *Pica pica* in central Alberta. *Canadian Field Naturalist*, 101: 108–110.

REESE, K. P. & KADLEC, J. A. (1982). Determining the sex of Black-billed magpies by external measurements. *Journal of Field Ornithology*, 53: 417–418.

REESE, K. P. & KADLEC, J. A. (1985). Influence of high density and parental age on the habitat selection and reproduction of Black-billed Magpies. *Condor*, 87: 96–105.

REYNOLDS, M. D. (1990). The ecology of spacing behavior in the Yellow-billed Magpie *Pica nuttalli*. Unpubl. Ph.D. Thesis, University of California, Berkeley.

RHAN, H., SOTHERLAND, P. R. & PAGANELLI, C. V. (1985). Inter-relationships between egg mass and adult body mass and metabolism among passerine birds. *Journal für Ornithologie*, 126: 263–271.

RICKLEFS, R. E. (1968). Patterns of growth in birds. *Ibis*, 110: 419–451.

ROACH, F. A. (1963). The Bullfinch – its past and present position relative to damage to fruit crops. *Proceedings of Bird Damage to Fruit Crops Conference*, National Farmers' Union, London, 1962.

ROBBINS, C. S., BYSTRAK, D. & GEISSLER, P. H. (1986). The breeding bird survey: its first fifteen years, 1965–1979. *United States Fish & Wildlife Service Resource Publication*, 157: 196pp.

ROLFE, R. L. (1965). Numbers of Magpies preying on a roost of Tree Sparrows. *British Birds*, 58: 150–151.

ROWHER, F. C. & FREEMAN, S. (1989). The distribution of conspecific nest parasitism in birds. *Canadian Journal of Zoology*, 67: 239–253.

SALVIN, O. (1859). Five months bird nesting in the Eastern Atlas. *Ibis*, 1: 302–318.

SCHARF, C. (1985). A technique for trapping territorial magpies. *North American Bird Bander*, 2: 34–36.

SCHARF, C. (1987). Sex determination of the Black-billed Magpie, *Pica pica*. *Canadian Field Naturalist*, 101: 111–113.

SEEBOHM, H. (1883). *A history of British Birds, with coloured illustrations of their eggs*. R. H. Porter, London.

SEEL, D. C. (1976). Moult in five species of Corvidae in Britain. *Ibis*, 118: 491–527.

SEEL, D. C. (1983). Breeding of the Magpie on Anglesey, North Wales. (Bangor Occasional Paper No. 15) Institute of Terrestrial Ecology. 19pp.

SELBY, P. J. (1833). *Illustrations of British Ornithology*. W. H. Lizars, Edinburgh.

SHANNON, G. R. (1958). Magpies' rapid replacement of dead mate. *British Birds*, 51: 901–902.

SHARROCK, J. T. R. (1976). *The Atlas of Breeding Birds in Britain and Ireland*. British Trust for Ornithology and Irish Wild Bird Conservancy, Poyser, Berkhamsted.

SHEDDEN, C. & FENWICK, M. (1988). Magpies, the black and white menace. *Shooting and Conservation*, winter 1988: 24–25.

SIMMONS, K. E. L. (1970). Further observations of food hiding in the Corvidae. *British Birds*, 63: 175–177.

SLAGSVOLD, T., SANDVIK, J., ROFSTAD, G., LORENTSEN, O. & HUSBY, M. (1984). On the adaptive value of intraclutch egg-size variation in birds. *Auk*, 101: 685–697.

SNOW, B. & SNOW, D. (1988). *Birds and Berries*. Poyser, Calton.

SNOW, D. W. (1958). *A Study of Blackbirds*. Allen & Unwin, London.

SOLER, M. (1990). Relationships between the great spotted cuckoo, *Clamator glandarius*, and its corvid hosts in a recently colonized area. *Ornis Scandinavica*, 21: 212–223.

SOLER, M. & MØLLER, A. P. (1990). Duration of sympatry and coevolution between the great spotted cuckoo and its magpie host. *Nature* (London), 343: 748–750.

STAPANIAN, M. A. & SMITH, C. C. (1978). A model for seed scatter-hoarding: co-evolution of Fox Squirrels and Black Walnuts. *Ecology*, 59: 884–896.

STEGMANN, B. (1927). Die ostpaläarktischen Elstern und ihre Verbreitung. *Annuaire du Musée Zoologique de l'Acadamie des Sciences de URSS, 1927*: 366–390.

STEGMANN, B. (1931). Die Vögel des dauro-mandschurischen Uebergangsgebietes. *Journal für Ornithologie*, 79: 137–236.

STONE, E. & TROST, C. H. (in press). Predators, risks and context for mobbing and alarm calls in black-billed magpies. *Animal Behaviour*, in press.

STUBBS, F. J. (1910). Ceremonial gatherings of the magpie. *British Birds*, 3: 334–336.

SWANBERG, P. O. (1951). Food storage, territory and song in the Thick-billed Nutcracker. *Proceedings of the 10th International Ornithological Congress*, 545–554.

SWENSON, J. E. (1980). Seasonal changes in habitat use and flock size by Black-billed Magpies along the lower Yellowstone River, Montana. *The Prairie Naturalist*, 12: 105–109.

TATNER, P. (1982a). The breeding biology of magpies *Pica pica* in an urban environment. *Journal of Zoology*, London, 197: 559–581.

TATNER, P. (1982b). Factors influencing the distribution of magpies *Pica pica* in an urban environment. *Bird Study*, 29: 227–234.

TATNER, P. (1982c). The density of breeding magpies *Pica pica* L. in an urban environment. *The Naturalist*, 107: 47–58.

TATNER, P. (1983). The diet of urban magpies *Pica pica*. *Ibis*, 125: 90–107.

TATNER, P. (1984). Body component growth and composition of the magpie *Pica pica*. *Journal of Zoology*, London, 203: 397–410.

TATNER, P. (1986). Survival rates of urban magpies. *Ringing and Migration*, 7: 112–118.

THOMAS, D. & RONNEFELDT, K. (eds) (1976). *People of the First Man: life among the Plains Indians in their final days of glory*. Dutton, New York.

THOMPSON, W. (1849). *The Natural History of Ireland*. Vol. 1. Reeve, Benham & Reeve, London.

TODD, K. S. (1968). Weights of Black-billed Magpies from south-western Montana. *Auk*, 85: 508–510.

TOMBACK, D. F. (1980). How Nutcrackers find their seed stores. *Condor*, 82: 10–19.

TROST, C. H. & WEBB, C. L. (1986). Egg moving by two species of corvid. *Animal Behaviour*, 34: 294–295.

TUCKER, G. (1989). Farmland birds in winter. *BTO News*, 162: 4–5.

TURCEK, F. J. & KELSO, L. (1968). Ecological aspects of food transportation and storage in the Corvidae. *Community Behavioural Ecology*, Part A, 1: 277–297.

TURNER, T. W. (1954). *Memoirs of a Gamekeeper*. Bles, London.

VADER, W., HANSEN, K. M. & NILSSEN, A. (1979). Schizochroic and non-eumelanic Magpies in northern Norway. *Fauna*, 32: 152–155.

VALVERDE, J. A. (1956). Notas ornitológicas sobre Santo Domingo de Silos. *Munibe* (Special Volume), 3–31.

VALVERDE, J. A. (1957). *Aves del Sahara Español*. Instituto de Estudios Africanos, Madrid. 487pp.

VANDER WALL, S. B. & BALDA, R. P. (1977). Co-adaptations of the Clark's Nutcracker and the Piñon Pine for efficient seed harvest and dispersal. *Ornis Fennica*, 49: 89–111.

VAURIE, C. (1954). Systematic notes on Palearctic birds, No. 5 Corvidae. *American Museum Novitates*, 1668: 10–12.

VAURIE, C. (1959). *The Birds of the Palearctic Fauna*. Witherby, London, pp. 148–152.
VERBEEK, N. A. M. (1972a). Daily and annual time budget of the Yellow-billed Magpie. *Auk*, 89: 567–582.
VERBEEK, N. A. M. (1972b). Comparison of displays of the Yellow-billed Magpie (*Pica nuttalli*) and other corvids. *Journal für Ornithologie*, 113: 295–313.
VERBEEK. N. A. M. (1973). The exploitation system of the Yellow-billed Magpie. *University of California Publications in Zoology*, 99: 1–58.
VERNER, J. (1985). Assessment of counting techniques. In: *Current Ornithology* (Ed. R. F. Johnston) Vol. 2. Plenum Press, London.
VESEY-FITZGERALD, B. (1946). *British Game*. Collins, London.
VINES, G. (1981). A socio-ecology of Magpies *Pica pica*. *Ibis*, 123: 190–202.
VON HAARTMAN, L. (1969). The nesting habits of Finnish birds. I. Passeriformes. *Commentationes Biologicae*, 32: 1–187.
VOOUS, K. H. (1960). *Atlas of European Birds*. Nelson, London.
WAITE, R. K. (1984). Sympatric corvids: effects of social behavior, aggression, and avoidance on feeding. *Behavioural Ecology and Sociobiology*, 15: 55–59.
WAITE, R. K. (1985). Food caching and recovery by farmland corvids. *Bird Study*, 32: 45–49.
WALTERS, J. (1988). Broedgegevens van de Ekster *Pica pica*. *Limosa*, 61: 33–40.
WARD, E. (1952). Some observations at a magpie roost. *British Birds*, 45: 403–405.
WARD, P. & ZAHAVI, A. (1973). The importance of certain assemblages of birds as 'information centres' for food finding. *Ibis*, 115: 517–534.
WHITAKER, J. J. S. (1894). Notes on some Tunisian birds. *Ibis*, 6: 78–100.
WITHERBY, H. F. (1920). *A Practical Handbook of British Birds*. Witherby, London.
WITT, K. (1985). Bestände von Elster (*Pica pica*) und Nebelkrähe (Corvus corone cornix) auf Berliner Probeflachen 1984. *Ornithologische Berichte für Berlin (West)*, 10: 154–175.
WITT, K. (1989). Do magpies (*Pica pica*) control the population of passerines in a city? *Die Vogelwelt*, 110: 142–150.
WOOD, J. G. (n.d.). *The Illustrated Natural History: Birds*. Routledge, London.
WOOLFENDEN, G. E. & FITZPATRICK, J. W. (1984). *The Florida Scrub Jay*. Princeton University Press, Princeton, NJ.
WYNNE-EDWARDS, V. C. (1962). *Animal Dispersion in Relation to Social Behaviour*. Oliver & Boyd, Edinburgh & London.
YARRELL, W. (1843). The Magpie. In: *A History of British Birds*. Vol. 2. Van Voorst, London.

Index